AMERICAN MARXISM

HOW A NEW COLD WAR DRIVES THE PROGRESSIVES' AGENDA

BY
WILLIAM REEVES

LIBERTY HILL PRESS

Liberty Hill Publishing
2301 Lucien Way #415
Maitland, FL 32751
407.339.4217
www.libertyhillpublishing.com

Unless otherwise indicated, Unless otherwise indicated, Scripture
quotations taken from the King James Version (KJV) – *public domain*.

Paperback ISBN-13: 978-1-6312-9532-4
Hard Cover ISBN-13: 978-1-6312-9533-1
Ebook ISBN-13: 978-1-6312-9534-8

To my parents: readers, writers, thinkers, characters,
and highly educated '60s intellectuals who believed faith,
family, and common sense came before their liberal idealism.
May they rest in peace.

TABLE OF CONTENTS

"Here, in the United States, we are alarmed by new calls to adopt socialism in our country. America was founded on liberty and independence—not government coercion, domination, and control. We are born free, and we will stay free. Tonight, we renew our resolve that America will never be a socialist country."

President Donald J. Trump, State of the Union Address on February 6, 2019

PREFACE

THIS IS NOT AN ACADEMIC RESEARCH PAPER WHERE the writer does not generate any new material and only cites one source after another after another and patches all the quotes into a quilt that supports a researcher's theory. Nor is it intended to be a biography of Karl Marx and his disciples. This is instead an unabashed collection of reflections, observations, and conclusions using frank and aggressive language that serves as a polemic opposition piece relative to the dangerous state of Marxism in America. It initially started out as a list of the 10, then 20 then 30 things progressives were doing leading up to and then during the 116th United States Congress and these seemed an awful lot like they were coming out of the Marxist playbook. To explain them all would require some historical perspective.

In pulling this together it became clear that the U.S. is in the midst of a new cold war. Not with the Soviets or the Chinese but a bloodless civil war where the expectations and understandings of social rules, cultural norms and economic realities are under a confusing and relentless attack from leftist agitators bent on transforming America. It's a battlefield where misperception often prevails and where fiction devolves into reality and perpetual hope and optimism devolve into fear and anxiety.

Piecing it all together has led me to conclude that modern-day progressivism, justice democracy, democratic socialism or social democracy—or whatever the Left calls it—is merely Marxism that's been repackaged to appeal to today and tomorrow's voters as a solution to society's ills. It is a rebranding of a tired political philosophy the Left hopes millennials and other impressionable Americans unfamiliar with the perfect failure rate of Marxism can relate to. Misperceptions lead to unmet expectations and distrust which then drives false assumptions about what direction America should proceed in as the 20s are upon us. This book is an attempt to clarify and bridge the disconnect the Left and Right have about who we are and what expectations we should have if we sincerely wish to build stronger relationships across all sectors of American society.

To be clear, I am first and foremost an anti-Marxist. I am conservative but not anti-liberal. Liberals and conservatives can coexist in America, and our country was founded on principles that relied on dialogue, deliberation and consensus building. Sadly, the far left is making this center-left and center-right collaboration extremely difficult because the progressives are trying to drag liberals further from centrist positions and into their corner while shaming independents, moderates, and conservatives into accepting if not outright adopting more left-leaning views. My goal is to showcase what the modern American left truly is–a divisive rather than unifying voice.

By way of background, I grew up in the American Rust Belt. My mother taught psychology and was a voracious reader, but she was not in the Rogers, Fromm, or Marcuse mold. She chose psychology as a major because at the time it was one of only a few professional disciplines where women were openly welcomed and like many professional women of her generation she was underpaid and underappreciated. My mother was a liberal who was captivated by the civil rights movement and the ideals of John F. Kennedy, yet was committed to her faith – she went to mass nearly every day – and felt people, and not government, can and should solve an individual's problems. Humanistic psychology wasn't her style. She wanted to help people, not convince them that abandoning God or embracing the welfare state was the key to one's liberation.

My father held degrees in journalism and fine arts, worked at a radio station and in his off hours would have been considered a community activist. He was probably more respected by the black community leaders he engaged with than the local working class Irish-American, Polish-American and Italian-American residents in our neighborhood who probably had a certain contempt for, rather than curiosity about, his intelligentsia ways. Later in life, he admitted that he purchased his 1968 VW Type 2 (aka the "hippie van"), so he could shuttle blacks from our, and other, precincts to polling places. They were very liberal in the intellectual and social sense, idealistic, and preferred that my siblings and I read or solve puzzles, rather than watch television. They taught us about the value of reflection, the purpose and need for ethical, responsible and moral behavior, and the need to expose behavior that isn't. Hence this book.

For a while, my parents rented out the third story of our home to a black family whom we got along with fine. When not volunteering in community work my father took a night job at a factory to not only help pay the bills but also to better understand a white and socially conservative blue-collar demographic that liberal activists desperately needed to vote blue to defeat Richard Nixon in 1968 and 1972.

My parents were heavily involved with the Model Cities Program—one of Lyndon Johnson's Great Society and War on Poverty programs, as well as social programs that represented a cross-section of the community's racial, economic and educational classes with the idealistic liberal goal to promote cultural programs for the benefit of inner-city residents.

We were not wealthy by any stretch of the imagination. In fact, we seemed to struggle. My father invested much of what he earned into the various social and arts programs he was advocating for and described us numerous times as working class or lower-middle class. They purchased an old three-story duplex home in need of repairs and took a mortgage of $71 per month. Despite the good they felt they were doing locally they decided to move to either New York City or Los Angeles where the arts cultures were at a scale more to my father's liking. We moved to California and settled in a modest apartment in Los Angeles's Westside— one of the most progressive enclaves in America—after my mother was able to secure a job in Los Angeles as an HR manager for a bank.

Residents of the Westside compared to towns like Buffalo, Cleveland, Detroit and Pittsburgh all voted blue then as now, but culturally and socioeconomically, they could not be more dissimilar. Whereas the Rust Belt was (and is) pro-union, benefitted from federal dollars going to the eds-and-meds industry, and had many wonderful public amenities and social programs to assist the urban underclass as well as the laid-off blue collar workforce, the citizens there did not hold the same left-leaning social or cultural views as Westsiders on such things as gun control, immigration, gay rights, welfare, the degree religion should play in one's life and government intervention in property rights. LA was a real culture shock for us. Our immediate neighbors included an openly gay couple, a divorced mom of two, and a family that emigrated from Iran, all demographics we never experienced. Local officials were very tolerant of homelessness, and seemingly nobody went to church—two things my parents found troubling. My father found work through the Screen Extra's Guild and appeared in several films and TV shows while trying to market his writings. Although he enjoyed the lifestyle and culture of the Westside and nearby Hollywood, he never hit the big time. It was simply too competitive.

When I went to college I majored in one of the most liberal of all professional majors - urban studies - which lead me into a career that requires me to meander through regulatory red tape set up by central planning bureaucrats in Sacramento. I married a non-white, non-Christian foreigner and have lived and raised a family in the most regulated and highly taxed state in the union.

I mention all this because by all accounts I should be a lifelong liberal Democrat, but Ronald Reagan's election profoundly influenced my values. Coupled with that was the disheartenment I saw in my parents through the 1980s. They felt that the utopia all the 1960's liberals had dreamed of was simply not working out. Cultural Marxism had hijacked the liberal agenda. By 1988 my father was voting red. For a conservative like me to offer meaningful and credible perspectives on leftism in America, one would have to have broad experience with people, policies, and programs that make up the traditional and modern Left. In hindsight, I was groomed by my parents to be a Democrat in the mold of the Kennedy dynasty. Certainly not in the activist, radical, or leftist anti-Vietnam War mold of Bernie Sanders or Saul Alinsky, but still fully left leaning.

The background was also included to preemptively counter what leftists who read this book will proclaim comes from a place of hate, racism, or white privilege which is their go-to trope when anti-Marxist material is published. It isn't from a place of hate at all. Leftists will insist that only a racist would oppose open borders, promote small government, or question the purpose and need for the United Nations, or that only an anti-Semite would mention Yiddish, AIPAC and communism, and only a privileged and ignorant right-winger would dare question, rather than blindly accept, the urgent need for nebulous and ever-evolving concepts like equality, environmental justice, diversity, or climate action.

It was challenging at many levels to write a book on this topic and keep it at a few hundred pages. How much background to give, how much emphasis should be placed on this or that, how much on economics and government and how much on psychology and sociology, how much history, current events, analogies or anecdotes should be added for color and how much frankness, humor and snarkiness to include in an otherwise serious essay. Dissertations in political science, psychology and sociology can and will be drafted in the coming years on both the latter-day progressive agenda and Donald Trump's impact on American politics because of the fascinating and complex nature of the material. Sadly, our nation has irreconcilable differences and is experiencing a schism that is playing out in a startling but currently manageable cold war. I'm optimistic that the divide can be bridged but I'm unsure if the chasm the Left has created can ever be filled in.

Its abundantly clear that we've dug our heels in and picked a side. Our side has the moral and legal high ground and their side is evil. As political columnist Doug McIntyre rhetorically asked, "What is a leader to do when there is nobody left to persuade?" The answer lies in normal people teaching our children American values and resisting efforts by the Left to indoctrinate them with nonsense. The deterioration of political discourse in the past decade and especially since 2016 reflects how sharply our society has turned from respectful dignity, ethical and responsible decorum and consensus building to increasingly vile, angry, partisan and ill-informed attacks full of projections, stereotypes and misunderstandings.

It was also difficult to draft this without using terms and phrases that might make people uncomfortable, or are defined or explained differently from what we're used to and this can be confusing. Discussion about citizenry and immigration, Christianity and atheism, racial and ethnic groups, anarchists and neo-Nazi's can be touchy topics to even mention let along dive too deeply into.

With the decline in union membership as a percentage of the workforce declining consistently since the early 1950s the drivers of Marxism for the past 70 years have not been blue collar factory workers but people in academia, intellectual elites, the arts and the media. Otherwise smart people who resent their lack of standing in traditional American society and see Marxism as a path to power for the intelligentsia. As a result, time was spent linking the philosophies of Marx to twentieth century psychologists, sociologists, writers, activists and political figures. The purpose was to add much needed context to landmark or controversial events in U.S. and world history like World War II, the Red Scares – yes, there were two, the counterculture of the 1960s and Zionism, and to better illustrate how this war is being fought.

Since my first allegiance is anti-Marxism and my second is to conservatism, I vote Republican. My life and views on the world have been shaped in part by an intersection of experiences with idealistic intellectuals, minorities, inner-city programs, local politics, unions, homelessness (and the mental health and drug usage issues tied to it), crime, atheism, and environmentalism among other things. As a capitalist who works in a conservative industry and gets paid to shepherd projects through regulatory processes, being able to understand the goals of the Left has been a key to my personal and professional success.

My hope is that my children, who live in a fast-moving and complex world that is under relentless pressure from the Left to fundamentally change America, and are too young to understand Marxism and its extraordinary failure rate, can gain a better understanding of what it really is and why it's such a threat to the American way of life. With any luck, they will think about the choices facing them every Election Day and intuitively be able to answer whether or not the advancement of Marxism is at the root of a candidate's agenda, or the underlying purpose of a state assembly or a citizens' initiative. The last thing we need in the coming generations are misinformed people who cannot tell a liberal from a progressive and inadvertently, or out of spite or irrational emotion, elect Marxists in disguise as Democrats into office to the detriment of America.

Finally, the reader may be unfamiliar with many historical persons and events herein, and may not immediately understand or agree with some of the contentions or conclusions. Again, please note that it comes from a conservative's viewpoint, but not from a place of hate, and hopefully this leads to thought provoking questions, respectful dialogue and reasoned counter arguments.

INTRODUCTION

WRITING ABOUT MARXISM IN A FEW CHAPTERS IS challenging. Countless books, essays, and dissertations have been written about Karl Marx, his philosophies and his impact on the world. Most people think of it as only being related to big government, high taxes, and high levels of regulation, as well as programs, and policies that emphasize public ownership of property, or the state over the citizen or the employee over the employer, and so forth. They don't know what the difference is between communism or fascism or what President Franklin Delano Roosevelt (FDR) thought of fascism (you'll be surprised). They don't understand exactly what the Germans, Italians, and Spanish were doing between World War I and World War II, or the role Communist Party USA played in confusing Americans. Nor do they realize exactly how the counter culture phenomenon of the 1960s actually began in the 1930s, and why conservative pushback to cultural Marxism since the end of World War II drives much of the Republican domestic agenda.

Writing about today's progressive agenda and its Marxist roots is just as challenging. Many of them actually think Marxism and socialism are somehow two different things. For many Americans, particularly those on the Left, Marxism is authoritarian, tanks, gulags, guns, uniforms, and factories, something cold and anachronistic that died with the fall of the Berlin Wall. Socialism, on the other hand, is seen as cool, new, friendly, and passive and comes with all the soft and warm fuzziness that a vacation in Europe offers. This book explains all of this.

WHAT THIS BOOK IS AND ISN'T

This is not a biography of Marx or his prominent mentors and followers, although descriptions of Marx and many key players in the history of the far left are included herein. This is more an examination of who and what motivated Marx, the basics of what he believed and what he tried to get across, as well as the neo-Marxists who carried the socialist torch and amended and implemented his ideology after he died. Additionally, this is about how and when the Marxists penetrated American culture, media, and academia, what they've been doing through the twentieth century and finally, why they behave as they do today.

Marx and his works have been studied ad nauseam. He is praised and vilified, loved and hated. He was largely responsible for increasing wages and improving working conditions worldwide and according to writer and historian Stephen Kotkin, responsible for perhaps 65 million deaths in his name from 1917-2017. Marx was never a politician or professor, just a publisher, writer, and radical. He relied on the charity of others for his survival and their talents to put his ideas in motion. His idea of how to implement socialism was called communism, and it wasn't easy to implement, let alone execute. Over the years, those who embraced his concept have merged his socioeconomic and governance theories with both the evolving and influential social sciences and cultural aspects of any particular nation to create a new way of living and thinking, not just a new way of working or governing.

OPPRESSION, MATERIALISM AND HUMANISM

If you can grasp at least some of the theories and purpose behind the following three concepts, you too can understand how the modern Left thinks and better predict how and why they'll respond in any given situation. These are oppression, materialism, and humanism. Basically, if an agenda item involves a suggestion of someone or something oppressing another, and/or places earth and science above heaven and faith and/or places the selfish desires of man before the selfless commitment to God, then chances are its Marxist.

I've yet to meet a person of any color or creed who hasn't gotten a raw deal now and then. Maybe they were screwed over, laid off, terminated, evicted, dumped, denied, or passed over. It happens. America is a wonderful place—the greatest country ever created—but it's not perfect. Heck, 50 percent of lawyers, some of the smartest and best educated people around, lose in the courtroom. For the most part, Americans are winners, but when we suffer a loss, we get up off the mat, the sun rises the next day, and we move on, confident that we've learned something and optimistic that tomorrow will be better.

But what about the few among us who don't like to win? The ones who get off the mat and rather than reflect and improve, they point fingers and plot revenge? The ones President Trump calls out and gets vilified for doing so. What if someone told you America isn't great at all, and it is simply an illusion maintained by a powerful patriarchy that needs to be marginalized, if not eradicated? Or, that you don't know how bad you really are or conversely how bad you have it? Or that our culture, also known as hegemony, is illegitimate? What if they claim the world will certainly end any moment now due to oppressive forces that urgently need to be stopped? What if they told you that you are being oppressed and you don't even know it? What if you are accused of being an oppressor, although you aren't, or that oppression is systemic and only a revolution will end it? What if they suggested that although you may think you're happy, you're really not?

If you heard that or felt that every day, you'd wonder what that person is doing.

What if that same someone then said your underachievement, inability to hold a job, or inability to make ends meet is not only unfair but not your fault—it is the fault of the oppressors! Or, that your failings are due to immoral or illegal forces inflicted upon you by oppressors rather than avoidable or self-inflicted? What if you are told the envy and hate you feel is not sinful at all, but normal and even justifiable—especially in a time of war, when resentful energy is needed to fuel a leftist cause.

What if you heard this stuff over and over again? You might start to think you live in a rotten and unjust place. That's the propaganda the far left is selling today.

Materialism is the belief that there is no spiritual world, mind and matter are the same, and everything happens due to interactions in the physical world. It's a reliance solely on physical things to explain the cosmos and to satisfy man, rather than a combination of physical and spiritual forces which the Western world faithfully lived by for 2,000 years. God doesn't satisfy man; money, a nice car and a big home do. It's a scientific perspective that dismisses the notion of God, and a soul, and therefore the concept of free will; and since there is no God, there is nothing beyond our temporal time on earth and no moral compass. Further, since we are nothing more than animals, smart and predatory, but just animals, we have a responsibility to share this earth with all life. This flies in the face of the traditional Christian worldview, which holds that man was made in the image of God and is above the plants and animals. Furthermore, per the Bible, the earth was created expressly for man's use and enjoyment. Of course, because Marxists and other children of the Enlightenment believe man created God, not the other way around, this is dismissed.

Humanism is materialistic in the sense that there is no God and there is no life beyond our temporal existence. And, since you are expected to be narcissistic, you should start living as you please to satisfy your need for fulfillment that spirituality once filled. The problem with materialism and humanism is that they cause people to live godless and morally bankrupt lives for the here and now. Material possessions are necessary to satisfy the needs in life. Lust and greed emerge. Selfishness and ruthlessness are the rule, and kindness and morality go out the window. As Vincent Miceli said in his 1971 book, Gods of Atheism, "Since man's future, according to communist humanism, is identified inevitably with the classless society, then the struggle for a communist victory justifies any means and any actions taken to further this absolute, historical cause."

The Left teaches that the world is a big, complicated and scary place, and all things considered it's too much to ask for people to rely on individual initiative and entrepreneurial spirit for success and prayer for hope and comfort. Taking accountability and responsibility for one's actions when we don't even know how and why things are happening is unfair. The Left offers a safety net if one is willing to pay a little more and sacrifice a few liberties for the comfort of being taken care of by someone who will never die or grow up and move away. Their pitch is: It's OK to be a scared child. Just let government become your big brother and everything will be fine. Whereas prayer and the love and support one's family and congregation once provided all the hope and inspiration one needed, the Left told everyone government is your only hope.

Leftists latch onto humanism because there is not just a godless element to it but a state element as well that takes away individual accountability and responsibility. Morals and ethics become fluid as time progresses and a group-think mob mentality dictating what is best for you and mankind prevails over a faith-based approach that relies on timeless and consistent values that are predictable and easy for individuals to comprehend. In the Leftist worldview, humanism is great because public agencies are tasked with being responsible for collecting and distributing resources throughout society, and being egalitarian in concept, the resources would be equitably distributed. The state, therefore, takes care of life's needs. The logic goes like this: Don't find happiness in your spirituality but find happiness in all the fun things your state provides—so long as you pay all your taxes, of course! This flies in the face of a conventional capitalistic society, where character, honor, morality and ethics are valued, and discipline, accountability and the rule of law prevails. A society where the needs of the individual are taken care of by himself and his family.

In short, humanists oppose a faith-based, profit-motivated society, and people like John Dewey and other American leftist intellectuals in the 1930s set out to define what they felt were key points and goals of humanism. These could be briefly summarized as follows: The universe was not created; Man was created by evolution; Religion was invented to explain nature; and Science disproves any supernatural power in the cosmos; God is a thing of the past; Religion only touches on things humans can grasp or experience; The fulfillment of human life is in the here and now, in a heightened sense of one's personal life; There shouldn't be any more religious emotions or attitudes; Man will learn to deal with crisis through his own knowledge, not God's; Man should have an organic rather than spiritual view of life; Humanism encourages self-worship and creativity; All associations and institutions exist solely for the fulfillment of human life; Acquisitive and profit-motivated society has proven to be inadequate and cooperatives are necessary; and finally, Humans should create a man-made utopia!

Humanists view oppression as the man using illegitimate power to put you down, and they view materialism as being there is no God, sin is okay, our jobs and our possessions define us, and we are one with Mother Earth. Humanism, according to humanists, is freeing yourself from the chains of religion and finding purpose and fulfillment as you live for yourself. It's all about me!

If you can grasp the oppression, materialism, and humanism concepts, you can begin to see how predictably focused the far left's narrative is: Oppressive forces are irresponsibly discriminating against or exploiting the world—its people, its economy, and its resources—to their selfish benefit, and this exploitation is done intentionally to the detriment of everyone and everything not a part of the oppressive class. Consequently, every action by the oppressive class is seen as creating or contributing to an existential threat that therefore requires urgent revolutionary reaction. This is why texts or spoken words, let alone direct actions, by President Trump freak out the Left. President Trump, in the eyes of the Left, is their poster child for the oppressive force: White, rich, straight, Christian, and anti-Marxist. Therefore, all the words he uses are a weapon to harm the oppressed.

The following explains 175 years of Marxism in one, albeit long, sentence. Since there is no heaven or hell, and since the capitalist man might destroy man's paradise (earth, not heaven) any day now, and since our lives are nothing more than systems of oppression and exploitation, oppressed people need to unite and wrangle power away from the oppressors—the aristocracy, the clergy, and the capitalists—in order for man to save the earth and achieve his ultimate potential.

Marx felt that history was nothing more than the story of oppression, sanctioned by the throne, the church, and the wealthy. These oppressors then used their illegitimate power to systematically rule over everyone else. He also felt that religious and cultural hegemony stymied man. Therefore, if the powerful could be overthrown, then humans could finally reach their full potential, free from all those inconvenient rules and draconian views the hierarchy forces upon us.

Modern-day leftist politicians and their allies in academia and the media believe behavior by the oppressive class needs to be controlled—and preferably—changed. By controlling their words, you can control their thoughts; and by controlling their thoughts, you can control their behavior. This is cultural Marxism at work—the intersection of political correctness and leftist political ideology.

POLITICAL IDENTITIES IN AMERICA TODAY

There are generally four main political identities in America today. From left to right, they are Marxists (the socialist/progressive club who are sometimes called left-liberal among themselves but we'll call them the far left), liberals (mostly moderate and left of center and who make up the "Democratic establishment"), conservatives (mostly moderate and right leaning and who make up the "Republican establishment" and include neoconservatives), and further to the right are pale-conservatives who make up what I'll call the far right. A big differentiator in foreign policy between an neocon and a paleocon is the former is interventionist and the latter is isolationist. Third parties and political organizations, both centrist and extreme, exist on both the Left and the Right, and tremendous misunderstanding prevails as to who and what exactly constitutes the far- and ultra-left and far- and ultra-right. Smaller third parties, like the Peace and Freedom Party (PFP), Green Party (both far left) and Libertarians (a weird mix of far right, moderate, and far left views) exist, while Independents (about 25–40 percent of the American electorate, depending on the poll) usually hold centrist views, and tend to be the ones who ultimately decide state and federal elections.

Far-left presidential candidate, Senator Bernie Sanders (I-VT), who will be 79 in November 2020, desperately wants to see a leftist elected president in his lifetime. Preferably it's himself, but I'm sure he'd be happy with any Marxist. He runs as an Independent but caucuses with and pretends to be a Democrat when convenient. Independents like

Sanders know there is no viable third-party path to the White House, so they expect the Democratic establishment to embrace views which are, frankly, in line with those of the PFP. Every four years, left-leaning third parties like the PFP and Green Party are told by pragmatists on the Left not to interfere with electoral politics, especially in swing states. In reality, if they had any patience or vision at all, people like Senator Sanders, U.S. Senator Elizabeth Warren of Massachusetts and U.S. Representatives Congresswoman Alexandria Ocasio-Cortez (AOC) of New York should spend the next generation—or two in the case of younger leftists like AOC—developing a third party to call their own. In their view, the PFP does not care for congressional bipartisanship between the major parties and cringes when a Democrat ever votes with a Republican. In fact, the PFP would love to have fence sitting left liberals break from the Democratic establishment and join their team once and for all. Why not?

Marxism has never been a major political force in America, but it has existed here since the late 1800s. As noted earlier, it can represent a few slightly different things, but it generally describes any economic, cultural, and political system rooted in a collectivist philosophy. The term is also used in the context of any system that advocates the emancipation of an oppressed class. Whether it's called democratic socialism, communism, fascism, Leninism, or Maoism, it's a collectivist and statist system that rejects religion and traditional Western power structures and is most commonly associated with the writings of Karl Marx.

Politics is not always clear and precise. Conservative commentator and writer John C. Goodman explained that an ideology is a coherent set of ideas about how the political world should function, whereas, sociology is a system of ideas and beliefs that are not necessarily consistent and may even be contradictory but are held together by people who flock together as one. American politics, because of the Classical liberal tradition carried forward by both liberals and conservatives, coupled with all the contradictions could, therefore, be seen as sociology rather than an ideology. In fact, Marx saw communism as a sociological phenomenon and thus a legitimate scholarly science. Examples of these contradictions are liberals who insist on strong secular schools but send their kids to private schools; want pristine parks but tolerance of and freedoms for transients; want a strong police force but tolerance, if not outright de-criminalization, of drugs and petty crimes; and want high regulation but complain about urban housing affordability. On the other side, conservatives want to keep blue-collar labor costs down, but rather than encouraging immigration, which puts downward pressure on labor costs, many support immigration restrictions.

KEY TERMS TO KNOW

For the purposes of this book, the following terms and descriptions will be used and some are essentially interchangeable.

Make no mistake about it, the views of AOC and her Justice Democrat Squad, along with Senators Sanders and Warren, are clearly Marxist. The other "Democratic" candidates who are or were running for president in 2020, with the possible exception of Vice-President Biden, hold many leftist ideals near and dear. Can these bad actors make so much of a difference, so quickly, to disrupt the conventional view of what a Democrat is? As the faces of the new left, the answer is yes, because it's turned out that they are representative of an increasingly and evermore hardline leftist movement in America. With more and more people embracing this repackaged brand of leftism, the worry we should all have is the lurching ever leftward of what was once a moderate, predictable, and reasonable Democratic party.

This book seeks to demonstrate that Marxism is dangerously alive and well in America, and it would be mostly unnoticed if not for President Trump. It is promulgated by a collection of players in academia, the arts, and the media who have joined forces with the far-left ideologues and misguided liberals in the political arena to not only embrace Marxism but to have it rebranded into what the American leftists call a "progressive" agenda. These leftists seek to push what they call democratic socialism or progressivism as a viable cultural, political, and economic model our society somehow needs to move toward. Through these relentless efforts, a long discredited and bankrupt state religion—one that most American's believe deservedly died with the fall of the Berlin Wall—has reemerged on the political scene to be the biggest threat to the American way of life.

Marxism is now the biggest threat facing America today. It encourages regulation, Godlessness, globalization, unfair trade deals, erosion of states' rights and divisiveness. The threat is bigger than illegitimacy, mental illness, drugs, gangs, immigration, and government program ineptitude. It's bigger than hurricanes and threats of nuclear missile strikes. Addressing it is more important than homelessness, Chinese intellectual property theft, union and pension reform, and litigation abuse/tort reform, and our national debt that are also serious issues facing citizens today. The reason is simple: These issues mentioned above impact many lives, and there are viable and stretch solutions not associated with Marxism that can address, if not fix, them. Marxism, on the other hand, is a deadly cancer, not a solution, and will negatively impact everyone's life.

Chapter 1

SETTING THE TABLE AND EXPLAINING A FEW KEY TERMS

FIRST, YOU NEED TO UNDERSTAND A FEW TERMS TO better grasp what socialism is, how it originated, where it came from, and why certain intellectuals latched onto it, and from there we can examine what the Marxists are taught. Hopefully this will give you, the reader, a better grasp on how they think and act.

Democrats make up most of the American political left. The Left can generally be broken into two camps: liberals and the far left. Liberal, not the "classical liberal" but the modern American liberal, will refer to moderate Democrats who are left of center, but who individually may hold right of center views on certain issues and, perhaps, even some far-left views. President John F. Kennedy and New York U.S. Senator Bobby Kennedy and President Bill Clinton fall into this category. I make this distinction because American conservatives also see themselves as classical liberals but certainly not modern-day American liberals.

Leftists, or the Left, will be used to describe those who are further out there on the left wing and support some far-left ideals. Marxist, socialist and progressive will be used interchangeably and sometimes collectively as leftist or the far left. The Associated Press describes the ultra-left

1

as those holding communist views or those who hold that liberal or socialist change can't come about from the present form of government. Progressives understand that to implement their agenda, fundamental change in how government works would have to take place. "Ultra-leftist" is rarely used by the media, but if you ever see it, this would be part of the far left as described throughout this book.

The media goes out of its way to make sure leftists like Senators Warren and Sanders are cast as "progressives" or part of "the liberal wing of the Democratic Party" (Former Vice-President Joe Biden is the liberal wing of the Democratic Party, not those two), as if progressivism meant progress in the right direction or something. This is not accidental. Republicanism is far closer to the classical liberal ideal than progressivism. Those on the far left generally want to distance themselves from being associated with Marxism under the theory, probably a correct theory, that America is not ready to elect a Marxist to the highest office in the land. However, the Leftists know America could inadvertently vote for a leftist candidate if he or she is carefully portrayed by the media as a liberal. If November 2020 comes and Senator Sanders is the alternative to President Trump, make no mistake that the mainstream media will portray him as the liberal alternative. President Trump is exposing this deception and casting these elements as the radical fringe of the Democratic Party, while showing how disruptive socialism can really be, and the Left resents him for this.

Many conservatives are "neocons," short for neoconservatives. These are center-right or moderate Republicans who, individually, may actually hold some left-of-center views. President George W. Bush and Vice President Dick Cheney were seen as neocons. Some neocon politicians are often pejoratively called RINOs or Republican in Name Only, and many of them and their constituents are often characterized as the "Never Trumpers." Ex-South Carolina Governor Mark Sanford, and Representative Justin Amash (I-MI), along with former presidential candidates Evan McMullin and Joe Walsh, and political commentator Ben Shapiro, are examples of "Never Trumpers." Many Libertarians who vote conservative are also "Never Trumpers," due to their position on border security. They are commonly in favor of open borders, gay marriage and the de-criminalization of drugs.

The neocon/Republican moderates and conservatives will be referred to as the Right. There are the paleoconservatives (paleocons), who advocate traditional American values and are considered by many on the Left as the faces of the "far right." The main difference between neocons and paleocons is interventionist versus isolationist. Pat Buchanan, Steve Bannon, and Alex Jones have been described as paleocons. The far right and alt-right or ultra-right are separate due to conflicting and confusing definitions by the Right and Left about what exactly the alt-right is. Neoreactionaryism, or NRx for short, which is sometimes called Dark Enlightenmentism, is a theoretical concept that certain Libertarian and conservative intellectuals came up with about a dozen years ago, advocating for less democracy and a return to a strong monarch and small bureaucracy. Something like this could be considered far right, due to its small government, anti-egalitarian leanings, and traditional views on religion and gender roles. At the same time, it has an alt-left aspect in its preference for a charismatic, great leader, seated for life, be it a king or some other authoritarian figure. The writings of Milo Yiannopoulos and Curtis Yarvin are written for IQ's north of 140 and are considered by the Left as part of the alt-right. The Left often characterizes ultra-conservative whites as the "alt-right," as a way to discredit small government leanings as being racially influenced.

Richard Spencer, who was once a self-described paleocon, is someone the media and academia characterizes as being part of the alt-right, but they're wrong—180 degrees wrong. Spencer claims not to be a neo-Nazi, but in listening to him, he sure sounds like a leftist National Socialist. He pretty much outed himself as a socialist, or at least a socialist sympathizer, in Dinesh D'Souza's documentary, Death of a Nation, as he appeared to show tolerance for "Socialism done right"—a collectivist system with a big authoritarian government. (It's unclear how socialism could ever be "done right," but that's beside the point.) There is no such thing as a partial socialist. Spencer and the neo-Nazis would be in the Marxist camp, although leftists go out of their way to deny any fraternal connection to fascism, but it's clearly on the Left end of the political axis. We'll dive deeper into this later, but an interesting argument could be made that antifa (leftists who fight other leftists because they think their leftist opponents are on the right) and Spencer (a leftist who some of his followers think is on the right but is really on the Left) are both part of the same zany alt-left wing of the Marxist camp.

THIRD PARTIES

The duopoly in our political system makes a viable third party particularly challenging. Americans always like fights between two entities, like boxers in a ring. There are two teams that play in the Super Bowl. Two teams that play in the World Series. There are cowboys and Indians, and cops and robbers and Republicans versus Democrats. Three feels odd. Like forming a coalition government in a foreign country. But I think this is where America is headed. First, there will be a schism on the Left where Marxists will split from liberals because the ideological differences between the two is far greater than, say, the Republican Party versus the Constitution Party. After seeing the Democratic Party erode, the Right will eventually split into two camps as well – a larger right-centrist group and a smaller Tea Party-like group of paleocons. Whether existing third parties will grow or be incorporated into newer movements is yet to be seen.

In theory, pure Libertarianism would be on the furthest of the far right on the x-axis of a political compass as it would have no government. But surprisingly, many modern Libertarians have left-leaning views on

drugs, abortion, criminal justice reform, immigration, and sexual identity, driven by a combination of humanism and beliefs about individual
liberties. Although they commonly vote conservatively, it's difficult to
pigeon-hole Libertarians as clearly on one side or the other, but we'll
tenuously consider them in the conservative camp because liberty, low
regulation and capitalism are important to them. Charles and the late
David Koch—mega fundraisers for Republicans and bogeymen for the
Left—are Libertarians and "Never Trumpers" who have been trying for
decades to rebrand Conservatism in America as the home for those who
support no borders, no tariffs, and no government regulation.

WHAT IS MARXISM IN A NUTSHELL?

Marxism is a basket of collectivist concepts that evolved before, during,
and after the time of a German named Karl Marx (1818–1883).
Marxism is generally thought of as a political, economic, and cultural
phenomenon, and not a specific government system. It's more like a
philosophy that takes the earthly form of socialism. In other words, the
implementing formats that advance the Marxist philosophy are forms
of socialism and each is situated on the far left of the x-axis of a political compass. These would include: democratic socialism, communism,
fascism, Leninism, Stalinism, Trotskyism, Maoism, etc. Collectively,
they are all forms of an atheistic and anti-capitalist public/cooperative/
collectivist order that socialism encapsulates, but Marx generally gets
naming credit for the entire concept because of his extensive and influential work on socialism and leftist economic theory that spanned four
decades. Not all democracies are the same. Not all monarchies are the
same. Not all brands of Marxism are the same.

Modern leftism adopted by the American progressive movement takes
on one of the main characteristics of Marxism: A grievance-based ideology, founded on Marxist ideals, driven by envy and resentment, and
motivated by actions that seek revenge for perceived injustices. Young

people in particular tend to gravitate toward an identity group, sort of a tribe of their liking based on race, sexuality, gender, or socioeconomic class; whereas people of past generations more likely identify with service groups. Now part of a tribe and rather than admitting to being envious of something, they turn the tables and try to explain that they're not vengeful malcontents but disenfranchised Americans, merely seeking justice. Justice sounds so noble! It sounds so fair! It sounds so righteous! Envy, on the other hand, sounds so sinful, mean and petty.

Envy is one of the seven cardinal sins in Christianity and is not the same as jealousy. Jealousy is a state of being and usually temporary and harmless. Envy is the insatiable desire for something you don't have that causes you to act irrationally, impulsively or dangerously in a quest to acquire or deny something from someone else. The energy from this envy fuels dangerous and counterproductive behaviors that bring about another cardinal sin—wrath—which is the hostility, anger and rage one feels to right wrongs, settle scores, or exact revenge. When the Left is confronted with the inconvenient truth or a harsh reality that their observations are wrong, their conclusions are false, their methods are violent, or their policies are un-American, they fly off the handle and double down by insisting they are not just in the right and the holders of moral superiority, but any judgment from the Right is coming from a place of hate and is therefore illegitimate. In other words, nuking the Left's narrative is dismissed as the oppressors hating on the oppressed.

WHAT IS SOCIALISM IN A NUTSHELL?

The idea of socialism and collectivism predates Marx, but in the early 1800s it was all theoretical and lacked a champion with a clear vision. It needed someone to pull it all together. If Marxism is the philosophical concept, then what we know today as socialism is the application. As noted previously, socialism is the implementing action of Marxism and it can take many forms, but there are some clear consistencies.

To explain this to young people, I use one of two analogies; one involving sports and one involving animals. For sports, think of the concept of socialism as the idea of a game played on a grassy rectangular field, with goals on each end. In some games, you can only score by kicking (soccer or Australian rules football); some by kicking and running (rugby); and some by kicking, running and passing (football). Each game has similarities, but none have anything to do with, say, tennis. Capitalist democracies could be the vision for a game played on a court with nets. Some games score points by striking a ball with your hand to a general or specific location (volleyball); others by striking a ball with a racket into a zone (tennis); and some involve tosses to a small, but fixed location (basketball). The other analogy is to think of our world as a zoo. Think of socialism as the scientific name for big cats with lions, tigers, jaguars, and leopards, all part of the cat club. Elephants, monkeys, and horses are mammals that also live in the zoo but are not a part of the big cat club. These species are the other political ideologies that exist in our worldly zoo.

As a sidebar, you might be wondering why I don't just recommend everyone read or watch Animal Farm, and the reason is that it only offers commentary on the rise of Stalinism and doesn't bother with the other strands of socialism. All the animals are Leninists or Stalinists and none are democratic socialists or fascists. For those unfamiliar with it, Animal Farm is a classic novel by George Orwell published in 1945, and the movie adaptation from 1999 is a good introduction for young people on the pitfalls of society embracing hardline Marxism. However, the story is only an allegorical depiction of the political and social consequences of the Bolshevik Revolution rather than an examination of socialism as a whole. More on this later.

It seems that when Americans hear the word socialism, they think of it as a way to solve social problems as in, "Let's solve our problems together as a society." It's not. Socialism is a system in which the means of production are owned and/or controlled by the state. Modern socialists, like American progressives, will say their platform goes beyond industry and commerce and includes a collection of economic, political, cultural, and environmental systems, revolving around equality and social justice and administered by the state and not private forces.

Conservatives will say socialism is all about envy, resentment, and control, with regulation and authoritarianism as the name of the game. It's a system that doesn't reward hard work but rather seeks an otherwise egalitarian society with limited or no individual rights and liberties, a system where the power over society is not in the hands of a meritocracy but in the hands of party loyalists, who may lack the business acumen to oversee any sector of the economy or industry or the managerial expertise to lead public agencies. Author Mark Hendrickson once wrote in Forbes.com back in 2013, "Leftist ideologues are chronic malcontents, constantly peeved that the world doesn't conform to their own ideal notions. Consequently, they sanctimoniously lash out, willing to tear down and tear apart society, condemning it for not being perfect, magnifying its imperfections while ignoring, if not despising, what is good about it." They hate America so much; they want to burn down the village to save it.

Forms of socialism can be traced to ancient Greece, but it really gained traction—in concept if not in practice—in Europe in the late eighteenth century with the French Revolution. It then spread across Europe, via the works of utopian socialists including John Stuart Mills (1806-73) and Henri de Saint-Simon (1760-1825) The prevailing issue of the day was control of land and the prevailing theories in the early days of socialism centered on transition of power from the church and aristocracy to the commoners. By the early- to mid-1800s, in no small part due to the efforts of social critics like Charles Dickens (1812-70) socialism's scope expanded from obtaining power to adopting public policies that had enough checks and balances in place to ensure nobody got left behind as the Industrial Revolution charged ahead. The problem is that motivation, incentive, innovation, entrepreneurship, and growth—the keys to a successful economy and the foundation of capitalism—are stymied in any leftist economic model. This is the opposite of the right Americans have to freely engage in commerce.

IS THERE A DIFFERENCE BETWEEN SOCIALISM AND COMMUNISM?

Not really. Is there a difference between a lion and tiger? Yes. But if you have a lion, tiger, and elephant in our zoo, and you asked a kindergartener, "Which one doesn't belong?" you'd get the correct answer. As a quick sidebar, to the Left there are meaningful differences between socialism, communism and fascism, which I'd describe as similar to the differences between what a defender, mid-fielder or forward does on the field, but for conservatives they're pretty close: A soccer player is a soccer player. As mentioned earlier, Karl Marx is the one most associated with socialism, but he didn't come up with the idea. He was one of many activists who sought to overthrow existing political systems in Europe, which centered on land ownership and control of resources, while guiding an economy under the approving eyes of the church and aristocracy.

Marx called his brand of socialism "communism" to differentiate his system at a time when various socialist theories floating around leftist intellectual circles were very similar. In simplest terms, Marx says in The Communist Manifesto, "(T)he theory of communism may be summed up in the single sentence: Abolition of private property." Somehow, intellectuals of the 17th and 18th centuries felt the church and aristocracy made people sad. Along came the Industrial Revolution, and suddenly it was the church, aristocracy, factory owners, bankers, and landlords who conspired to make people sad. Marx, like any other megalomaniac, effectively said, "You're sad whether you know it or not, so listen to me and not your priest, landlord, or boss."

Marx's version of socialism is what he called "communism." In his system, communism has two steps: an initial phase where the proletariat (the workers) rises up (violently if necessary) and (temporarily) takes control of the government, and a second (permanent) phase that would happen sometime later, where the proletariat would relinquish control, and there'd be no government, no borders, and no markets. A true communal world where there would be no more wars, corruption, exploitation, or imbalances.

The Soviets, led by Vladimir Lenin (1870-1924), took it through the first phase and implemented proletariat rule. But, despite calling their system "communism," the Soviets never fully implemented Marx's grand plan, because people like power if they have it and don't want to voluntarily give it up. Lenin was a fan of a radical named Sergei Nechayev (1847–82), who was a nihilist and author of Catechism of a Revolutionary (1869). Nechayev wrote these gems about leftist revolutionaries saying, "The Revolutionist knows only one science, the science of destruction," along with, "The revolutionary despises public opinion. He despises and hates the existing social morality in all its manifestations. So, for him, morality is everything, which contributes to the triumph of the revolution." This type of violent philosophy is what drives leftist anarchists like antifa. It suggests anything and everything that contributes to the triumph of the revolution is, therefore, moral. Nikolai Bukharin, a buddy of Lenin and fellow radical Leon Trotsky, even suggested that assassinating a ruler is not only not murder–it's not even a crime. I presume he implied assassinating a ruler in Western Europe and not his buddy Lenin.

Lenin brought together the theories of Marx and the immoral and hedonistic views of Nechayev to create his state. He and Stalin knew that with no government, there would be no need for egotistical leaders, drunk on political and social power, to yield, and no government-run markets to generate cash to pay political favors or influence other corrupt officials. Lenin and Stalin were not about to relinquish power. The same went with Hitler, Mussolini, Franco and the Kim dynasty in North Korea.

The Marxist/proletarian political parties in Western Europe–and in America pre-1932 – were, for the most part, marketed as labor parties. The pretext, of course, being worker's rights. Hitler's fascists were socialist, but he had issues with the communists in Germany because he felt they took orders from the Soviet Union and fundamentally objected to the economic aspects of fascism. Consequently Soviet sympathizers were, therefore, traitors. One of those issues related to loyalty. Because Marx did not like borders, the communists are loyal to no country, only an ideology. Hitler wanted socialists to be loyal to their country rather than to an ideology centered in Moscow. He believed communists were only loyal to an ideal but National Spcialists could be loyal to an ideal and a country. Hitler felt your identity as a worker should be linked to all other workers in your country and not your classification or trade. As an example, a welder in Germany should have kinship with a German factory manager and not a machinist in England or construction worker in France. He wanted socialism to work but simply could not trust the communists to be loyal to Germany. The same was true with Mussolini in Italy where Il Duce wanted a brand of socialism for Italian speakers.

Again, socialism and communism are fundamentally so close that one by one definition a single word differentiates them. For orthodox Marxists, they define socialism as the first or lower stage of communism, based on the principle of "from each according to his ability, <u>to each according to his contribution</u>" while the second or upper stage communism is based on the principle of "from each according to his ability, <u>to each according to his need</u>".

TROTSKYISM VS STALINISM VS BUKHARINISM

Left, center and right. In the American political perspective, all three of these men held Marxist perspectives that are on the far-left of how we view the political spectrum. But in the Marxist world view, these represent left, center and right, and it's important to understand this nuance because this is what people like Senator Sanders and AOC, particularly AOC, think about Joe Biden. AOC's mindset reflects how many voters in radically far-left places San Francisco and Manhattan view the political landscape. To them, starting at a firm position on the far left and moving rightward there's great (Marxist), good (liberal) and acceptable (moderate Democrats) and everything else is on the ultra-right fringe and therefore bad. AOC sees Biden's platform as too far to the right of her Marxist orthodoxy and she's claimed that in any other country Biden would be part of an opposition (right-wing) party.

To the Soviets of the 1920s and 30s, they had orthodox (left), moderate (center) and hybrid (right) leaders and saw most political ideologies in America as far-right. Nikolai Bukharin (1888-1938), and later Josef Stalin (1878-1953), argued that socialism could be built just for a single country, even an underdeveloped one like Russia. Marx had doubts about the viability of communism in an isolated and agrarian society like Russia. In his view, socialism needed to spread from developed countries to less developed countries, not the other way around. He reasoned that communism needed to start in a fully developed nation, where capitalism and industry had matured, while socio-economic classes emerged, and all the accompanying problems capitalism caused were manifested. Lenin held the more orthodox Marxist view that revolutions should spread to other countries.

Bukharin felt a certain degree of capitalism was good for communism. This is where China eventually headed, and Bukharin was branded as the right-winger. Leon Trotsky (1879-1940) and Lenin (the intellectual left-wingers) subscribed to Marx's idea that the revolution needed to focus on workers, without the need to worry about entrepreneurship or economics, and be able to spread the collectivist and egalitarian dream internationally. Trotsky believed that a communist state, led by blue collar technocrats unfamiliar with budgets, management, bureaucracy and military science would be no match for capitalist rivals who might be tempted to invade a nascent communist nation. Hence, socialist revolutions were needed in other, preferably adjacent, countries. Stalin, the centrist, appreciated Lenin's interpretation of Marxism but drew from Bukharin's ideas. Stalin succeeded in building something Marx probably wouldn't have expected or approved of doing – building a wall around a militarized communist council of nations. His motto was, "Socialism in One Country."

WHAT IS FASCISM IN A NUTSHELL?

Much more on this later, but don't be fooled. Fascism is socialism. Do not believe otherwise. AOC made a fascinating remark about President Trump one day in saying that, "For a president who seems to care so much about socialism, he really doesn't seem to give a damn about introducing fascism into the United States." Huh? Fascism is, perhaps, the most misunderstood word in American politics, in part because leftist politicians, the media and academia don't want to correctly define what it is. It's not a conservative, Republican, right wing, or President Trump thing. Fascism is socialism with borders. It's a Marxist political system, developed by two Italian socialists: Benito Mussolini (the "father of fascism") and Giovanni Gentile (the "philosopher of fascism") and implemented in a handful of countries (namely Italy, Germany, and Spain) across Europe in the 1920s and '30s. Some people think it was started by a German named Friedrich Nietzsche (1844-1900), due to his commentary on master societies versus slave societies, but he was a philosopher and not the architect of a political party. Mussolini and Gentile were political architects who saw fascism in a full and glorious Marxist context – a political, cultural and economic transformation of society.

Mussolini was the charismatic politician and pro-military army veteran. Gentile, the teacher, writer, and philosopher, was the brains and he began writing about ways to improve Marxism in the late 1890s. Together they sought to permanently change Italian society.

The fascist movement was officially founded in 1914, and by 1922, the National Fascist Party with Mussolini as Prime Minister and Gentile as Minister of Education had taken control of Italy. The fascists were socialists but felt Marxism as a doctrine wasn't workable. Gentile tweaked the Marxist concept to appeal to the identity of the entire Italian speaking population, rather than the plight of the proletariat class. When the Great War (World War I) came and the proletariats fought for country rather than against capitalism and the aristocracy, socialism was at a crossroads. Somehow Marx had miscalculated something. Marx wrongly assumed that workers would not join the fight and instead use the cover of war for revolutions by blue-collar workers across Europe. He never imagined workers preferred country and culture over nebulous things, like class identity or esoteric concepts, like worker empowerment.

Even before World War I, Gentile felt socialism could work, if the definition of the oppressed class was expanded to be an oppressed people. He understood that to ordinary Italians, God, geography, culture, hegemony and family—things orthodox Marxists had issues with—were too important to dismiss, so he came up with a new-and-improved brand of Marxism he knew the masses would accept. Instead of class conflict, as the textbook primary driver of any socialist revolution, the fascists felt the key to successful socialism was nationalism. If everyone felt they were part of the revolution (white- and blue-collar), it would finally work! Gentile believed that socialism with borders, corporate syndication and a nationalist and highly-policed culture, working within the existing hegemony, was the best path forward.

What Is Capitalism in a Nutshell?

Capitalism can convey an economic model, or refer to a type of national governance structure, but for the most part it is an economy driven by private citizens and not by a public bureaucracy. The simplest way to explain capitalism is to call it an economic system, whereby the exchange of goods and services is in the hands of the basic economic unit (the family) and privately-owned business, both large and small. The public realm can, and does, play a role in the economy of a capitalist nation. The U.S., Hong Kong (for now), Singapore, New Zealand, Japan and Canada are capitalist nations, although Hong Kong as an administrative region and Singapore as a city-state are somewhat unique. These contrasts with other predominant economic models some countries use that is a Marxist collectivist and central planning representation calling for government control—if not outright ownership—of property and the economy. North Korea is the most obvious example of a state that employs central planning.

In theory, it's conceivable for an extreme Libertarian political and economic model to exist, whereby there is no state to regulate the economy or tax the citizens. But, for all intents and purposes, the state can, and does, have a role in a modern capitalist economy. Republicans want that role to be small, and Democrats want that role to be big. Progressives want it to be really big! The far right wants it to be really small. In a country as large and as economically diverse as the United States, some amount of a mixed economy is necessary to cover national defense and transportation needs, as well as protecting the banking and investment industries. How much government involvement is the right amount is the primary difference in political philosophies these days.

WHAT IS A CONSERVATIVE IN A NUTSHELL?

American conservatives were the custodians of the American liberal ideal brought forth in 1776 and so eloquently explained in the 272 words of Lincoln's Gettysburg Address. Conservatives, despite what the Left would have you believe, are not opposed to progress, science or new ideas. Conservatives believe that change and innovation require careful thought, particularly in the context of the constitution. Conservative beliefs are generally tied to traditional Christian teachings, the Puritan work ethic, and respect for private property, the rule of law, and personal liberties.

Conservatives also believe certain inherent but important values consistent with what our Founding Fathers laid out need to be passed down to subsequent generations to ensure that the republic can continue to flourish. This passing along of the cultural hegemony is what the cultural Marxists are at war with. The Leftists want young people to reject what their parents and pastors are teaching them. Conservatives, of course, are not backing down and naturally take offense at the tactics used by the cultural Marxists.

Conservatives understand that America is a constitutional republic and not a democracy. They are pragmatic, value initiative and hard work, and believe in entrepreneurship, free trade, and freedom of association, among other things. Conservatives believe in school choice and equal opportunities but are not foolish enough to expect equal outcomes. Conservatives believe change comes from within after great reflection and consensus building, not through a mob mentality. Leftists believe change comes from changes in the environment—or the courtroom. Leftist concepts, like egalitarianism, or nebulous matters, like world peace or climate injustice, are not conservative values. As for those who don't know, the normally liberal Ninth Circuit Court ruled that climate is not guaranteed under the constitution.

WHAT'S THE DIFFERENCE BETWEEN "THE LEFT" AND "THE RIGHT" IN POLITICS?

Right vs. Left originated in France in the eighteenth century when people who supported the king sat on the right side of the chamber, and those who preferred more liberal policies sat on the left side. Those on the right saw hierarchies, meritocracies, and national autonomy as logical and necessary, and generally preferred the status quo. In their opinion, individual rights—and God-given rights—trumped collective needs, and when it came to social issues, care for the poor was the responsibility of individuals, their families, and their church. Productivity (work, commerce, income generation, etc.) was the individual's responsibility, not the state's. Those on the left wanted change and saw existing hierarchies as illegitimate byproducts of chance (being born rich), force, or capitalist exploitation. But, in any case, the Left maintained that power was bestowed and validated because of the aristocracy, church, or capitalism. They sought faster, and more disruptive legislative, judicial and social change and the writings of the early socialists reflected this mindset.

In the European – and San Franciscan–political perspective, everyone is, well, socialist, so they view political parties the way the Russians of the 1920s did, which is in the context of left (the ideologues and the orthodox), center and right (commercial interests, but within the confines of socialism). In the parlance of American politics, all of socialism is on the far left regardless of how patriotic, capitalistic, militarized or authoritarian it is. In America, the Right or right wing is the domain of anti-Marxist conservatism. In Europe, socialism can be on the Left, middle or right, but in America it's impossible for socialism to be anything but the far left and within the far left it gets divided up further. Orthodox Marxism is the far left of the far left and fascism would be the far right of the far left. This nuance explains why AOC claimed that in any other country, European ones specifically, Vice-President Biden would be, in her words, on the other side, the right wing. As for the

17

purposes of this book, left and right are from the American perspective, not from the European socialist perspective.

That distinction between right and left still holds true, but today it's less about pro-business on the Right versus labor on the Left. It's gone beyond the "change the world" mentality of the Left versus the Right's mentality of just fixing a few things in America. Its citizens of the U.S. for the Right versus citizens of the world for the Left. Its unity and faith on the Right versus tribalism and secularism on the Left. It's an internal locus of control – what's in our control–on the Right versus an external locus – what's out of our control–on the Left. It's an obsession with the perceived oppression in the areas of income, gender, sexual inequality, and environmentalism that have become far more political hot-button topics than political inequality to the Left. Those on the Right see wealth as justifiably earned due to entrepreneurship, intelligence, sacrifice, risk taking, hard work, and so on and so forth. Those on the Left see wealth as a byproduct of the luck of your birth coupled with an exploitation that is both disproportionate and unfair, especially to the less fortunate around the world. Hence the Left has a desire for not just national wealth and resource redistribution and rebalancing, but internationally too.

Another distinction between the Left and the Right is that conservatives believe the three key documents that established our nation, also known as the Charters of Freedom (aka the Declaration of Independence, the Constitution of the United States, and the Bill of Rights), have secured all the freedoms and rights a person needs—of the people, by the people, and for the people. Furthermore, because these are by and for the people, many on the Right believe the government and courts do little these days but misinterpret the Charters of Freedom and in doing so, constrict, or even take rights away. In short, the fight to secure the foundation by which our nation was built from a territorial and a policy perspective was fought and won against the French in the mid-1700s and the British in the late 1700s. These rights were codified in the bitterly debated U.S. Constitution (1789) and debate and refinement continued almost immediately afterward resulting in the Bill of Rights (1791).

This isn't to suggest that conservatives are against social or constitutional change. Progress, in the view of the Right, should be evaluated at the state level, and be reasonable and measured. Constitutional amendments are a serious matter and those that have merit have received broad conservative support with 27 out of 33 being approved. All states, whether they were liberal or conservative leaning, ratified the Thirteenth Amendment ending slavery. Thankfully, ridiculous constitutional amendment proposals like the abolition of the Senate in 1911 by Socialist Party member, and mentor to Eugene Debs, Victor Berger (S-WI) and a $1 million maximum wage cap drafted by leftist U.S. Representative Wesley Lloyd (D-WA) in 1933 were promptly shot down.

Lastly, it's important to explain why the Left deliberately tries to confuse the meaning of far-right and who resides there. And, to be blunt, it involves deliberate attempts by the Left to distance themselves from fascism. By way of quick background, with Lenin's death in 1924 the Soviet Union was at a crossroads. As for Americans, there was no distinction since it was communist versus communist versus communist. But for the Soviets jockeying for power, the three sides were extremely diverse. Again, sort of like politics in modern San Francisco. Hundreds of shades of blue. Orthodox Marxists like Trotsky saw themselves as the Left Opposition and focused on working people and class struggle. The Left was intellectual and philosophical. Josef Stalin was seen as a centrist who intended to implement a highly bureaucratic command economy system and needed to borrow from the Left and right oppositions to facilitate his statist model. Those who viewed capitalism as an economic necessity, like Nikolai Bukharin and his New Economic Policy supporters, were the Right Opposition.

This distinction is important to understand, because it helps explain why leftists, since at least the 1930s cleverly, but still erroneously, describe Nazi's as right-wing. The German government under Hitler, with its interdependence and capitalist industry, is what the Soviets, and their allies at CPUSA, would describe as Right Opposition, or right-wing socialism. Therefore, from the viewpoint of Soviet communists, yes, Nazism would be on their right, because it resembled Bukharin's Right Opposition model. However, duplicitous leftist sympathizers in America, like Bella Dodd in the 1930s and 1940s, capitalized on Moscow's portrayal of the Nazi's as right-wing socialists and concocted a message to the American people that dropped the word socialism and suggested fascism would be on the far-right of American politics. It was cast as sort of a 180-degree alternative from communism, which simply wasn't true. CPUSA told us that Communists were our friends and since fascism was their rival it should be America's rival too. In short, don't believe the Leftists. Fascism is what I would describe as the far-right of the far-left.

Another error-filled way to distance themselves from fascism is a belief by some in academia that right versus left is not measured or character-ized by size of government but size of (in)equality. They see the extreme far left as a horizontal society, where everyone has equal political and economic power and the ultra-far right as having an inequitable hier-archy, where no two people have the same amount of money or power. The fallacy of this lies with them not recognizing that in the largest pos-sible government model of the ultra-far left, everyone has equal power and status, because everyone is a soldier in the Red Army. Everyone is a soldier in the revolution. Big government supposedly makes everyone equal, but does it? Is everyone equal in China? Of course not. In a the-oretical ultra-far right society there is no leadership, let alone govern-ment, beyond the head of your household and maybe the pastor of your church congregation. Theoretically, it is horizontal, because everyone has equal political power, because there is no government and equal, or near equal, economic power, because most everyone is a farmer or otherwise living close to the land. To argue that Nazi Germany had little or no government, the hallmark of a far-right political model, is silly. I could make a counter argument that the biggest social, political and economic inequalities in the world exist in far-left big government China. Again, to avoid pesky inconveniences, the proper way to look at left versus right is the size of government, not the size of economic and/ or political inequality.

WHAT IS A PROGRESSIVE IN A NUTSHELL

The classic ideal of liberalism our founding fathers embraced, respected the autonomy of the individual and the pursuit of economic opportunities through open and fair marketplaces, as well as civil liberties enforced through the rule of law, private property rights, scientific exploration, and experimenting with new ideas, among other things. America's great liberal experiment then expanded to include the advancement of an environmentally conscious and pluralistic society that flourished through cooperation and tolerance of different races and creeds. The story of the American liberal experiment is not complete. And, as I mentioned earlier, liberals and conservatives can coexist, but people mix up the idea of social and intellectual progress with the political ideology of progressivism.

Progressives are not liberals. Egalitarianism, relentless regulation and mandates, confiscation, humanism and open anti-Christianity, infringements on civil rights, central planning, globalism, militant feminism, violent protests/dissent, identity politics, infanticide, collectivism, the dismissal, if not the destruction, of the grand narrative—also known as post-modernism, and censure and shaming through political correctness through speech, thought, and behavioral controls—known as cultural Marxism, are progressive trademarks, not liberal trademarks. The majority of responsible liberals reject most, if not all, of these concepts, and this is what distinguishes JFK and President Johnson from Senators Sanders and Warren. JFK was a liberal. Senator Warren is a Marxist. The progressives are on the fringe of the Democratic Party. They are on the far left of the x-axis, and being leftists, they are, by definition, Marxists.

Some progressives proudly self-identify with Marx, but most progressives will ignorantly claim they aren't Marxists at all. They will say they're nothing more than enlightened American liberals, who just want stronger social safety nets, more government control of the economy, higher taxes and more left-leaning social and regulatory policies than the liberals of yesteryear. They may see liberalism as too centric, or they may feel the liberalism of their parent's generation didn't work or didn't go far enough and needs to be tweaked.

Others will say that Senator Sanders isn't a socialist at all, because he doesn't want to control the means of production. But that's inaccurate. He is a socialist and here's how to respond to that one: The government is responsible for 38% of our GDP. That alone means the government controls the means and production of a lot of goods and services being produced every day. The federal budget is about $4.8 trillion per year and when you consider Senator Sanders' Medicare for All (M4A) proposal, which may cost $40 trillion, $50 trillion or maybe $60 trillion over 10 years, you're talking about doubling the federal budget. Then, if you add in the Green New Deal you're talking anywhere from $16 trillion (Senator Sanders) to $94 trillion (AOC) over 10 years and then you can see how the government triples in size. So, to claim that Senator Sanders' proposals do not control the means of production in American society is disingenuous. Of course, private industry will still exist, but Senator Sanders' agenda will pretty much become the single biggest part of the American economy.

Two things usually give them away as Marxists and not liberals. First, they have a tendency to embrace a form of big tent, come-one-come-all intersectionality, with people and ideals, and all the accompanying gripes and grievances that requires them to embrace, and stay faithful to the core tenant of leftism, which is the battle for the oppressed versus the oppressor. Endorsement of taxpayer-funded abortions or sex-change operations, decriminalizing drugs and theft, and open borders are examples of inflexible policy positions that Marxists expect their adherents to abide by. Another thing to look for is that everything they demand, or otherwise fight for, is in the name of the oppressive class. Once limited to a description of working-class laborers (i.e., employed people), the oppressive class is now every social, economic, and identity group that is not part of what the Leftists call the patriarchy.

You can't be a partial Marxist. Marxism is largely based on promises that will be delivered upon after full investment by its adherents and an eradication of the oppressive forces that are holding those goals back. Nearly all leftist thought (income redistribution, racial and environmental inequality, Godless secularism), nearly all leftist priorities (taxes, socialized medicine, social programs, a borderless world), and nearly all leftist behavior (social justice warriors, militant feminism, the Green New Deal, antifa, etc.) is rooted in one or more basic Marxist concepts that promises heaven on earth.

When you look at their views in one or all of the dimensions discussed herein, you see how progressives are seeking to advance Marxism. In short, progressives are in fact Marxists, who want to break down (if not at least seriously rework) the capitalist system in the name of income redistribution, break down the Christian norms in the name of humanism and social equality, break down our constitution and judicial system in the name of social justice, and break down our methods of commerce in the name of environmental justice.

So, for the purposes of this book, the terms leftist, progressive, social democrat, democratic socialist and Marxist are one and the same because, well, they are alike. The only remaining difference between liberalism and leftism/progressivism/Marxism is that liberals still place some value on truth and Judeo-Christian ideals. Think of JFK, who put God, honor, liberty and country ahead of his liberal platform. Progressives don't do that.

Chapter 2

THE ORIGINS OF SOCIALISM

AS MENTIONED EARLIER, KARL MARX DID NOT invent the idea of socialism. Up until Marx and his buddy Frederich Engel's seminal 1848 pamphlet, The Communist Manifesto, the concept of socialism had been debated theoretically in leftist circles for decades. But, he and Engels generally get credited with its origins because they crystalized a great deal of it in one infamous publication.

The unofficial father of socialism was a Frenchman named Henri de Saint-Simon (1760–1825), but others shaped the collectivist thought process prior to Marx, including Immanuel Kant (1720-1804), Georg Hegel (1770-1831) and Ludwig Feuerbach (1804-72). Marx and Engels, of course, came up with their more groundbreaking and comprehensive version of socialism, calling it "communism," in 1848. Later, during the 1850s and '60s, Marx developed a close-working relationship with a German contemporary named Ferdinand Lassalle, who is often associated with modern democratic socialism. Marx also relied on Lassalle for financial assistance.

Interestingly, Marx and Engels wanted to distinguish their new-and-improved vision of socialism from other prevalent collectivist concepts of the time, so they called it "communism." The biggest difference being the socialists of their day foresaw an inevitable, yet peaceful proletariat assumption of power, but a purpose and need for—rather than the eradication of—the bourgeoisie class, in this new power paradigm. Marx and Engels knew the powerful wouldn't voluntarily relinquish power, so The Communist Manifesto called for a violent takeover by the proletariat, if necessary, and another step to be taken afterward—a borderless and stateless egalitarian society, where there was no private industry, private property, or profit to be made.

They theorized that once the proletariat assumed control and people realized how peaceful and good an egalitarian society was, they would declare it a success and voluntarily step down as leaders. What people don't realize about communism is that Marx saw it as big government (the initial proletariat takeover stage) and later no government (the full-blown communist stage). This is impossibility, of course. To this date, no nation that has ever experimented with Marxism has gotten past the first stage, because once the great proletariat leader of the so-called oppressed is in place, they don't want to step down. Do you think Stalin, Hitler, Mussolini, Franco, Kim, Castro, or Mao would have ever voluntarily stepped down? So, to sum it up, the end goal of Marx's vision was a utopian society with no bourgeoisie, no crime, no religion, no corruption, and no war. The thinking being if everyone basically had the same exact things and the exact same rights and the exact same expectations and the exact same obligations, there would be no need for government, because everyone and everything in that egalitarian world operated fairly. Over the years, Marx added to it and refined it a bit, but for all intents and purposes, he is the name and face of socialism.

Since leftist thought is rooted in the principles that Marx and Engels drafted, it's really the same stuff; just different flavorings have been added. You can tell the difference between a tiger, lion, leopard, and jaguar by looking at them, but scientifically they are all really just big apex predators of the Panthera genus. Saint-Simon's brand of socialism, which called for all workers – both blue and white collar – to rise up against the rich, Marx's communism, Gentile's fascism, Leninism, and Democratic socialism have different spots on their fur, but deep down, they are all the same: big predatory cats of the Marxist genus. Leftists, socialists, communists, progressives, or however they want to describe themselves are, deep down, big cats. They aren't a collection of diverse animals in the zoo, with one being an ape, another a horse, and another an elephant.

Dickens and the Birth of the English Socialist Movement

As you would expect, Marx was greatly influenced by what he was seeing and reading about in Europe during the mid-1800s. This was during the early years of the Victorian era (1837–1901) when industrialization was changing not only England but countries across Europe, from rural agrarian societies to urban industrial centers of banking, commerce, and density. If you can imagine for a moment the London that Charles Dickens described in A Christmas Carol—overcrowding, poverty, and disease infestation, contrasted against the wealth being created by a growing industrial economy, you can see how Marx's writings, like those of Dickens, were designed to put a spotlight on the plight of the working class.

Marx, looking to advance his anti-Christian and anti-capitalist agenda, pounced on the bleak circumstances surrounding the underclass in Victorian London. He viewed the social condition as a direct result of the wealthy exploiting the working class. The only way, he thought, the working class could ever emancipate itself was through revolutionary change. He made the leap that not just 1840s London, but maybe all of history was the story of class struggle. In other words, every event in history can be viewed through the prism of an oppressed (person, class, race, etc.) group, fighting against their oppressors. This is obviously not true. History is the story of brave, bold, and heroic people of all races and all classes and all genders surviving natural disasters, famine, and neighboring tribes to create flourishing villages, communities, towns, states, and nations. Human history is the story of perseverance, commitment, collaboration, friendship, and teamwork—not envy and revenge. The Leftists, of course, would have you believe otherwise. So, to them, the world has never been more than some underdog fighting back, every single day in every single village, since the dawn of man.

WHERE DID MARX GET HIS IDEAS?

There's an old saying that goes: Birds of a feather flock together. Marx read Dickens's work and hung out with fellow, like-minded radicals, who tended to study and discuss the same materials, from the same sources, as part of an unofficial socialist society. Socialism wasn't something dreamed up by Marx, but he was committed to turning it from a theory into an actual social science. Unlike many intellectuals who influenced Marx and had teaching positions to attend to, he was the one with the time (he didn't work) and resources (Engels and Lassalle bankrolled him) to sort through all the socialist ideas and concepts from various sources and, thinking like a wannabe lawyer-philosopher might in an age where scientism and humanism were gaining influence, tried to assert that his leftist ideology was a science. Kant, Hegel, Hess, Bauer, and Saint-Simon were some of the many influences in young Marx's life.

NAMES TO KNOW: GEORG HEGEL

Georg Wilhelm Friedrich Hegel was a German philosopher, who was himself greatly influenced by fellow German philosopher Immanuel Kant (1724–1801). As a sidebar here, philosopher is a big word that means: someone who has too much time on their hands and a pen and paper nearby. Ironically, philosophers of the 18th and 19th centuries complained that man was spending too much time contemplating his purpose; yet that's all they ever did—contemplate man's purpose. Guys like Hegel reasoned that instead of man thinking what he was told to think about, from family, community, church, and so on, these sophists claimed man should instead think about what leftists had to say. Because, then, as now, leftists know best. Although they wrote thousands of pages of material, I can sum up Hegel, Hess, Feuerbach, Marx, Engels, and the whole lot in one sentence: "Stop listening to your priest, your king, your landlord, your father, your mother, or your boss, and start listening to me!"

As a seminary student, he developed a dislike for restrictions, which begs the obvious question of why would anyone join a seminary, if they didn't like strict rules, God, hierarchy, and patriarchy? He spent his downtime daydreaming about how cool the French Revolution was and the broad change it promised for the rest of Europe. My hunch is that Hegel's goal in life was to have everyone read his work, so he could bask in his own brilliance. But, success eluded him. For decades, he bounced around from one tutoring or teaching job to another, and finally, when he was in his 50s, while serving as the chair of the Philosophy Department at the University of Berlin, he found his calling as a popular lecturer to students who took copious notes of his theories on philosophy, religion, and history. The notes these students took were later published and read by academics, like Bauer, who then forwarded them on to people like Marx.

Hegel's theories are extremely esoteric, but he made two significant contributions to Marxism. The first, which really struck a chord with Marx, was that a thing could not exist without its opposite. In other words, you can't grasp the concept of up without also understanding the concept of down. Hegel studied the tensions that arose between conflicting interests one finds through the world—freedom versus authority, science versus religion, slave versus master, and so on and so forth. One could study these conflicts and contrasts by using the dialectic method of identifying the issue, negating it, and coming up with a solution.

This is how modern American Marxism works—find a problem (real or imagined), scream that the world is going to end as a result, and negate, discredit and/or criticize any source that could negatively impact the narrative and, thereby, gain sympathy for the cause, and finally coming up with a synthesis (aka a promise, however impractical or ridiculous) on how to fix it. The class struggles between workers and business owners, the rich and the poor, the aristocracy and the peasants were dialectic issues Marx strove to solve.

The second major contribution of Hegel is the idea that it is legitimate to conquer or destroy that which was not fully realized. Fully realized in the humanist worldview signifies societies that embrace materialism and godlessness and not fully realized indicates societies that, in the eyes of the Left, are intellectually disingenuous, illegitimate, or evil. This Hegelian view forms the basis of why leftist revolutions are justifiable and its view drives progressivism today. America is illegitimate, because belief in religion and, in particular, Christianity, American Exceptionalism, perpetuation of the patriarchy and devotion to capitalism are considered character failings, moral shortcomings and structural deficiencies, which Marxists need to shine a light on and destroy.

EARLY EUROPEAN SOCIALIST MOVEMENTS

Leftists claim that socialism can be traced back to the dawn of time and found in the teachings of Plato, Aristotle, and, for crying out loud, Jesus Christ. They suggest it's the way people have really wanted to live since the dawn of time but organized western religion (Christianity) and capitalist exploitation got in the way to create a semi-functional but unfair and dystopian world. In the early 1800s, after the French Revolution, several French leftists were actively influencing labor and socialist movements, and word began to spread throughout the Western hemisphere about socialism. The appeal in France centered on the abolition of private property and power taken from the aristocracy and church and delegated to the people. Saint-Simon, who greatly influenced Marx, is generally credited with socialism, as he was the first to recognize the urgency to satisfy the social, political, and economic needs of workers.

By the 1820s, groups in the U.K. and France began to self-identify as being part of a utopian socialist movement, where cooperative and collectivist ideas were advocated, but implementation proved elusive, perhaps because of the resiliency of their aristocracy (i.e., not falling like the French). Many German philosophers took keen interest in this revolutionary movement. How could it work in Germany like it did in France? The German aristocracy held out much longer. Emperor Wilhelm I (1797–1888) considered himself chosen "by the grace of God" and not the people, which I'm sure would have annoyed the heck out of people like Saint-Simon and Marx. A ruler coroneted by the patriarchy (bad!), validated by the hegemony (bad!), anointed by the Church (bad!), catered to by the merchant class (bad!), and blessed by God (bad!).

EVOLUTION OF GOVERNANCE

For most of human history, leadership of the tribe, nation, or empire was the purview of strongmen, military dictators, emperors, kings, and theocrats. Honor, courage and virtue were considered aspirational traits. For most of western history local and state leadership was defined by commitments to honor and respect for church dogma. Bravery, courage and, yes, even individual dominance, often prevailed over intelligence or pragmatic ideals. In the late 1700s, state governance took a sudden and dramatic turn, when intellectuals in the American colonies formed a civilian constitutional republic and named it the United States of America. The concept of a group of commoners, merchants and scholars, but none of royal blood and elected by a predominantly agrarian population to run a nation was fascinating, but still implausible in Europe. Commoners just didn't create states. It never happened except in the U.S. This concept of creating a republic ex nihilo, Latin for out of nothing, was unique in world history and extraordinary. I'm going to attribute its implementation to then prevailing belief that decentralized America Christianity was above aristocracy or theocracy – whereas in Europe the centralized church partnered with the aristocracy to rule–and the relative ease of private property ownership, entrepreneurial opportunity and gun ownership.

In the nineteenth century the honor culture model began to change to a dignity culture. In the U.S. this was driven by the respect for law and self-restraint. To gentlemen of that era not all conflicts needed to be settled with a duel. In the 1850s, 75 years after the American Revolution, there was still no nation like the U.S. In Marx's time, there were more emerging democratic structures, which took root in retaining a monarchist identity with traditional customs and gender roles. Leadership would be the king's role as he was still seen as honorable and dignified, with moral and ethical behavior the job of the church, and legislative decision-making a parliament's role. Marx, having issues with authority and power, felt it was impossible for the common laborer to ever gain effective representation in government, because he did not own land or control the means of production. Since workers outnumbered priests, business owners, and landowners, he envisioned a scenario where sheer numbers were the differentiator. And, he designed a more radical branch of political thought, which advocated state-based (worker) governance. The emergence of Marxism eventually changed Europe, and through the efforts of progressives, Marxism is seeking to change America, too.

THE COMMUNIST MANIFESTO

By the time Marx and Engels published The Communist Manifesto in 1848, the words socialism and communal or communism were fairly well known in Europe, but were loosely defined, and there wasn't much in the way of clear distinction between them. The term socialism tended to be favored by Protestants and atheists, who sought to solve social problems together as a society and, perhaps more importantly, wanted to distance themselves from the Roman Catholic Church's Right of Holy Communion (i.e., communism sounded like communion). Socialism sounded respectable and classy to the intellectuals, while the poor and working classes tended to favor the word communism. The Paris Commune was a workers' revolt that managed to rule Paris for two months in 1871, after a power vacuum was created at the end of the Franco-Prussian War. But, it wasn't until the Bolshevik Revolution in 1917 that the word communism came into use and became associated with an official government philosophy. However, these communists who made up the Bolshevik Revolution were proud socialists, and this is lost on people in the 21st century, who think communism and socialism are not closely related.

NAMES TO KNOW: KARL MARX

To say Karl Marx was intelligent and well-read is probably an understatement. To say he was a disturbed individual is probably also an understatement. Marx felt that only perverted societies in need of being destroyed had God as its foundation. Marx's apologists know that if his actual and true goal for a world-wide, violent brand of revolutionary anti-Christianity became the narrative on socialism, it would be discredited. (Anti-Christianity is by definition Satanism, so these two words will be used interchangeably herein.) The Left now, as then, goes to great lengths to keep a large and telling part of his personality hidden, as evidenced by the fact that Wikipedia, the modern-day Encyclopedia Britannica, makes no mention of his open and strong anti-Christian opinions and contempt for his fellow man.

When confronted with that inconvenient truth, leftists tend to downplay or deny his peculiar personality. Rather than admitting he was a Satanist, who wanted to drag humanity into hell with him, they describe him as an enlightened atheist. Rather than admit he wanted the eradication of Christianity from civilization, they describe him as a social scientist and humane savior of mankind, as well as a guiding voice to what would be later called humanistic psychology. Rather than admit his philosophies egged on violent anarchists like Sergey Nechayev, Mikhail Bakunin and Pierre-Joseph Proudhon, while he dreamed of sitting back and watching the world burn, he is described as some sort of social commentator and critic, who merely used shock and awe tactics, like Charles Dickens did, to draw much-needed attention to the daily ills seen in the industrial cities of early Victorian England.

The appeal of Marxism for many people, then and now, lies in the notion that it has the answer to social, cultural, and political issues outside of the dreaded patriarchy and hegemony the various Christian churches and Western governments upheld. Namely, I'm poor, because I'm oppressed. I'm politically disenfranchised, because I'm oppressed. My prospects are bleak, because I am oppressed. By neglecting any self-reflection and personal accountability and deflecting any and all shortcomings, failures and underachievement back onto the shoulders of the oppressors, rather than oneself, a person could be cleansed of responsibility. Akin to being absolved of sin. To the Left, Marx is portrayed as a good person, who came up with several wonderful strategies to liberate the poor, the marginalized, and the exploited. Marx was, in fact, a bad guy. There is no evidence he actually wanted an everlasting global brotherhood of peace-loving people, free of the shackles of state, religion, and capitalists. He and his fellow anarchist collaborators were architects of a very dark agenda that has seen tens of millions of people die in his name.

By way of background, Marx came from a family of rabbis and was raised in western Germany. His father Herschel was a lawyer who realized his career and social standing would increase if he distanced himself from his Jewish heritage so he baptized his entire family as Protestants, including Karl, when he was six. Marx was an ethnic Jew, who enjoyed a comfortable, upper-middle class childhood, and his father, now going by the name Heinrich, called him his favorite son. Young Marx took a stab at poetry and drafted a few pieces, praising Christ, but he found there was little public interest in his work. His poems just weren't that great. Something must have happened in his later teenage years that scarred him for life. Perhaps, it was getting picked on, because he was a Jew. Perhaps, it was the rejection of his writings, or maybe it was that he was an unlikable person. He began to hate people and religion.

At about age 18, he had abandoned his faith—much to the chagrin of his father, who felt his son had become a demon. According to many of his collaborators, associating with him was on his terms. He was an angry and frustrated young man, who got into fights and used the word destroy so often in his essays, it became his nickname in school. Mikhail Bakunin, one of the leading anarchist thinkers of the nineteenth century and one-time close friend of Marx, observed, "One has to worship Marx in order to be loved by him. One has to at least fear him in order to be tolerated by him. Marx is extremely proud, up to dirt and madness." Karl Destroy Marx. A man you must fear in order to be loved by him. How charming!

He called mankind "human trash" and had particular contempt for those who found peace and happiness in religion. In his manuscript titled, Critique of the Hegelian Philosophy of Law, which was drafted in 1843 and published in 1844 when Marx was 26, he wrote, "The abolition of religion as the illusory happiness of man is a requisite for their real happiness."

Most leftist intellectuals concluded that God didn't create man. Man created God. To be clear, Marx, at least in his early years, wasn't an atheist. Atheists believe God doesn't exist, but he held that God did exist. In fact, God was the evil one who needed to be destroyed—not the devil—and hell would be a great place for us to all end up going. He felt the church used God to do nothing more than perpetuate the status quo, the so-called patriarchy, which in his mind was to keep the rich, rich (and in power), and the poor, poor (and in submission). Marx sought solace in writings and philosophies that not only questioned religion but advocated for its eradication, even if it sealed his eternal fate, to which Marx wrote, "Thus heaven I have forfeited, I know it full well. My soul once true to God, is chosen for hell."

His fiction, fantasies, poetry, or whatever it was, had little marketable value. Being a Jew in Christian Germany probably didn't help his psyche. In addition, his publishing of revolutionary materials caught the eye of the authorities, and he was on the run by his mid-20s. From this point on, he committed himself to sociology and economics. He squandered all the money his father was providing him while at college, so he needed to change schools and their relationship soured. His father did not support his son's radical leanings or open anti-church convictions and held out hope that the demon that possessed his son would be exorcised out of him. However, by then, it was too late. The younger Marx developed an issue with parental authority and never reconciled with his father, who died when Marx was 20.

Marx had no vision to serve mankind, and the Left will never find any evidence that he did, because, well, he never did. On the surface, he wanted to be a respected philosopher and social scientist, but deep down, he was an obsessive and difficult person to work with. He desperately wanted credibility and power, but it was elusive until years later. Now, without his father's financial support, unable to sell his mediocre writings, and incapable of make enough by publishing underground anarchist pamphlets to fund his party lifestyle, he needed to find his purpose—and new patrons. By age 24, he found one in Friedrich Engels (1820-1895).

Marx met Engels in 1842, and by 1844 they were close friends. They fled Germany and later France, due to their radical endeavors, and settled in Brussels in 1845. Engels soon moved to England ahead of his friend, while Marx finally landed in London in 1850, where he lived the last 33 years of his life. Marx was unwelcomed in Germany, rarely went back, and died stateless. He was a fan of Dickens and the social novels he and others wrote in the 1830s and 1840s, which depicted the wretched lives of the urban poor and the lack of responsibility the wealthy took to solve the social problems they (the capitalists) were causing in the Victorian era. A Christmas Carol, for instance, focused a spotlight on the lack of attention the wealthy were paying to the plight of the urban poor.

THE MIDDLE CLASS AND THE SOCIALIST CAUSE

Charles Dickens (1812-70) did not write Oliver Twist (1838), A Christmas Carol (1843) or Hard Times (1854) for the poor's reading enjoyment. He wrote these to get the attention of the middle class. Dickens' father had spent time in debtor's prison and this played a role in his feelings about social status. He felt the rich would take no interest in his social commentary, while the poor were illiterate and living and dying in dire poverty every single day anyway. But, the middle class, in the minds of the early socialists, was thought to be the key to changing the political and economic status quo in England. The Reform Act of 1832 started the ball rolling, by shifting power in the House of Commons from countryside landowners and urban merchants to city residents. The concept of putting the power into the hands of the common people, at the expense of the wealthy, was a major shift and gave optimism to the socialist movement.

The early socialists felt that if conscientious middle-class citizens in large cities were elected to parliament, the Leftists needed to make sure these new politicians knew of the issues facing the poor. The thinking was that if social novelists, philosophers and sociologists like Marx could generate enough sympathy from the middle class, then finally society's ills could be addressed. This tactic explains why 175 years later, the Leftists in America always mentions the middle class in all their narratives. The rich don't care; the poor can't do anything about their lot, but the middle class, yes, the middle class! Their commitment (taxes and votes) will be the difference in how the world is changed.

Conservatives typically use the term Americans to refer to our fellow citizens, as in "my fellow Americans", without specific reference to any class, race, or geographic subculture, such as southerners, mid-westerners, or Texans. But listen carefully during a Democratic rally or political debate. The Left rarely uses the word Americans, because they don't necessarily want to appeal to all Americans (nor risk insulting residents of Ecuador, who the Left feels should also be called Americans). So, to them, every issue must be framed to appeal to a class of Americans perceived to be oppressed—whether it is race, gender, sexual orientation, blue collar labor, immigrants, and so on and so forth. Just like the Leftists' writing and babbling in Europe two centuries ago, the Leftists want to court the middle class's sympathy to permanently shape the political debate in their favor.

There is no evidence that Marx met Dickens, but according to Dickens' biographer, William Richard Hughes, Marx wrote to Engels about the Victorian novelists saying, "(they) have issued to the world more political and social truths than have been uttered by all the professional politicians, publicists and moralists put together."

NAMES TO KNOW: BRUNO BAUER

In 1835, at age 17, Marx enrolled at Bonn University to study law, but he spent too much time drinking and running up debt. His father, Heinrich, paid off his debt on the condition that he enroll in Berlin University, where the social scene was less distracting. While there, Marx came under the influence of an instructor named Bruno Bauer (1809-82), who introduced Marx to the writings of former Berlin University professor Georg Hegel, who had died just a few years earlier, as well as Ludwig Feuerbach. Bauer was so outspoken and radical that he was censured and later banned from teaching. He professed, among other things, that the New Testament was Greco-Roman fiction and forgery, and religion was oppressive, thus responsible for the miserable state of people.

When Heinrich Marx died in 1838, young Karl was cut off financially, yet he managed to finish his doctoral thesis at the University of Jena. Now looking for work, he asked Bauer for help in getting a teaching position, although to no avail. But, they kept in touch. Despite being unemployed himself, Bauer was still busy voicing controversial opinions. In 1843 he wrote "The Jewish Question", which prompted Marx to respond in 1844 with his controversial reply titled, "On the Jewish Question." Bauer kept in touch with Marx for years, but the key takeaways for Marx, Engels and the neo-Marxists that followed in the later part of the nineteenth century were that religious demands are incompatible with the rights of man and Jews wouldn't have political emancipation without abandoning religion and advocating for a secular state.

MARX'S VIEWS ON PEOPLE

Karl Marx was an equal opportunity hater. In Declan Hayes's 2007 book, God's Solution: Why Religion Not Science Answers Life's Deepest Questions, he notes how Marx felt there were good and bad races. "The bad races, the non-whites, were simply too unenlightened." He somehow sensed the U.S. of the 1850s was more progressive than Europe and yet was in favor of slavery, because it was the purest form of socialism. Without it, American industry would fail, and the economy and culture would regress back to farming-based patriarchal society from the 18th century. In 1848, Marx wrote that the Germans were "stupid," the Slavic people were "riffraff" and the Russians, Czechs and Croats were "retrograde races" and "ethnic trash." The Jews and Chinese were "peddlers" and "beating is the only means of resurrecting the Germans." Perhaps, most shocking and certainly something you'd probably never hear a leftist admit, Marx felt slavery was a perfect form of socialism, because it created a cradle-to-grave obligation for an oppressed class that the rich needed to bear. Part of the hypocrisy on the far left is their devotion to Marx, despite his hate-filled views.

NAMES TO KNOW: MOSES HESS

In Cologne, around the age of 20, Marx met a French-Jewish philosopher named Moses Hess (1812-75). Hess was the one who originally introduced Engels to Marx in 1842. Nobody today makes a living as a philosopher. There are lecturers at colleges, who teach philosophy. But, back in the day, there were people who vented and complained all day and somehow found a following. Philosophy was considered the pinnacle of intellectualism. It was a soft science but still a science. Men like Marx wanted to be known as philosophers and scientists, not anarchists. What was once called philosophy is now blogging. Hess, like Marx, had contempt for aristocracy and religion and was a firm believer in an emerging leftist idea called socialism. He was also a racist and an anti-Semite and anti-Christian, so it's not surprising they found each other and took a liking to what the other had to say.

Hess adored Marx. He found him more tenacious than himself and saw Marx as the demon who would "give the last kick to medieval religion."

Georg Jung, a friend and contemporary of then 25-year-old Marx said, "Marx will surely chase God from His heaven and will even sue him." Eradicating Christianity from civilization was Marx's primary goal, and Hess wanted Marx to take his anti-Christian passion and channel it into the still-evolving socialist theory. Socialism became the vehicle to convey the destructive radicalism of Hess, Marx, Bauer, Engels and the others to the masses.

Marx and Hess, while both Jews, certainly had no compassion for their ethnicity. Marx wrote the anti-Semitic book called On The Jewish Question in 1844, at age 26, and in it he blamed the state of the modern capitalist world on Judaism, which in his view, had money as its god. His 1856 article published in the New York Tribune blamed wars on Jewish capitalists who steal the treasures of mankind. Interestingly, it was not uncommon for Jews who adopted socialism to rail against Jews who retained their capitalistic or religious views. In fact, the Frankfort School, for example, was made up entirely of hard-left, humanist and anti-capitalist Jewish intellectuals more interested in political, religious and cultural emancipation than their faith. Ruth Fischer (1895–1961), a Jew who founded the Austrian Communist Party, at age 23 in 1918, and later served in the German Reichstag (the lower house of Parliament) during the 1920s said, "Squash the Jewish capitalists, hang them from the lamp posts; tread them under your feet."

MARX'S INTELLECTUAL CIRCUS

Besides Hess, Engels, Bauer, Proudhon, Lassalle and Bakunin, Marx took an interest in the unconventional. So, to that crew, without God around, everything is permissible. Marx sported a beard, as was common in his day, but he wore his hair long, which was unusual—except for the followers of apocalyptic English prophetess Joanna Southcott (1750–1814). Southcott was a housekeeper, who developed a surprisingly large following by claiming to hear voices from God. She later claimed they were from Satan, but nonetheless, she was quite a sensation. The timing of these sudden prophecies, which she began receiving at age 42, is suspicious, because they occurred during the French Revolution, when fear was paralyzing England, because radicals were beginning to talk of a similar revolution in England. People soon began believing everything they heard. Among many things she claimed was that a woman would be the next messiah and then later said she, herself, was God's wife and would give birth via immaculate conception at age 64 to a reincarnated biblical character named Shiloh.

Southcott never became pregnant, never had the baby, and died shortly thereafter. However, before dying, she also claimed that a mysterious box in her possession held the key to world peace, but it contained nothing more than an expired lottery ticket and some household junk. She has been described as being just about everything from an early feminist, a madwoman, a prophet, and a high priestess of the occult. Southcottian sects existed in England, Canada, and the U.S. as late as the 1970s, as they prepared for a day of judgment in 2004. Marx biographer Richard Wurmbrand was convinced that Marx, like other leftist intellectuals interested in the counterculture of the day and who took a shine to her fantasies of apocalypses and raptures, was a follower of Southcott.

A lot of other self-styled prophets and mystics took notice of Southcott's inexplicable popularity. After her death, a man named John Ward (1781–1837) emerged as the new face of the Southcottians. Among other things, Ward claimed to be both Jesus Christ and Satan (at the same time) and made a name for himself by railing against government, landowners, and the church. Does that sound familiar? Although they never met, Ward's mix of chutzpah, apocalyptic warnings, and anti-establishment got Marx's attention. Despite having been dead for decades, the Southcott followers never disappeared, and it's probably not a coincidence that, in time, the Southcottian cultists were embracing communism. Gee, I wonder how that happened.

So here you have Marx associating with an apocalyptic communist cult, while hanging out with his devil-worshipping buddies, which included Russian anarchist Mikhail Bakunin (1814–76) and Frenchman and socialist thinker Pierre-Joseph Proudhon (1809–65). What could possibly go wrong? The occult and Satan were symbolic elements for the socialists, the anarchists, the malcontents and the revolutionaries. They saw Satan as a rebel, a free thinker and emancipator. There should be no surprise then that the anarchist group antifa has Satan's trident as part of their logo. Proudhon, who also sported the Southcott hairdo and who Hess introduced to Marx, claimed Marx "worshiped Satan," which should be of no surprise. Proudhon was full of blasphemous statements about God. Another close friend of Marx's was a German poet named Heinrich Heine, who felt forgiveness was necessary, but not until one's enemies are dead. In an age long before the Internet, how did these creeps find one another?

By the 1850s, the entire leftist intellectual circus seemed to revolve around Marx. Men like Hess, Marx, Bakunin, Proudhon, and Heine weren't looking to help mankind. These were a group of weird anarchists and agitators with axes to grind, who wanted to be famous as revolutionaries or in philosophical circles like Hegel or scientific circles like Darwin. They wanted political, social, and economic studies and theories to be considered real sciences. They were a new breed of dangerous revolutionaries who sought a war on the patriarchy by using their pens to deceive and confuse people. They believed in God but denounced and hated Him, and their writings openly challenged the supremacy of God and, by association, the Christian-capitalist world order. So, with friends like this, who needs enemies?

Marx had such a knack for finding great friends, he must have also enjoyed a great family life too, right? No. Marx never reconciled with his broken-hearted father, Heinrich, who referred to Karl as "the demon," and he broke off contact with his mother. He never worked after leaving the publishing business at age 24 and mooched off an uncle he didn't like, as well as Engels and Ferdinand Lassalle for most of the rest of his life. Marx fathered at least seven children and was so broke that his family lived in an apartment with no furniture. He lost two children to suicide and three others to malnutrition, probably because he spent his money on alcohol, postage to send his writings to Germany and New York, and failed investments. He lost one son-in-law to suicide, and another one chickened out at the last moment.

Despite the modern left's insistence that he was a humanist, materialist, and atheist, he carried some sort of left-handed path status in the underworld where he lived, as his wife, who, by the way, left him three times, referred to her husband as "High Priest and Bishop of Souls." He was an alcoholic, who railed against capitalists of his day who kept proletariat mistresses, yet he had an affair with his housekeeper, proceeded to get her pregnant, and told his lackey, Engels, to take the fall for the sake of his relationship with his remaining children.

When his wife died, he didn't go to the funeral. And, when his mother died, he traveled to Germany, not for the funeral, but to check on any inheritance he might be able to pocket. When his supportive uncle died, Marx's only comment was related to any inheritance he might be entitled. He was a paid informant for Austrian authorities but was on the lam from the German ones. Marx lived illegally in England under various aliases such as "Mr. Williams" to avoid political enemies, debt collectors and deportation. And, finally, he was buried at the notorious Highgate Cemetery in London—to this day a mecca for wannabe vampires, vampire hunters, black magicians, ghost chasers, mystics, occultists, grave robbers, and other misfits. A nice guy, who ended up in an even nicer place, huh?

NAMES TO KNOW: FREDERICH ENGELS

Frederich Engels was Karl Marx's BFF. He was German and grew up in a family that owned textile factories in Germany and England. His wealth allowed Engels a lot of time to travel, write, edit Marx's works, and most importantly, finance Marx's lifestyle. Engels was a smart guy with a knack for writing and editing, but he lacked business sense. Despite his father owning the business, he was never promoted above an office clerk and eventually quit the family business to spend his father's fortune on Karl Marx. He was the epitome of the beta male, who was enamored with Marx and gained his own level of notoriety by being Number 2 in Marx's cult of personality. Just being associated with Marx made Engels famous in leftist circles. Deep down, he probably wanted to be the Leftist revolutionary but knew he didn't have the passion to drive the bus, so he was happy playing second fiddle to a buddy.

Spiritually, Engels grew up a devout Christian but was influenced by a German liberal philosopher and Berlin University professor named Bruno Bauer, who steered the former away from God around age 19. Bauer was friends with Engels and Marx for a while, until they had a disagreement over some technical matters of communism. But, they remained on the same page with their anti-Christian rants.

Engels was so impressionable that he bought into the idea of socialism after just one meeting with Moses Hess. After Marx and Engels laid out their vision of communism (and the hate and resentment that came with it), Hess came away impressed. Hess saw their work as a more marketable and overarching way to smash the status quo than an anti-Christianity slant. Hess felt it strove for the same thing—an abolition of all the false truths and morality brought about by religion. Again, these guys weren't out for the love, peace, and general goodwill of mankind. In Anti-Duhring, a book written in defense of communism, which had come under attack by fellow German and socialist theorist Eugen

Duhring, Engels wrote, "Universal love for men is an absurdity." Why love your fellow man when hate is so much more effective?

WHAT DID ENGELS CONTRIBUTE BESIDES DEVOTION TO MARX?

People sometimes ask for an example of how the writings of Marx and Engels impact our lives, because they find it hard to believe any aspects of Marxist labor theories actually exist in America today. I've done a lot of work in Riverside County, California. Riverside County covers more than 7,300 square miles and has a population of about 2.5 million people. Physically, it's the size of New Jersey and is home to more people than 15 states, plus the District of Columbia. And, with 22,000 employees, it has dozens of different departments and agencies that need to be meandered through by the housing and construction industry to obtain all final approvals to build roads, parks, office buildings, stores and homes.

Obtaining a building permit for a large project can be a years-long process in California. One of the frustrations is working with a County employee and then being told that person no longer works in the department you need clearance from, because they have been transferred and we'd have to deal with a new employee transferred from elsewhere, who assumed the old employee's place. The new employee lacks the background and experience to complete the necessary tasks at hand. The time it took just to get the previous employee up to speed has quite often already caused significant delays, and now there is a new employee and a new learning curve. Then a year or two later, that person departs to work in another section, and you'd have to again work with someone else, while they get up to speed.

What does this have to do with Marxism, other than the fact that these agency workers are part of a very employee-friendly public sector union?

Engels believed that, deep down, every worker has interchangeable talents, and by eliminating or discouraging specializations, you somehow enhance the talent of the workers while ending up with true equity in the workplace. He assumed it would be easy and fulfilling to be a tailor one year, an engineer the next, a janitor the following year, and maybe a banker the year after that. (And you wonder why his father wanted him out of the family business!)

His theory centered on the idea that if everyone had the opportunity to do whatever they wished, they'd never get bored, and there would no longer be any divisions of labor. By eliminating these divisions, certain social classes couldn't monopolize certain positions or careers any longer. In theory, let alone in practice, this doesn't make much sense. A guy pushing a broom on the factory floor may never be capable of becoming a supervisor on that same factory floor, so why even suggest it might be a good idea for the two of them to swap jobs?

In practice, this would be absolutely preposterous, because what if 10 million people decide to become bakers one year, and nobody wants to make shoes? In Engel's mind, the government has an obligation to create 10 million bakery jobs and an obligation to think ahead and tell people not to plan on buying new shoes next year. That, my friend, is the basis of what's called central planning!

Engel's theory defies common sense and didn't age well, as skills in the workplace have evolved. But, that didn't stop public sector unions from giving it a shot. Leftists will try to shout you down if you rightfully claim that no two people have identical skills, IQs, motivations, or ambitions. Some people are better with numbers and others with words, while others work well with people, and others are more withdrawn and prefer to work alone. Some people won't care for a government-mandated demotion. That's totally normal, but not to the hardliners. In Engel's bizarre egalitarian world of conformance, uniformity, and interchangeability, you can't have individualistic profit and career motivations, because it blows up the interchangeable employee model.

This hasn't stopped many large public agencies from trying it. Public employees are employed for the sole purpose of serving the public and most do a great job. By negotiating union contracts that allow public-sector employees to bounce around from one department to another does a disservice to the public, who relies on experience and specialized talent.

Chapter 3

WHAT IS MARXISM?

WHEN SOCIALISM WAS EVOLVING IN THE EARLY 1800s, and before Marx's ideas became widespread, it tended to focus initially on land ownership – as land was a huge part of the power structure–- and not long after through political reforms and the works of Charles Dickens and others the socialists began to focus on the living and working conditions of the poor. Concurrently, there was a political movement incorporating some of the liberal and scientific elements of the Age of Enlightenment that held promise for early socialists in the U.K and U.S. This was known as the Whig Party, and four of their candidates served as U.S. President—all between 1841 and 1853. These were William Henry Harrison, John Tyler, Zachary Taylor, and Millard Fillmore.

The Whigs were not socialists but were the first political party to take a page out of the Age of Enlightenment and put science and progress at the forefront of their agenda. Among other things, the Whigs believed (1) the legislative branch of government (the House of Commons in the U.K. and Congress in the U.S.) should have more power than the Executive Branch (the King in England and President in the U.S.), and (2) specific to the U.S., business and life in cities on the East Coast should be a priority and westward expansion in the 1800s was wrong.

The Whig's base was urban voters in the northeast, who wanted more attention placed on issues facing cities. (Does that sound familiar, 170 years later in 2020—the House of Representatives wanting more power than the President and the world revolving around voters in New York City?) Ultimately, the party fell apart in the U.S. in the late 1850s due to their inability to agree on whether they should support or oppose two big issues of the day: Catholic immigration from Europe and slavery.

Few, if any, progressives in America today know what Whiggism was about, but the concept of it would strike a chord with leftists because it holds that there is an inevitable progression toward a more liberal, enlightened, scientific and democratic society. The Whigs of Marx's day believed the world was getting smaller and would get better as time went on, once science and liberal thought reached every corner of the globe. Whigs, like the progressives of today, saw themselves as intellectuals and portrayed those who advanced their secular and scientific-based agenda as heroes and those who opposed it as villains.

As a sidebar, one of the shortcomings of having a Whiggish worldview is the blind acceptance that science of today, philosophies of today, and attitudes of today are better than yesterday. What this does is cause people to judge the past, in light of the present. This is why many people of today, particularly young leftists, judge past generations and our Founding Fathers so harshly. As an example, leftists of today might believe George Washington was a bad man, because he should have known that slavery was wrong, and since he kept his slaves rather than freeing them, he was worse than bad; he was evil. Junipero Serra and the Spanish missionaries of past centuries were trying to save souls by converting, forcefully if necessary, the Native Americans to Catholicism. That was their purpose. Saving souls was doing God's work on earth. Serra's legacy of the California missions and spreading Catholicism throughout California is truly remarkable. A leftist of today might counter that Serra was a bad man because he should have known he was oppressing people and forcing them to do something against their will, all for the benefit of a fairy tale.

I bring this up because Dickens, Marx and the enlightened and socially conscious intellectuals of the day had four cracks at having one of their own in charge of the U.S. government, yet historians have routinely identified the four Whigs as the lowest-ranked presidents ever. But the dream lives on in modern-day leftists, who hold the same fantasies as to where the world is heading as the Whigs of the 1840s. Progressives today believe that, despite the persistent resistance by conservatives in the flyover states, America is inevitably moving toward a more tolerant, godless, globalist, and scientifically-oriented, leftward agenda. So, stop fighting it, you deplorables! Even today, leftists (like the Whigs of 175 years ago) portray those who advanced their causes as heroes (President Obama) and those who oppose it (President Trump) as villains.

THE INTERNATIONAL WORKINGMEN'S ASSOCIATION

Marxism is collection of statist political theories that evolved from a theoretical philosophy on social class empowerment, into a failed state religion for every misguided country that ventured into it. It's a broad concept like a game played on a grassy pitch or a genus of large cats. Marxism as a politically active movement can probably be traced to 1864 and the founding of the International Workingmen's Association (IWA) in London. (Marxism as a cultural revolution and not just a worker's empowerment movement began evolving a few decades later.) The IWA was a collection of leftist activists, mostly anarchists and trade unions, with the goal of establishing socialist and labor parties and setting labor policies across the industrial world.

When Marx died, many of his followers were hopeful that it could somehow take root somewhere. Anarchists in the late 1800s were hopeful that Russia could be that place. Eventually, by 1985, 33% of the world was living under hardline Marxist rule in 17 countries. In the 100 years since 1919 40 nations have tried communism and today, there are only six that remain under Marxist control – China, Vietnam, Laos, North Korea, Venezuela and Cuba. Yet, 156 years after the IWA fired the first shots at world democracies, it manifests itself in a threatening brand of American leftism, mixing economic Marxism, cultural Marxism, and latter-day European democratic socialism.

Venezuela is the most commonly cited example of Marxist failure these days. It went from the richest South American country to one of the world's poorest in about 10 years. Marxist policies, especially economic ones simply don't work. FDR and his Keynesian New Deal–style mixed economy from the American 1930s is effectively the furthest leftward we've gone economically toward Marxism, although I can argue that we are close to blowing past this, if enough of the wrong types get elected.

President Trump has become the face of a broader conservative pushback to a larger role of the government in the economy. He is pushing back as hard as possible to minimize the mixed-economy concept and avoid what Senator Sanders and his ilk believes is an inevitable, possibly in our lifetimes, full transition from a Christian-based capitalist nation to a socialist one, where the government controls the majority of our economy. U.S. Government spending, as a percentage of GDP, averaged 37 percent from 1970 to 2016, with a low of 33 percent in 1973 to a high of 43 percent in President Obama's first year in office in 2009. In Europe, it's 50 percent or more, and if you leave controls of fiscal policy to Democrats, it will creep toward, and probably past, that figure. The larger the percentage of government, the more reliant on government certain Americans become.

Marxism needs other people's money to force its overreaching programs on society. Margaret Thatcher once said, "Socialism is great until you run out of other people's money." Senator Sanders and other leftists believe more government involvement in our lives, government having a bigger role in the economy, and government having even more regulatory authority over economic output, is a good thing, because it would bring about more fairness and accountability. Government growth is actually bad for the economy. Obviously, high taxes and more regulation stifle the economy and enable failed Marxist policies to take a bigger role in society. As the economy fails, the Leftists will try to jump-start a stagnant economy with a centralized planning model, Keynesian demand-side policies, such as those forced on us by FDR. The point is: If someone talks about a bigger role of government in our economy, this is a Marxist. No question.

PROGRESSIVISM AND CHRISTIANITY

For understandable reasons, leftists prefer to use softer terms, like atheist, humanist or secular rather than anti-Christian or satanic. For the sake of twenty-first century readers who may not understand the semantics here, being anti-Christian is by definition, in normal Western thought, satanic. You can be Buddhist, Muslim, Hindu or an atheist. There is nothing wrong there, as these are not satanic theologies. Being actively anti-Christian, like Marx and his buddies, is satanic, because to oppose God is to be against him. And, Satan is the one leading the fight against God.

On college campuses, anything goes, but the Left has always recognized that Satanism is outside the Overton Window in the context of open political discourse, so they tend to describe Marx in more palatable terms: atheist, humanist, materialist, intellectual, philosopher, and so on and so forth. Until Anton LaVey came along in the 1960s, Satanism was more of a literary movement in an underground secretive society, rather than a religion practiced in broad daylight. But, for the purpose of understanding what Marx was really up to, you need to wrap your mind around how much resentment intellectuals in Europe had for the church during Marx's day.

In Marx's time, increasingly radical left-wing political ideas had been spreading in Europe, beginning with the fallout from the French Revolution. Because the European monarchies needed the church to keep social order, and since church yielded so much economic, moral and political power, Satan was appealing to radicals, since he was interpreted as having rebelled against the tyranny, patriarchy, hegemony and everything else that was imposed by organized religion.

To the Leftists in the mid-19th century, including Marx, there really was a heaven and hell, and Satan was a real entity who stood for the struggle against tyranny, injustice, and oppression. He represented rebellion, revolution, liberty, individualism, and free thinking. Satan endorsed radical thought and sinful behavior. And, for decades, the Soviets openly praised Satan as a symbol of their revolution—freedom from oppression, freedom from moral judgment, equality for all, and so on and so forth. If you ever wondered why the Russians are so untrustworthy, even 30 years after the fall of communism in Europe, just consider that some cultural remnants of the Soviet days (God is bad, and Satan is good) are hard to shake.

The thought of Satan as a rebel, the patron saint of misfits and outcasts, and symbol for the struggle against tyranny and injustice appealed to Marx and other radicals of his era. These early socialists were actively seeking to undermine the hegemony of Christianity in Europe, and Satan represented the outrageous radicalism they sought. Marx believed the common man couldn't do much on his own, unless it was sanctioned by the church or a capitalist patron (a boss or landlord). The local parish church kept communities in line and served as the morality police, and the court system was controlled by the aristocracy. In Marx's time, there was no Church of Satan or internet to exchange or codify their anti-Christian ideals. But, the prevailing tenets they held were that morality was a construct of the weak, meant to control the strong; everything that stands in your way is a lie created by the weak, who can't or won't fight you; and as an animal and not a higher being, you should satisfy your basic instincts to gather resources and dominate others.

Marx's hang-up with Christianity, besides power and cultural hegemony, was that in the traditional Christian worldview, the inequality of outcomes is a result of personal choices. Suffering, poverty, and the like were not caused by society, nor were these society's problem to fix. They were the result of poor choices, meant to be handled first by you, then you and your family, and finally you, your family, and your church congregation. Suffering, as a result of life's choices, was common but thought of as a virtuous character-building opportunity. (Few today see suffering as tied to virtue or character building, but back in the day, this is how responsible Christians thought.) Contemplating God was how you were supposed to spend your day and securing a seat in heaven was more important than whether you died at age 50 or 90, or became rich or famous, or whatnot. Christians have always held that pain and hunger are consequences of behavior, and pain and hunger generally teach us to behave differently. Suffering wasn't desirable. Nobody wants to suffer or wish it upon another but suffering without losing faith was a chance to earn brownie points with God.

Young Karl Marx, probably because he could not accept that his life choices weren't working out and probably believing his financial woes were, of course, not his fault, chose the anti-Christian path of materialism. This theory held that suffering and poverty were the result of everyone but you, and the only way to rid yourself of suffering and poverty was to eliminate the spiritual and capitalistic aspects from your daily life. Marxists love this. Nothing is ever your fault, and you always look to the government for solutions.

Since Marx's day, the Left has eliminated accountability and maintained that they need to change the economic and political paradigm to give the poor what they need—health care, housing, criminal reform, opportunities, and so on and so forth. The Satanists' primary issues with Christianity were: (1) the idea that man was in God's image and thus above Earth and the animals; and (2) the matter of free will as the ability to restrain your animal desires and make conscious decisions. It's the soul, the ghost in the machine, the little voice that tells us what's right and wrong and what the outcomes of those choices would be. It's sold or abandoned when one accepts Satan in their life. Free will is what sets humans apart from animals.

Marxism is materialism, which says we are shaped by our environment and not moral choices, because there is no soul in play anymore. Be the alpha animal you were born to be, say the materialists. There is no free will, because you don't have a soul saying "No" or "Don't" or "Maybe that's not a good idea." The Left sees free will as an impediment that limits human potential, because guilt and responsibility come with it. Contrast this with Christians, who view free will as the one thing that gives us our greatest potential. To the Left, as everything is deterministic, there is no need for free will and therefore no need to take or assign moral responsibility or feel guilty about anything that espouses the cradle-to-grave mentality, where government will take care of it for you. Suffering and poverty were once moral shortcomings or lessons to be learned from but are now looked at as physical and biological phenomena, rather than spiritual and moral ones. In their view, tigers don't feel any remorse for killing a foe or their prey, because they do what tigers do. And, in Marxist orthodoxy, you shouldn't feel any remorse over your choices either.

GLOBALISM IN THE 1800S: SAME THEN AS TODAY

As mentioned previously, Karl Marx was influenced by many scholars and philosophers, including Emmanuel Kant and Georg Hegel. Kant was an influential German philosopher, who believed the key to a utopian world order, where perpetual peace prevailed, would require like-minded individual states that operated under a broad international governing organization. (The Soviet Union's annexation model operated under this theory.) Marxism cannot survive if there are enclaves where the dissenters (the capitalists, the religious, and the conservatives) could emigrate to and thereby live in capitalist exile. If you could sum up Kant's main contribution to Marxism, it's the idea of one-worldism—the idea that the world would be a nicer place to live if everyone was living under the same peace-loving ruler.

Hegel was another German philosopher, who made a case that crushing lesser, not fully-developed (in the progressive context of cultural and intellectual development) societies was permissible. It is therefore legitimate to conquer or destroy that which was not realized in the eyes of the Left. The American left believes the American experiment of a Christian-based constitutional republic founded on individual liberties and capitalism has been a failure. In their view, the American Founding Fathers were all white Christians, who apparently created an illegitimate society vested in social, economic, and environmental injustice. And, it was thus, not fully developed and therefore, illegitimate. Destroying America the Founding Fathers created is, therefore, permissible.

SOCIAL DEMOCRACY AND THE POLICY OF APPEASEMENT

Although Germany and France probably had more leftist radicals per capita than Belgium or England, London was a Mecca for European leftists like Marx and Engels, largely because they could live in safe exile, away from political turmoil on the European continent and the German and French authorities who disagreed with their ideas. (I find it ironic that Marx was against enclaves, where people of non-conforming views could live safely in exile, but that's exactly what he did.) In Europe, in the late 1800s and into the early 1900s, Marxist thought was mesmerizing to many but was seen as more a theory of certain unemployed intellectuals, with way too much time on their hands, like Marx, than a serious political movement. That was until the Bolshevik Revolution in 1917. Shortly afterward, fascism became a reality in Italy; then, it appeared in Germany and later Spain.

Socialism grew in western Europe (particularly in the U.K.) in the years between the two World Wars, not because of the appeal of Bolshevik or Gentile Marxism, but because of the sudden and real fear that if the underclass could overthrow the monarchy and parliament of Russia, perhaps the English or French underclass could do the same. Thus, began a policy of appeasement toward labor parties and their Marxist handlers across Western Europe. Germany took a different path—embracing the fascist brand of socialism as a reaction to the post–World War I implications imposed by capitalist U.S., UK, and France to the west and the more impractical and untrustworthy communist system favored by intellectuals in eastern Europe and adopted by Lenin for the U.S.S.R.

There are American leftists today who believe, as the British did in the 1920s, that the underclass needs to be fed a steady diet of food stamps, subsidized housing, and other perks, from cheap, if not free, Internet as a form of social insurance policy, analogous to bread and circuses as was the case in ancient Rome. Marxists capitalize on a fear held by white elites in urban America of being overthrown by the black and brown underclass in major American cities. Again, Marxism plays on emotions and fears. The theory Marxists employ goes like this: Wealthy whites— those less likely to own guns and perhaps more passive and more fearful of urban violence by the underclass—will be willing to pay more in taxes to fund programs that raise the underclass up and out of poverty as an insurance policy to preserve order in society. Bread and circuses have been replaced with 99-cent cans of beans, cheap (and increasingly more legal) drugs, and free Internet.

THE PROBLEM MARXISTS HAVE WITH RELIGION

Russian writer and philosopher, Fyodor Dostoyevsky, often gets credit for saying, "Without God everything is permissible", but whether it was him or Marx, it spoke to the moral nihilism that arose in Russia during the mid-1800s and was meant to explain that nothing is inherently right or wrong. Right and wrong is only in the eyes of the assigner. In the eyes of anarchists, assassinating the Czar would, therefore, be perfectly alright.

Christianity was a major cause in the development of the Western world, and the Puritan work ethic is a major cause of the success of capitalism in America. Frugality, honor, virtue, ethics, discipline, deferred gratification, and modesty, coupled with hard work, were the foundations. Hard work was a sign of grace, and heaven was only for those who worked hard. Catholics (through good works) and Protestants (through hard work) saw that individuals could serve themselves and the good of society, through the trading of marketable skills. It was understood that hard work was a virtue, and the more successful you were, the more virtuous you must be.

It cannot be overstated that for hundreds of years, Americans understood that life on Earth was temporary and full of hardships, wars, and illnesses. Facing these issues head on was a regular part of life and a great opportunity to earn a seat at the table in Heaven, where life was everlasting. This is a big reason why conservatives emphasize individual accountability for one's predicament in life.

Freedom is based on individual liberties, coupled with universal expectations of ethical and moral behavior it derives from Christian fundamentals, rather than any form of governance, as it rightly transcends bureaucracy, structure, and regulation. In theory, America could survive on guidance from the Bible. In fact, most communities in America did just that for hundreds of years, since the Pilgrims landed. For nearly all of American history, the Bible was the most important book in America. Almost everyone in every town and in every county had a Bible. For conservatives, it still is the most important book in America, but for the Left, it most certainly is no longer useful—it's dangerous!

The Left would love to eradicate religion permanently from American life. Asking Americans to voluntarily give up religion isn't going to happen. If the Left really believes Christianity is just a package of illusions, the opium of the people, they surely must know that it is a very strong aspect of our culture. You simply can't explain the American hegemony without mentioning Christianity. This annoys the Left, because Christianity and our constitution are the two things that are bulwarks, keeping the Leftist revolution under thumb. It's not unheard of for religions across the globe to adapt to evolving customs and norms. Christianity in America is not averse to progress or change, but the systematic abandoning of religion to achieve political goals is an unacceptable attack on America itself.

Progressives, like Marx, reject religion. To latter-day Marxists, Christianity is particularly problematic because many of our laws and customs derive from Christian values. Karl Marx had a major hang-up with authority, power, and, in particular, Protestantism and Roman Catholicism, because they served as a theological framework for Western governments, whether they be monarchy, parliamentarian, or democratic. Saul Alinsky, an activist from the 1960s, heaped praise on Lucifer as a rebel, who succeeded in breaking away from the oppressive establishment – heaven. As a matter of fact, Alinsky wished to go to hell after death as it would be, in his words, heaven for him. Lucifer, being the unofficial patron saint of outcasts and misfits, is the quintessential 1960s countercultural Marxist hero—an individual the man kept down but had the strength and willpower to liberate himself. Lucifer and Alinsky—the oppressed misfits—are a match made in hell.

The Bible and the Left (not classical liberalism here; I'm talking about modern leftism) are as opposed as any two worldviews can be. While there are people who are both liberal and religious, and probably a handful who are Christian and Marxist, those who claim to hold a Bible-based worldview are nearly always conservative. In a half-hearted effort to appeal to American Christians, progressives package their left-wing positions (unimpeded immigration or homeless rights, for example) and wrap them in a few verses from the Bible (helping the poor) to tug at heartstrings and garner sympathy. As for conservatives, if you are poor, homeless, addicted or whatever, you, your family, your neighbors, or your church have a duty to help lift you up—not the government.

The Roman Catholic Church has moved far to the Left over the past 50 years or so, but has not renounced capitalism. Leftists often try to point out that capitalism is in conflict with church teachings on aspects of equality, charity, fairness, and social justice. Indeed the church teaches the three theological virtues of faith, hope and charity but these can be best executed in the realm of capitalism where opportunity prevails and not collectivism where initiative and motivation go to die. In 1991, Pope John Paul II answered this question in his encyclical Centesimus Annus, or "the 100th year" in celebration of the 100th year of an encyclical titled Rerum Novarum, by Pope Leo XIII, in 1891. He wrote: "if by 'capitalism' is meant an economic system which recognizes the fundamental and positive role of business, the market, private property and the resulting responsibility for the means of production, as well as free human creativity in the economic sector, then the answer is certainly in the affirmative."

In Western civilization, distribution of alms for the poor was the job of the church or a charitable entity, obviously funded by parishioners and the community at large. But, along with the reception of charity, came obligations, sometimes unwanted obligations, but it was the price the homeless and destitute paid for a warm meal, some cash, or a bed. As an example, to get a meal, the destitute had to go to a church service or give up a vice—at least for an hour or two. At the turn of the 20th century, the progressives found it reasonable for the poor to trade faith for food. Today this isn't the case. They resented the moral judgment that was passed onto people who were generally viewed as living immoral life-styles. They despised the notion that ministers and community volunteers working in skid-row missions and not politicians or judges could decide what is virtuous and what isn't. (This helps explain why there is such a knee-jerk reaction to conservatives being appointed to state and federal courts.) On virtually every important matter in life, there is a conservative Bible-based view and a secular leftist view, and the Bible and Marxism will always be diametrically opposed.

For nearly 2,000 years, Western civilization held the traditional biblical view that people, regardless of their place of origin, regardless of their religion, and regardless of their socioeconomic status, were inherently bad. Left to their own devices, people would do selfish and terrible things. Catholic baptism didn't make people good. Accepting God and being born again in the Protestant manner didn't automatically make people good. The Christian view is that deep down, even if we are born with a soul—a ghost in the machine capable of moral guidance—people are naturally selfish, envious, lazy, and susceptible to temptation. Questionable behavior, dangerous behavior, bad behavior, and evil behavior, therefore, comes from our failed nature. As a result, moral guidance needs to be codified and taught to young people. The Left believes that human nature is not the source of evil. In their opinion, people aren't evil. Capitalism, patriarchy, poverty, religion, nationalism, racism, or some other external cause, endorsed or promulgated by the oppressor class, is the cause of all evil.

Another biblical position that has the Left and Right at odds is whether the Earth was created for the benefit of man (Christianity), or if man is a byproduct of evolution and intended to coexist with nature and, thereby, has a duty, as earth's smartest animal, to be the custodian of it (Marxism). I'm not suggesting that Christians can't or shouldn't care about nature, only that nature is in second position on this planet behind humanity and its resources serve man. Christian conservatives hold the position as stated in Genesis 1:26, that man has the dominion over all the earth and all the animals. The Left-wing view is that man is just another part of nature. If there is a God, it's Mother Nature. This is a big reason why there is so much angst among the Left about climate change/global warming. Humans are harming nature (i.e., ourselves, our animal brethren, and our God), and this is morally wrong. Conservatives hold the traditional Christian position, in that they see the earth and its resources as separate from man and a means for our use and enjoyment. Here's a news flash: Science is an observation, not a truth.

PETA does a great deal of admirable work on behalf of animals, but like any activist organization, they are prone to say and do some peculiar things that are actually harmful to their credibility. As an example, calling your dog a pet is offensive to them. Not offensive to PETA. Offensive to your dog. They are now asking mankind to refrain from something called speciesism, which is the commonly-held belief, by most of mankind, that all animal species are inferior to humans. This blather resonates with the Satanists, who believe humans are nothing more that intelligent predatory animals. Equality, even among the species.

The full verse of Genesis 1:26 (King James Version) reads as such, "And God said, Let us make man in our image, after our likeness: and let them have dominion over the fish of the sea, and over the fowl of the air, and over the cattle, and over all the earth, and over every creeping thing that creepeth upon the earth". This passage is meaningless to the godless, but the God-given dominion over Earth's resources is obviously a major problem for the Leftists and a good reason for environmentally obsessed leftists to discredit Christianity. To suggest that man has the divine right to use Earth's resources for himself is a non-starter for the Left and makes bridging the political divide on environmentalism and the purported causes of climate change (and solutions) difficult, if not impossible. Unless, of course, religion—and specifically the inconvenient language of Genesis 1:26—goes away.

Author, educator, and political commentator, Dennis Prager, does a great job of explaining the conflicts between biblical teachings that have been a major part of our cultural hegemony for 400 years and modern leftism. The attack on conventional Christian teachings can be traced to Enlightenment thinkers, even before Marx, and these attacks continue today. Christianity simply isn't going away anytime soon, and this infuriates the Left. Prager, and most Christian conservatives, hold a "God-based moral code" that stands for a reasonable standard for moral and ethical behavior, and it's clearly at odds with progressivism.

Among the things Marx resented is the biblical view that holds that man is created in the image of God, and therefore is formed with a soul—a conscience that's capable of telling us what's right and wrong. It's an immaterial spirit, helping to guide us and save us. Marx, like most people living in the 19th century, believed in God and that heaven and hell existed. He felt humans needed to reject God (not just ignore God) and actively rid themselves of their soul to achieve their personal greatness. Marx felt that with any luck, humans would fall into the pit of hell with him following behind, laughing all the way, but first there is work to be done. The modern left-wing view on man, his purpose, and his habitat is seen as atheistic, but it really is anti-Christian and closely mirrors the obsession Marxists have held for more than 150 years: man is purely a material being—a compilation of earthly elements and nothing more.

Although modern Christians recognize humans as being mammals, they still hold the prevailing belief of Genesis 1:26 that humans are above animals and are not on some Darwinist eat-or-be-eaten, survival-of-the-fittest crusade. The Bible teaches that we have a ghost in the machine—that soul, that conscience, that little voice— and therefore humans have free will. We can, therefore, choose to do good deeds or not. The orthodox Marxist view is that human beings have no free will, and, therefore, humans have no true self control. The modern Left sees everything we do as determined by needs, our environment, our impulses, and everything else in our genetic makeup. The Left maintains that it's our uncontrollable instincts, our families, our friends, our neighborhood, our police, and our schools, rather than free will, which explains both murders and kindness. This is obviously a major disconnect between how the Left and Right views behavior and accountability.

Prager writes about another important aspect of Christianity that made its way into the American value system relates to the traditional view that God made order out of chaos. Chaos requires thought, logic, organization, and compartmentalism. And, Christians believe that's exactly what God did, and we're glad he did. He separated the earth from the sky, the land from the sea, humans from animals, man from woman, and so on and so forth. Round pegs go into round holes, not square holes. One such example that has become a major topic these days relates to gender. In the Christian view, there is only male and female and there are no alternative genders. Race and ethnicity is also not discussed in the Bible. Male and female is thereby the only distinction in humans. Because of the cultural Marxist commitment to 71, and counting, different gender identities, the Left can't stand any aspect of our cultural or governance structure that is based on absolute biblical teachings, and they are outwardly trying to eliminate the single male-female gender binarism.

Another thing Prager emphasizes in the traditional Christian view that wisdom begins with acknowledging God. And, from wisdom, you get leadership, rules, guidance, and order. The beauty of Christianity is that it offers answers and provides moral guidance and structure, so that social order and proper behavioral norms don't need to be recreated village by village, town by town and society by society, if everyone accepts Christian wisdom. There would be consistency and uniformity on moral issues. The Catholic Church stuck with Latin as its official language until the 1960s, because of a desire for everyone across the world to hear everything consistently. For those who don't know the biblical readings in a Catholic church on any given Sunday are the same in Peru as they would be in Italy. The secular view is that God is unnecessary for those things, particularly wisdom. Furthermore, the Leftists strongly believe that God is actually destructive to wisdom. As Prager has said, wisdom in the Leftist worldview comes not from organized religion, your family, your minister, or your mentor, but instead from leftist intellectuals residing in the most secular of American institutions—universities.

Universities being the center of scientific study have held the key to advancing the Leftist ideology. The thought process being if science can be seen as the generator of facts, then these facts could become truths by which we live. This is a big reason why Marx wanting his theories accepted as a science is not seen as subjective or conditional like faith, because it's easier to tie truths to science than to faith. The disconnect here, between right and left, is that some facts and some truths are a matter of faith that science could never prove out and the Left will never accept. In their opinion, smart people do not rely on faith, they rely on truths. They ironically say smart people are open-minded, but ignore that it takes an incredibly open mind to believe what you cannot see or touch. Open-minded to the Left means believing what can only be seen or proved scientifically. That actually sounds limiting and closed-minded to me. Can something you cannot see or touch be a fact and a truth? Why not? Science is not incompatible with Christianity, but again, science is just an observation, and not necessarily a truth. For example, $1 + 1 = 2$ is a fact and a truth, but $2 = 1 + 1$ is a fact, although not the truth, as two can also equal five minus three. The message to take away here is that science does not necessarily mean truth.

REJECTION OF CONSERVATIVE VALUES

Marxists reject traditional American values, because they are rooted in conservative thoughts on work, religion, law and order, and family. The Left views conservative social and cultural policies as draconian, harsh, unnecessary, and vindictive and therefore repressive. Marxists recognize an opportunity here to indoctrinate more and more young people. They appeal to millennials by pointing out that traditional conservatives (i.e., Christian views and Republican views) reject homosexuality, godlessness, abandonment of family obligations, drug usage, hedonism, extramarital sex, and so on and so forth. As Christians often say, "With God, anything's possible." According to Dostoyevsky and Marx, "Without God, everything is permissible."

The biblical view is that the nuclear family is the basic unit of society—a married father and mother and their children. This is the biblical ideal, but certainly other family structures can thrive and create healthy communities. Marx wanted to dismantle the family unit, because it inhibited adult-working productivity and kept humans tied to landlords and church. If everyone was single and the state raised the few kids that were produced, our society would advance to the point of being "fully realized", as Hegel would suggest. Far from it, actually. Our society would regress into tribes of immature adults, acting out, like irresponsible teens.

THE MARXIST ASSAULT ON THE FAMILY

In Marx and Engel's, The Communist Manifesto, they call for the "abolition of the family." They believed the family, as the standard economic unit in any capitalist society, is where patriarchy and capitalism worked in tandem to produce a world of alienated workers (male and female), who were unwilling and unable to change the class paradigm, because they were simply instruments of capitalist production, limited by family roles and duties. Because men controlled their wives, daughters, and female siblings at home, they, meaning men and men alone, rather than the state, dictated state production. Marxists don't like this, and feminist theory largely grew out of the concept that women needed to break free from those traditional roles. And, if it required Marxism to make that a reality, they were for it.

Shortly after they took power in 1917, one of the first things, the communists did was to make divorce quick and easy. Whereas it used to take years for a woman to successfully petition for a divorce, the commies made it possible to have a full, unconditional divorce in less than a week. Soon divorces outnumbered weddings. Liberating women from their husbands to work in the factories brought about unintended consequences, most notably, the abandonment of children. Orphanages became overrun. Street crime and truancy increased. Abandoned husbands no longer had reason to come home from work, and alcoholism and prostitution skyrocketed. Churches that had previously provided a safe haven for the poor to get back on their feet were shut down as religion became outlawed.

MARXISM EMBRACES GODLESSNESS AND NIHILISM

Marxism embraces not just godlessness but Satanism, materialism, nihilism, and the like, because they remove spirituality, purpose, and reason from our lives. Marxists have spent the past 170 years redefining or eliminating theological truths that people took for granted, such as the idea that heaven existed and was a wonderful place to spend eternity. Karl Marx had a disturbing hang-up with authority, power, and the Christian world order. He loathed Christianity and the way it guided the moral structures in European nations, to the point where he became a Satanist, bent on eradicating Christianity from our lives.

Marx spent his life criticizing and complaining about everything and anything that endorsed the status quo. Although he was the champion of the workers of the world, he himself didn't work. He instead wrote fantasies and esoteric philosophical essays on psychology, sociology and world destruction, while living in safe exile in London, ironically in a stable, capitalist democracy. You want to talk about the ills of an idle class, according to Wurmbrand, he lived for decades by milking "six million francs" from his buddy Engels.

You'd have to wonder why intelligent men would rather plot the downfall of Western civilization, than channel their intellectual energies into banking, trade, commerce, or the performing arts, but never underestimate the twisted fantasies that unemployed daydreamers like Marx and Engels and anarchists like Bakunin can conjure up. Yes, some of Marx's contemporaries, like Darwin (1809–1882), were actual scientists, although their pretext wasn't a bona fide scientific pursuit, but instead the elimination of poverty or advancement of human rights and the destruction of a Christian capitalist system.

Men like Darwin were doing profound scientific work, and deep down, this is how Marx wanted to be remembered. Marx was excited over Darwin's landmark 1859 book, Origin of Species, calling himself an admirer of Darwin's work. Marx felt Darwin's work could help him tie the natural sciences with his social science – class struggle. Marx and Engels wanted to be seen as scientists too. And, they sought to advance a humanist and science-based (natural and social) worldview, rather than the much more prevalent spiritual-based worldview. (Interestingly, because Marx wrote in German and hung out with other German exiles and his occult congregation, while living illegally under the alias Mr. Williams, he was therefore relatively unknown around the

U.K. during his lifetime. So, it's believed Marx knew of Darwin but likely not vice versa.)

Marx embraced Satanism around age 18, while still living in Germany. (Satanism being, of course, the same as anti-Christianity.) He never disavowed it and was seen self-performing occult rituals when he was near death. Marx apologists deny this and try to claim he was just a humanist or atheist or a young rebel, who had issues with his father and Christian patriarchy, or that he went through an immature phase like all teens do. Ah, no. He absolutely was and seemed to have lived his life making everyone around him miserable. He was a disrespectful son, a manipulative friend, and a terrible husband and father. He was an angry and unfriendly man, who just wanted to watch the world burn.

Satanism holds that humans are not above animals, as Christianity teaches, but just another animal living in what they would term a Darwinist world—survival of the fittest. This world would be free of Christian morality and constraints, where we can be what we are: highly intelligent but still predatory animals that should live for today (not for your salvation), fulfill our instinctive needs, and kill or be killed. Satanism, on its own, would never be taken seriously by respected members of society, so Marx and his followers tried to convey a message that people's identity and purpose weren't determined by God, your family, and free will but instead through a mix of historical, scientific, and material conditions.

Marx certainly found an audience for his social and economic work that he didn't have for his poems and fiction. Until he came along, logic, reason, and human behavior were viewed through the prism of Christian values, morality, and purpose. A legacy of Marx is that logic and reason are no longer seen as gifts from God, but human constructs intended to enable and control society through the means of production. Before Marx, everyone understood that love, truth, and beauty flowed through

God, but the Marxist revolution sought to wash away any semblance of metaphysics. In his opinion, the elimination of God would lead to the new classless and egalitarian society, devoid of all those religious thoughts that prevent us from being the animal we deserve to be, as well as a society devoid of the opium of the people and all those pesky metaphysical illusions people blindly follow.

It would be hard to argue the Marxists haven't largely succeeded in taking God out of our daily lives. The Bible has lost its place as America's most important book. Fewer and fewer people are going to regular church services. Even fewer ponder their salvation. In the satanic worldview that Marx adopted, Christian morality is nothing more than rules, with no basis in nature and created by the weak to control the animal within us. Has anyone ever wondered why the Russians and Chinese are so inherently unethical? Has anyone ever wondered why Western investment in Russia is so risky or why getting truthful information out of China is so difficult? It's because religion and the morality it teaches—and held them up to be—was eradicated from their societies.

One last thought on science and Darwinism. Marxists are the ones who value science over spiritual beliefs: evolution over creation, facts over faith, and so on and so forth. But when it comes to certain convenient political touch points, such as gender identity, all of a sudden science is out the window. If Brian, living in California, wants to be a woman today, he is legally a woman, and tomorrow he can become a man again. It's magic! Science be damned, even though the Left professes to be "all about science." I suppose the identity of the oppressed class, on any given day, is somehow unsettled science?

Chapter 4

PRE-WORLD WAR I: EARLY PROGRESSIVISM AND NEO-MARXISM

SINCE THE 1890S, PROGRESSIVISM HAS PROMOTED activism on social causes and the redistribution of wealth. This unattainable objective demands an ever-growing, invasive, ponderous, and inefficient centralized government. Early Progressivism was seen as separate from socialism but is still part of a broader neo-Marxist movement that arose in the decades after Marx died.

Through the nineteenth century and into the twentieth century, many varieties of socialism emerged, based on Marx's concept. Some, like fascism and Stalinism, had a few refinements, but they are all similar at their core—like big cats—and collectively are called Marxism. At the turn of the twentieth century, Western Europe preferred the democratic socialist model, and in the 1910s central, southern, and eastern Europe adopted more workable versions of Marxism (fascism) or more orthodox versions (Leninism). Nonetheless, they are nothing more than refined versions of Marx's socialist vision.

In the U.S. the first seeds of Marxism were planted in 1872, when the International Workingmen's Association (IWA), a collection of left-wing anarchists that had Marx and Bakunin as its figureheads, moved its headquarters to New York City. Founded in London in 1864, the First International, as it was also known, soon split into two camps – the reds, who favored Marx's approach to systematic revolution involving authoritarian elites and factory laborers and the blacks, who favored Bakunin's violent anarchism by the poor. The IWA saw post-civil war New York City as a safe zone, far from disapproving governments in Europe and home to increasing numbers of European immigrants and newly emancipated black slaves, as well as a growing industrial economy.

Once in the U.S., they established a political party called the Workingmen's Party of the United States and later renamed it the Socialist Labor Party of America. Membership was small, and tended to communicate among each other and back to Europe in their native languages, which, in hindsight, helped limit the IWA's influence on pre-World War I politics. The rival Social Democratic Party of America was founded in 1898 and a year later, some members of the Socialist Labor Party joined with the Social Democratic Party to create the Socialist Party of America in 1901.

Progressivism was an outgrowth of Marxism's entry into America's political landscape around 1890, and the movement lasted for about 20 to 30 years. The basis of progressivism was a desire for more government oversight, regulation and control. In their view every aspect of modern urban life, from housing to transportation to factories to banking to politics, needed urgent reform and oversight. It was the first attempt to use government as a vehicle to re-shape American lives. Modern leftists will contend that progressives of that era were a bipartisan mix of Republicans and Democrats and the progressive's political party was separate from any of the socialist parties that arose at the time. My contention here is that progressivism, as a movement, was, nonetheless, rooted in Marxism. Because leftism has no base in America, the progressives' agenda centered on quality of life in northern American cities and consisted primarily of women's suffrage, workplace safety (including child labor laws), public education, and immigrant rights, rather than on economic or cultural deconstruction. Progressivism was a movement, but for a short period it was an actual political party that earned the nickname Bull Moose.

There were progressives on both sides of the political aisle, but the more vocal ones were moderate Republicans who took sides with two-time Republican President Teddy Roosevelt and split from President William Howard Taft's agenda. Taft was a Republican, who was considered a progressive, but he was an administrator and lacked the leadership skills and charisma of Roosevelt. Roosevelt, a former Republican, ran as a progressive in 1912 and secured 88 Electoral College votes but lost to two-term Democratic President Woodrow Wilson (also a progressive), who was instrumental in establishing the League of Nations after World War I. The Progressive Party ceased operations in 1916, but progressive activism continued turning towards the socialists.

NEO-MARXISM

After Marx died, dozens of sociologists, psychologists, philosophers, and other humanities types, fascinated with our boy Karl, had way too much time on their hands and began to fill in some of the holes they saw in his theories. But how and where? On college campuses and in newspapers of course! American factory workers were interested in pay and working conditions and not in the esoteric matters of political party creation. Intellectuals needed to carry the torch. Philosophy was never a big American thing. Most Americans were well versed in our Constitution and the Bible, but softer sciences like psychology and sociology were emerging sciences only the intelligentsia cared about. The only way a secular view of society could be advanced, outside the disapproving purview of the church, was under the auspices of knowledge and enlightenment across college campuses and through the news media.

There has always been a sort of pervasive anti-Christian prejudice, which existed in intellectual circles and not just Europe, but the U.S. as well. Religion simply didn't fit in with the materialist, humanistic, and scientific agenda in the intellectual circles, which resided almost exclusively at universities. Universities began to consider these softer majors as sciences, which gave intellectuals a forum and a level of credibility they did not previously enjoy.

Because most of the Leftist agitators and anarchists were European, it shouldn't be a surprise that a German named Victor Berger (1860-1929) and Frenchman named Eugene Debs (1855-1926) became the initial faces of American Marxism. Berger founded the Social Democracy of America organization in 1897 and later the Socialist Party of America in 1901. He was the first Socialist elected to Congress and, like leftists today, had a reputation for intolerance of dissenting opinions. Debs emigrated from France to Indiana as a youngster and was an activist and socialist after being introduced to it by Berger. He ran unsuccessfully for president five times, including once while in prison. Debs promised that, "no man will work to make a profit for another." He is held in such high regard among American Marxists that Senator Sanders put a portrait of Debs up at City Hall in Burlington, Vermont while he was mayor there.

Russian immigrant Meyer London (1871-1926), who lived in the predominantly Jewish Lower East Side of Manhattan, had the most political success and served in congress for three terms over six years, before and after World War I. London's father was an anarchist himself and published the radical Yiddish weekly newspaper, Morgenstern, out of a small print shop on the Lower East Side. Socialism in the 1880s and 90s wasn't as well known in the Russian Empire as it was in Western Europe, but it was growing. Russian Jews, like London, were decidedly anti-Czarist and took a shine to the Marxist message they were hearing on the street. London had gotten into trouble in Russia and had to escape the country and he successfully immigrated to the U.S. at age 20 in 1891. Almost immediately, he associated with German leftists, who also lived on the Lower East Side. Collectively, they found Marxism's promise of an egalitarian and inclusive society with labor unions being the driver of social change very appealing. Yiddish newspapers and other correspondence became a trusted medium to convey Marxist news to and from Eastern Europe and New York.

The New School for Social Research in New York (now known as "The New School") was deliberately set up in 1919, to provide a platform for leftist professors who may have been unwelcome at more conservative schools. They saw benefit in bridging orthodox Marxism with other, more human-based, intellectual concepts that explained the human condition, such as psychoanalysis, existentialism, and sociology. They were big on analytics too. The most famous neo-Marxists were probably Antonio Gramsci, the father of cultural hegemony, and Herbert Marcuse, the father of cultural Marxism. The primary idea put forth by the neo-Marxists is that revolutions do not need to be bloody. Revolutions can be won, using cultural re-appropriation.

WHAT IS CULTURAL HEGEMONY?

Merriam-Webster defines "hegemony" as the, (1) "preponderant influence or authority over others," and (2), "the social, cultural, ideological, or economic influence exerted by a dominant group." Modern leftists define hegemony today as "too many people who have the wrong views," but hold that thought as we go back to the early 20th century, when one man caught onto something.

After the French Revolution, more and more Europeans began to criticize Christianity, and one of the ideas these materialists put forth was a notion that man could be perfected ("fully realized" as Hegel would put it), if his environment was sufficiently changed. The belief among a growing number of European intellectuals was that one could achieve greatness if he or she stopped wasting time contemplating God. Soon, a consensus was reached on the Left that spirituality was nothing more than a construct of the bourgeois; however, a few Marxists felt there had to be something they were forgetting. Marxism was not taking hold; therefore, something more than an economic revolution that took root once religion was abolished was needed.

NAMES TO KNOW: ANTONIO GRAMSCI

An Italian and dedicated Marxist named Antonio Gramsci (1891–1937) began to think that power wasn't always wrapped up solely in what he felt were the repressive elements of society—military, political, and/or theocratic bodies. Power, he proposed, is actually the result of a confluence of civil forces that collaborate together to keep the status quo. Gramsci was the first to propose that the media, the arts, the church, the courts, and the schools, as well as the bourgeois in the banking and manufacturing industries—the common sense of society—stood to benefit from an unspoken hegemony that strove to keep society, and specifically the working class, in line. The rationale being that everything should work when everyone is on the same page. Yes, the legislature and military were the faces of the nation, but the real drivers in any society were its influential citizens and institutions that gave the nation, and by extension the military and legislature, their credibility. These forces work together to create and sustain a superstructure that is difficult, but perhaps not impossible, for anarchists to penetrate.

Marx and his followers believed religion was nothing more than an illusion, created by capitalists, to maintain and keep political and economic power. Gramsci broke from conventional Marxist thought, when he realized Marxism wasn't just an economic system designed to replace a capitalist one and dependent upon the rejection of Christianity, but more importantly it could be a cultural movement. He felt advanced societies didn't need violence to keep order and that people, not the military officers, not the captains of industry, not the theocracy, but just plain, ordinary people outnumbered the elites and could change the balance of power, if the revolutionaries could change the hegemony.

Gramsci believed that the working class could change the hegemony by promoting a counter-hegemony that challenged the normalization of capitalist exploitation and establishing a new culture and new set of values. The whole concept of the counterculture of the 1960s was not an American idea birthed out of the Civil Rights movement or opposition to the Vietnam War. The groundwork for the counterculture movement was laid out by Gramsci decades prior. It was developed by a Marxist, decades earlier, in an Italian prison.

Gramsci was convinced that if enough people could put forth a compelling counternarrative, one popular enough and with enough moral credibility that people across the entire economic spectrum could buy into it, then maybe, just maybe, you could undermine the existing hegemonic narrative. The moral leadership aspect was the key to uniting enough of a cross-section of society to create a credible counternarrative to help change the existing cultural hegemony. If all goes well, all sectors of society are engaged and eventually converted into accepting a new narrative, one that supports the Leftists' vision. Gramsci was popular with Italian communists and with the Frankfurt School but certainly not with fascists who felt the existing Italian cultural hegemony (Catholicism, etc.) needed to remain intact.

Gramsci died when he was just 46 and yet was a major influence on countless leftists, including the founders of the Frankfurt School, a Marxist think tank consisting of about 20 neo-Marxists that was established in 1923. The members of the Frankfurt School found comfortable refuge working out of the halls of what was then the University of Frankfurt—before it was renamed the Goethe University Frankfurt—and operating as the "Institute for Social Research," because it allowed them the ability to easily cross reference other scientific disciplines. Their focus was on the softer sciences, rather than the physical sciences or technical trades. Interestingly when they moved to New York City in the 1930's they changed the name of their journal from the bureaucratic and technical sounding Magazine of Social Research to the friendlier and more academic sounding Studies in Philosophy and Social Sciences.

The Frankfurt School agreed with Gramsci that changing the narrative first through nonviolent manners, rather than rushing to dismantle the economic and political condition, was the key to the Marxist revolution. These academic types, consisting mostly of sociologists and psychologists, focused their writings and research, not on the typical Marxist matters of economics and the plight of the working class, but instead on how to manufacture bloodless cultural revolutions to achieve the same socialist aim. The Frankfurt School was the body that brought us "political correctness," the counterculture phenomenon of the 1960s, and identity politics.

GRAMSCI IN PRACTICE TODAY

Here's an example of where Antonio Gramsci's theory on how to change cultural hegemony is actively being used: There is an anti-Israel movement known as Boycott, Divest, and Sanctions (BDS). Similar BDS methods were used against South Africa for decades, and eventually, after enough persistent international effort over many years, Apartheid was eliminated. BDS in the Israel-Palestinian conflict serves the same purpose. BDS is not an official organization but more of a tactic used by a loose collection of leftists and Palestinian sympathizers, who are seeking the destabilization and delegitimization of Israel. The near-term goal being the delivery of economic pain to every Israeli household, with the end goal being the establishment of an official Palestinian state or, better yet, the eradication of the Jewish state.

Since a civil war started by the Palestinians would be hopeless, the BDS movement contends that a civil war would need to be bloodless. Gramsci's theory would hold that the Israelis have constructed a strong and sustainable cultural hegemony through various pro-Israel institutions and players that aren't going away without significant and persistent resistance. In order to deconstruct it, the revolutionaries would need to challenge the existing narrative by bringing economic pain and shame from human groups, influential citizens, multinational corporations, and foreign governments. Because the cultural hegemony in Israel is so strong, it has been difficult for the BDS activists to make much penetration, but that's not stopping them from trying.

Back here in the U.S., the contrast between secular, intellectual and open borders versus religious, conservative and nationalism with borders largely explains why so many Jews in America have ethical issues with President Trump's wall, the U.S. Embassy's relocation to Jerusalem, Benjamin Netanyahu and the Likud's position on the Palestinian situation, and therefore they join with other liberals in supporting the BDS movement.

Thankfully, members of the U.S. House of Representatives, on both sides of the aisle, saw the truth behind the BDS agenda and resisted the pressure from the Left wingers in the House by voting 398–17 in July of 2019 to condemn the BDS movement. Of course, three of the four Squad members (AOC, Rashida Tlaib, and Ilhan Omar) predictably voted against the resolution, but the takeaway was an overwhelming bipartisan win against what is nothing more than an attack on the cultural hegemony of Israel.

Chapter 5

BETWEEN THE WARS: FASCISM, COMMUNISM AND THE INTELLIGENTSIA

BENITO MUSSOLINI WAS A PHILANDERER AND HAD no interest in religion, but instead of the abolition of religion, the fascists saw Catholicism as the part of the Italian national identity. So, they installed a single-party, highly regulated, and authoritarian government, where Italians as a whole were told they were the oppressed people. At the time, a portion of northern Italy, as well as adjacent countries with large Italian populations, like Slovenia and Croatia, were part of the Austro-Hungarian Empire, while Corsica, Nice and Savoy were controlled by the French. The fascists wanted Italian speakers to be ruled by Italians.

Hitler, intrigued by Italian fascism and the eugenics of American progressives, ran with the same concept, except for the religion part. Labor unions and management were given no choice but to set aside their disputes and work together for the common good of the country. All work, all production, all investment, everything associated with industry and commerce needed to be for the good of the nation, with big government (i.e., thuggish storm troopers were there to make sure nobody steps out of line). This is what several 2020 Democratic presidential candidates are seeking—Wall Street and big business are teaming up with labor unions (or else) to put what they characterize as the common good first—with stringent and unforgiving government oversight, of course.

THE GENESIS OF COMMUNISM IN THE U.S.

The period right before World War I brought the formation of the Fasci Rivoluzionari d'Azione Internazionalista in Italy in 1914, the Bolshevik Revolution in 1917, the establishment of the opposition Communist Party of China in 1921 and the formation of Communist Party USA (CPUSA) in 1919, after a split from the Socialist Party of America following the Bolshevik Revolution. The First Red Scare came about in reaction to the Bolsheviks and was fueled by the rise in patriotism American's felt following World War I. Laws such as the Espionage Act in 1917, the Sedition Act of 1918, and the Immigration Act of 1918 were enacted to address fears of labor unrest, anarchy, or a Bolshevik-like revolution and to get rid of violent immigrant anarchists like Luigi Galleani. Galleani followed Karl Marx's buddy Mikhael Bakunin's strategy of insurrection known as collectivist anarchy. His group was tied to domestic terrorism, including the deadly Wall Street Bombing of 1920 that killed 38 people.

It's impossible to tell the story of Marxism in America without discussing the influence Jewish immigrants had on the Leftist movement. Although people from many different nations and ethnic heritages advanced Marxist theories Marxism really resonated with Jewish intellectuals. Even Victor Berger, the first Socialist elected to Congress, was Jewish. In full disclosure, I'm Catholic but ethnically I'm one-eighth Jewish and the Ashkenazi in me is keenly aware of the historic marginalization and persecution of Jews in Western civilization. Refusing to acknowledge how widespread, influential and important Marx's message was to them would be disingenuous.

I'm familiar with both liberal and conservative viewpoints taken by those in the Jewish-American community. As you can imagine, I'm very sympathetic to the conservative Jewish positions and I'm outnumbered, but that's OK. AIPAC's message resonates with me, while J Street's doesn't. Ellis Island was processing nearly 900,000 immigrants per year by 1914 and leftist sympathizers from throughout Europe were all over New York. Fear was spreading that these immigrants, who were mostly poor and with many familiar with Marxism, might overrun the U.S. At its height CPUSA was linked to nine daily newspapers and opportunity knocked as immigrants familiar with Marx flooded New York City. From 1922 to 1988, they had an influential leftist mouthpiece in the daily Yiddish paper, Morgen Freiheit.

Jewish immigrants to America in the late 19th century and early 20th century considered Yiddish (also known as Judaeo-German) their native language. And, it was common but not required for Yiddish to be spoken in the home and among friends and business associates. The native language, be it German, French or English, was spoken to gentiles. Marx spoke Yiddish. My Jewish great grandmother spoke Yiddish. The researchers from the Frankfurt School, who ended up at Columbia, spoke Yiddish. Approximately 11 to 13 million European Jews spoke Yiddish before the Holocaust, as it was once a major European language, and widely spoken throughout Germany, Ukraine and Belarus.

For many Jews, Yiddish was seen as secular and international as compared to Hebrew, which was seen as a holy language, reserved for ritual and prayer. Many secular Jewish intellectuals associated Hebrew with religion, conservatism and Jewish nationalism, known as Zionism. In the early days of the Soviet Union, Yiddish was seen as a worker's language and Hebrew was seen as being part of the bourgeoisie. In the 1920s, Yiddish was promoted as the language of the Jewish proletariat in the Soviet Union. The official Belarusian state emblem had the motto, Workers of the world, unite, written in Yiddish.

The Jewish population in New York City rose from about 80,000 in 1880 to 1.5 million in 1920, making them an influential economic, cultural and political voice. CPUSA, founded in 1919, and with initial membership more than 50,000, recognized the Jewish influence over the textile industry in New York City and saw a marketing and outreach opportunity in a sizable audience of Yiddish-speaking immigrants settling in Manhattan. In the days long before television and the Internet, newspapers, along with books, were a major conduit for information to be exchanged. But books took forever to get printed, while dailies were, well, published daily. By affiliating with a Yiddish newspaper, CPUSA could align sympathetic Yiddish voices in Manhattan with those on the front lines of Marxism in Eastern Europe. So, with 45% of America's Jewish population living in New York City at the time, with New York having a tradition of high union penetration in the nation's then largest workforce, and with Columbia, NYU and the New School offering leftist intellectual opportunities in a safe haven far from the Nazi's, it's no coincidence that the Frankfurt School's diaspora landed in Manhattan. Like it or not, New York City became the headquarters for communism in America.

Impossible you say. New York City was and is the capitalist center of the world! True, but by the 1930s New York had become the center of leftist thought. Their numbers weren't great, but their influence was great. The following is from a 2017 article Maurice Isserman wrote for the New York Times titled, "When New York City was the Capital of American Communism":

"Immigrants, many of them of Eastern European Jewish background, provided the main social base for the party in New York City in the 1920s: As late as 1931, four-fifths of the Communists living in the city were foreign-born.

In cities around the country, from Detroit to Seattle to Los Angeles, Communists began to play a visible and effective role in politics, both local and national. But nowhere were they as successful as in New York.

By 1938, the party counted 38,000 members in New York State, about half its national membership, and most of those lived in New York City. Communists were increasingly native-born (although many were the children of immigrants). Party-organized mass meetings in the old Madison Square Garden were packed with as many as 20,000 participants; the annual May Day parades drew tens of thousands, too."

I find it humorous that the author used the word "was" in the title, as if New York City ever ceased being the capital of American Marxism.

After WWII, attitudes about communism changed, for the better, in America. The Communist Control Act of 1954 banned the Communist Party and it went underground. In 1989, the U.S.S.R. cut off funding and although it no longer exists as a political party, it still exists as a "political organization," with a membership between 5,000 and 10,000 and operates its headquarters out of an office in, of all places, Manhattan.

It's disingenuous to talk about Marxism in America and not touch on how and why it resonates with many in our minority communities. It's economics for some and for others it's more of an intellectual pursuit: ethics, secularism and political and cultural emancipation. Most Jews were happy being American citizens and American capitalists. Most found liberalism, rather than communism, to be the right fit for them and others are conservative. For some Jews, who leaned further to the Left in the first half of the 20th century, it was was about more than just ethics and intellectual aspirations, but also personal safety. Communism and not the Democratic or Republican Parties resonated most with their ethical views on equality, fairness, the free movement of goods and services and the eradication of racism and religious discrimination they saw in America. Jews, with their history of being persecuted, were certainly never in favor of state religion, borders or walls and many found Marx's promise of a secular and borderless world free of oppression appealing. Absent a Marxist third party to vote for, many minority groups, and not just those in the Jewish community, historically joined with liberals in voting for Democratic candidates.

NAMES TO KNOW: JOHN DEWEY

In 1933, and not to be outdone by the Leftist German immigrants, who were infiltrating Columbia University, an American leftist named John Dewey and 33 of his lefty buddies signed onto what was known as the Humanist Manifesto (1933). It was later labeled the Humanist Manifest I, after it was expanded into a Volume II (1973) and later a third volume called Humanism and its Aspirations (2003). Per Columbia's website, Dewey taught there from 1905 to 1930 and, "His arrival made Columbia's philosophy department arguably the strongest in the country." An atheist, Dewey was a fan of Kant, as well as a traveler, who wrote glowingly of communist Russia. He disagreed with some of Marx's philosophies and Stalin's methods but was a committed leftist. The groundwork he laid at Columbia paved the way for the arrival of the Leftists from the Frankfurt School.

I find it humorously ironic that Dewey was an atheist, and yet a federal judge ruled in 1987 that secular humanism was a religion on the grounds that it was essentially a dogma, being taught in some public schools. A man who didn't want religion created one.

FASCISM AND WHY IT'S ON THE FAR LEFT

To understand why people wrongly believe fascism is on the far right, you need to understand the disinformation campaign the Leftists in the west used, going back to the early 1930s, to confuse the public about fascism. I am not a fan of fascism, and I can hear it now, "Only a racist fascist or a leftist activist on the lookout for it would know so much about fascism!" I'm neither. Consequently a big challenge I've had is convincing left-leaning people that they have been deceived by their own kind about what fascism really is. Fascism is a left-wing thing not a right-wing thing, and two key aspects need to be jointly explained. First, the far left qualities that make it a left-wing thing, and secondly, how and why the intelligentsia has successfully deceived Americans into believing its somehow close to American paleoconservatism when in reality it is much closer to the world Senator Sanders and his antifa storm troopers desire.

George Watson, in his 1998 book, The Lost Literature of Socialism, speaks to the political misunderstandings the west always had about fascism. Watson wrote, "By the outbreak of civil war in Spain, in 1936, sides had been taken, and by then most western intellectuals were certain that Stalin was left, and Hitler was right. That sudden shift of view has not been explained, and perhaps cannot be explained, except on grounds of argumentative convenience. Single binary oppositions—cops-and-robbers or cowboys-and-Indians—are always satisfying." Correctly explaining Spain as a Left versus Left civil war in 1936 wouldn't advance any political goals of leftist intellectuals who saw Soviet socialism as good and Italian, Spanish and German socialism as bad. They therefore desperately needed Americans and Brits to see the Spanish Civil War not as good socialism versus bad socialism, but words Americans could relate to: Freedom versus tyranny and good versus evil. They largely succeeded. By the time World War II rolled around most Americans recoiled at the thought of fascism despite having no clue that it was socialist, only that it was tyrannical and evil.

HOW AMERICANS WERE FOOLED

The Nazi phrase Blut und Boden, or blood and soil, was intended as a slogan to reinforce the purpose and need for a specific, defined place, rather than the concept of a borderless, and internationalized nomadism that communists advocated. What the Germans were saying is, our brand of socialism (fascism) is better than your brand (Soviet communism) and we're going to implement our brand in a homeland, rather than globally. Leftist intellectuals were really caught off guard by fascism, particularly in Germany. Bella Dodd, writing in School of Darkness, said of her visit to the University of Berlin in 1930, "In Germany, I frequently discussed the rising tide of conflict, but on one thing professors and students alike were agreed — that fascism could never come to Germany. It was possible in Italy, they said, because of the lack of general education — but, such a thing could not happen in Germany. Two institutions would prevent this: The great German universities and the German Civil Service." Boy, were they wrong!

For many of them, until the late 1920s and early 30s, there was nothing that suggested fascism would sweep Europe as the preferred socialist governance model. Leninist Communism was much more preferable to the intelligentsia. Fascism represented socialism with borders, whereas the Leninist version of Marxism represented socialism without borders. Fascism was dropping anchor and rejoicing in a nation's history, while Leninism was forgetting history and thinking only of progress. Fascism was socialism within the historical hegemony and patriarchy. Leninism was socialism under a new order. Fascism resonated with members of society, who were defined and bound by cultural norms and customs and were happy with walls and barriers. Leninism resonated with the academic and secular types, who were terrified of homogeneous and exclusive enclaves. Fascism was industry making profit in the name of the nation. Leninism was about the dismantlement of capitalism. Fascism was about all the people – the Italians for example – being oppressed and having enough. Leninism was about certain people – the proletariat–being oppressed and having enough.

Perhaps worst of all, especially for Jewish intellectuals, the hijacking of socialism by the fascists in Germany presented a life and death problem: There was no need for, let alone a role for, Jews in this unnerving brand of socialism. The persecution of Jews, but also Roma and other marginalized groups allowed the American Left to cast what was happening not as a cultural, religious or ideological matter in Eastern Europe but as a worldwide humanitarian crisis driven by inequality, discrimination and hate that demanded the attention of American Christians. Why? Because American military might was the only thing that could eradicate fascism. But there was a problem. Many American Christians were not willing to die in a war to save marginalized ethnic, religious and cultural groups or the communists. Something more was needed: An appeal to America's ego. Fascism was dumbed down for Americans and redefined by intellectuals as a uniquely evil and authoritarian dictatorship bent on world domination. Americans were rightfully appalled at the human rights abuses, but more importantly WE dominate the world - militarily, ethically, spiritualy and culturally - not those cocky Germans.

Communism's very survival depended upon fascism's defeat. The Soviets were desperate to counter the Nazi's and they turned to leftist allies in America for help. Through relentless propaganda from Communist Party USA, and sympathy from Hollywood, the media and academia, Americans were deceived into believing Brand A of socialism was different from and better than Brand B of socialism and Americans began to see communism favorably. FDR, although initially supporting the fascist movement in the early 1930s as a better brand of socialism worth looking into, switched sides, as WWII approached, after strong political support in 1936 and 1940 from certain leftist groups, who feared fascism was hijacking the socialist cause.

89

This propaganda was done through a method known as gaslighting. Gaslighting is often associated with manipulative behavior seen in abusive relationships, but the term is commonly used today to explain relentless political propaganda by one group seeking to influence another. In general, political gaslighting is a form of psychological manipulation where a group covertly sows seeds of doubt in a targeted audience. A single individual is usually not effective in gaslighting a large group because hearing something once from one person is not the same as hearing it constantly from multiple sources. It requires coordination and relentlessness by likeminded ideologues who attempt to permanently convert points of view by making a target group question their memory the judgment or their understanding of something. The goal is to wear them out over time and indoctrinate them so convincingly that it makes disagreement impossible. My contention is that the American Marxists gaslighted the American public so convincingly about fascism in the 1930's that unwinding that lie is extremely difficult.

NAMES TO KNOW: BELLA DODD

Bella Dodd (1904-69) was an Italian immigrant who earned a master's degree from Columbia and a Law Degree from NYU. The youngest of 10 children and growing up in poverty, she saw communists as the only political party that cared about people. As a teacher, lawyer and union activist, she was one of the most influential CPUSA voices of the 1930s and 40s in America. An agnostic, she travelled to Rome in 1930, after getting her JD and found Italian fascism, with its obsession about public order, train schedules and sanitation and their little regard for poverty, appalling. Dodd was expelled from CPUSA in 1949, converted to Catholicism in 1952 and became a vocal anti-communist. In 1953, she testified before the U.S. Senate about widespread communist party infiltration of labor unions and before the U.S. House's Un-American Activities Committee.

In 1954, Dodd wrote an alarming tell-all book titled, School of Darkness. It was a biography and exposé on what CPUSA was up to in the 1930s to secure support for the communist's anti-fascist agenda. It started in 1932, with Washington's recognition of the U.S.S.R., which gave credibility to leftist movements on college campuses and in labor unions. Basically, CPUSA went on a full-blown misinformation campaign, to ensure American support for the Soviets over the Nazi's. CPUSA hoped to one day be a viable third party and it didn't want American's equating one socialist concept with another, so they decided to deliberately confuse the situation. She and others believed that the Soviets and Americans were going to enter 100 years of peace and prosperity, but those darn Italians and Germans got in the way. Along came those rotten fascists, who threatened to end the communist dream and replace it with a different socialist vision. That was a terrifying and very real possibility, so the Soviets and CPUSA hatched a plan: convince Americans to be repulsed at the mere mention of fascism, even if they didn't know what it actually was.

The following excerpt, from School of Darkness, explains the most successful political lie ever brought upon Americans, which is: the fooling of Americans into thinking fascism is right-wing and somehow a polar opposite alternative to leftism, when it's really a left-wing movement.

Dodd wrote, "Since 1932, the Communist Party had publicized itself as the leading opponent of fascism. It had used the emotional appeal of anti-fascism to bring many people to the acceptance of communism, by posing communism and fascism as alternatives. Its propaganda machine ground out an endless stream of words, pictures, and cartoons. It played on intellectual, humanitarian, racial, and religious sensibilities, until it succeeded to an amazing degree in conditioning America to recoil at the word fascist, even when people did not know its meaning."

Consider this analogy when explaining this to young people. You have a zoo with a tiger, lion, elephant and donkey, and the tiger and lion don't get along. The lion comes up to the elephant and donkey and says, ignore that I sort of look and behave like the tiger. I'm a friendly horse and you need to beware of that monstrous tiger over there. He's bad. The elephant and donkey, unaware of the old limerick, The Two Cats from Kilkenny, which suggests that each cat thinks there is one cat too many—and being too dumb to let them fight to their mutual deaths, so there wouldn't be any – nod their heads and say, yeah, I'll take your word for it. The lion, who now identifies as a horse, then says to the elephant and donkey, let's fight him together. Me from the east and you from the west. Together, we will put an end to Panthera predators and have 100 years of peace.

This is the America that the American Marxists want, one that blindly accepts disinformation as truth. I can't resist repeating Dodd's words: recoil at the word fascist, even when people did not know its meaning.

When Mussolini and Hitler rose to power, the socialists in the U.K. and America took notice. Harold Nicolson, a Democratic Socialist and member of the House of Commons, concluded that fascism was militarized socialism. As mentioned above, Communist Party USA, in wanting to side with Stalin and not Hitler, of course, began to portray fascism as being right-wing. Socialists, unfamiliar with Gentile, had no explanation for fascism. They reasoned that it couldn't be socialism. It was, but they desperately didn't want it to be. At first, it was intriguing. FDR loved the idea of socialism, within the existing patriarchy and hegemony, and the thought of labor and private industry being 100% in line with government goals. Then, all of a sudden, it was threatening, because the communists said so? If I had a time machine, I'd tell our government that we should have fought both of them.

To FDR, it looked like the Italians were onto something. Gentile had, in fact, created what he called the most workable form of socialism, so FDR reasoned that, maybe the American left could learn a thing or two. Rexford Tugwell (1891–1979) was an American economist, leftist, and advisor to FDR, who studied, among other places, under Columbia's noted liberal theorist John Dewey. He was all in on FDR's New Deal programs and took a trip to Italy to see what Mussolini's and Gentile's brand of socialism was all about. He came back impressed and claimed, "Fascism is the cleanest, neatest, most efficient piece of social machinery I've ever seen. It makes me envious." Mussolini expressed great pleasure in the validation Tugwell bestowed on fascism in his report back to FDR and even proclaimed, "FDR is one of us! He's a Fascist."

What's odd, given fascism's socialist roots and the mutual admiration society that was FDR and Mussolini, is that if you watch enough CNN or MSNBC, you'd be convinced that fascism exists on the right side of the political compass. The idiocy of this is the denial on the part of the Left that conservatism is about small government, coupled with individual liberty and the antithesis of big government authoritarianism that is fascism. The further to the right you go with a political ideology, the larger the personal liberties are, and the smaller the government is, to the point where the extreme edge of the right (the "far right" as the leftists explain them) is actually an ungoverned society, where families and church congregations become the economic and political units. On a political compass, the far right is not the domain of a large and highly militarized authoritarian regime. This is the domain of the far left, and the best contemporary example is the Kim regime in North Korea.

Fascism, like its cousin Leninism and its father socialism, is on the left side of the political spectrum, and there are minimal differences between the three. Each is Marxist, and each is about extensive government control. They differ slightly in their national and global focus and tactics, but they all seek the same thing: control. Theoretically, the neo-reactionaries would rather entertain a monarch than a president, if forced to make a choice. But, truth be told, the far right does not want control by any dictator or any government. Perhaps leadership by a king but not authoritarian control. Why can't the Left understand this? I think a lot of them do but saying so deviates from the misinformation in the Leftist narrative.

If you want to have your mind blown away for a moment, ponder this thought: The outrage mob known as antifa, the self-described anti-fascists, are actually fascists who are fighting to portray the antithesis of fascists (the libertarians, conservatives, paleoconservatives, etc.) as the actual fascists and themselves as not, while at the same time doing battles in the streets with the neo-Nazis (fascists), who may not even know that Nazism is leftism. In other words, you have leftists (antifa) who don't even know they are fascists, fighting other leftists (the neo-Nazis), and each side (both the antifa and neo-Nazis) wrongly thinks is on the political right.

NAMES TO KNOW: GIOVANNI GENTILE—THE PHILOSOPHER OF FASCISM

The Left doesn't seem to know their history, either. The philosopher of fascism was an Italian named Giovanni Gentile (1875–1944). Gentile was an influential Italian writer, teacher, and philosopher of his time and was named the Minister of Public Education at the beginning of Benito Mussolini's regime (1922–43). He was a "neo-Hegelian" who rejected individualism and believed all meaning flowed through the state. Gentile was a committed socialist and Hegelist, who was influenced by Marx; however, he felt Marxism, due to its position on the worker-manager dialectic, wasn't the best way to set up governing systems. He felt there needed to be sort of a yin and yang public and private balance to serve the state, and Marx's goal of state ownership of everything wasn't going to work as Marx envisioned it.

94

When Gentile began writing in his mid-20s, Marx had already been dead for nearly 20 years. By that time, different philosophers had picked and chosen the aspects of Marxism most appealing to them, but nobody knew how to make it work. Marx thought the great European war he predicted (World War I) would be the impetus for wholesale change across Europe, but it wasn't. Workers rallied around and fought for their particular flag.

Gentile was against the liberal individualism he saw in America, because it allowed for the ideological composition of congress to change too easily. As an example, in 1888, Republicans held the House, then, over a four-year period from 1890 to 1894, the Democrats went from holding a huge majority, with 238 seats in the U.S. House of Representatives, to holding a startlingly few 93 seats. In 1910, after 16 years of increases, the Democrats finally regained the majority by picking up 58 seats. But, by 1914 the Republicans had recaptured the House again by picking up 62 seats. A socialist, Victor Berger (S-WI), was elected to the House in 1910, then voted out in 1912 and another was voted in during the 1914 mid-terms and voted out by 1918. These monumental ideological swings did not go unnoticed. To certain Marxists in Europe, like Gentile, the advancement of society required tenure and continuity and they understood that a single-party system was the only way to prevent political turnover every two or four years, like they saw in America.

Gentile saw the failure of the parliamentary democracy in Europe as driven by plutocracy and ignoring the interrelationships that exist between the individual, corporations, society and government. Working within the framework of socialism, he proposed that individual and corporate interests were to be incorporated into the stato etico or ethical state. The thinking being that public and private interests are an interdependent yin and yang and collectively, they constitute the state.

95

Most Americans don't know who Gentile was, but he was a devoted Marxist who wanted to come up with a more practical way to implement Marxism. See, up until 1917, Marxism was, for more than 60 years, mostly just a theory leftist intellectuals in Europe debated. Sure, there were a handful of labor parties here and there, but nobody knew how to implement and sustain it. That was until the Bolsheviks came along. The Russians implemented Marxism as Lenin interpreted it, but Gentile felt Marxism, without better implementation mechanisms and sustainability safeguards, would fail, sooner or later. Basically, he thought there needed to be a different and more practical approach, and he came up with an idea.

Gentile strongly advocated a version of socialism that had a public commitment to the greater good and a private commitment to the nation. The yin and yang, where a highly taxed and highly regulated private side could make money, and maybe a lot of money, but could only serve state purposes. Everyone, every business, no matter what you did or worked on, needed to be on the same page, working on behalf of the glory of the nation. Small business, large industry, banking, commerce, all of it, serves the public.

Gentile spent several years advocating for his brand of Marxism, until he found a charismatic champion for it: fellow Italian, Benito Mussolini. Gentile called his brand of Marxism "fascism," and it was adopted by Mussolini, who formed the Fasci d'azione rivoluzionaria in Italy in 1914 and took power in the early '20s, and later by Hitler in Germany and Franco in Spain. According to D'Souza, Gentile saw fascism as socialism with a nationalist twist. I like to call it socialism with borders. Up until that point, socialist theory was never linked to patriotism. It was, "workers of the world unite," not, "patriotic Italian speakers unite." Socialism was always thought of as a movement, for and about angry workers, demanding change. But what if it was happy workers and happy factory owners, who wanted to hold hands and change to a socialist society? Workers and industry working in unison for the public good. Impossible? It happened in Italy, Germany, and Spain. If anyone says Mussolini or Hitler are "right wing," they are misinformed, which is what Communist Party USA wanted. Hitler was an open and dedicated socialist, who was all in on Gentile's concept. Mussolini thought Gentile was brilliant and named him the Minister of Public Education.

Gentile saw promise in bringing Marxism to Italy, but it needed to be refined, and he needed a charismatic champion to fight for him. Like all socialists, even to this day, they view any and all brands of Marxism as democratic. He believed there was a right type of democracy and a wrong type, and the right type would have to be appealing and popular enough to have a voluntary and complete submission to the state by the populous. The wrong type is "liberal democracy," practiced in countries like the United States. ("Liberal" in this context, meaning classical or Western democracies, with institutions, laws, and systems, centered on liberty and personal rights, not liberal as in progressive or leftist.)

As noted earlier, Gentile found the style of democracy in America as being too easy to change. He did not see the composition of Congress, from liberal to conservative and back again, as a balance of power but a disruption. And, he saw the American system as too selfish and too individualistic. The proper type of democracy, the right type of democracy, according to Gentile, was "true democracy." This is where individuals— through their consent, resignation, and submission on Election Day— permanently would subordinate themselves to the state. This is what AOC wants: consent by the oppressed classes on Election Day to be the servants of the state. There would no longer be opposing political parties, because the individual has abandoned the right to that choice to the state and for consistency and efficiency sake, the state wants and needs a single, unified, unopposed ruling party. (Can you say "California"?)

Gentile wanted to create a new form of socialist community that, in the words of Dinesh D'Souza, felt like a family, as in "we're all in this together." Everybody in the family shares the same last name and the same political party, right? The government would be the parents, and the citizens would be the children. Through the government, the people will, because they are loving family members, all take care of one another. Hitler's Germany used this approach: we are all the same, and if you look and believe differently, you are obviously not a part of the German family and are not welcome. Conservatives became wary when Democratic politicians used phrases like "we're all in this together," "government is here for us," or "government exists to provide for us." We're all in the same boat, because we are all part of the same family. Those are out of Gentile's playbook for a unified fascist nation.

Gentile thought fascism was not only socialism in its purest form, but socialism in its most workable form. Whereas Marx sought to mobilize people on the basis of class, fascism mobilized people on their national identity, as well as their class. In other words, fascists are socialists with a national, rather than labor or economic, identity. The Left finds this hard to believe, because it flies in the face of their narrative. To the Left, national identity sounds like something only conservative white Americans would want, what the Left calls "white nationalism." Therefore, by definition, conservatives are racist until they repent or prove otherwise. Since Hitler was an evil fascist, full of anti-Semitism and hatred for outcasts and other minorities, fascism needs to be forever, even if wrongly, linked to white conservatives, to advance the bizarre narrative that conservatism is, at its core, fascism.

In the fascist mind, but not conservative mind, the state tells everyone how to think and how to act. In fascism, there is no such thing as opposition parties nor dissenting opinions, and all private action should be oriented to serve society. With fascism, there is no distinction between private and public interests. In their system, the administrative arm of society is the state (rather than the family, church, and local community government in the conservative mind-set) and to submit to their Marxist utopian society is to submit to the state.

Gentile's philosophy parallels the modern American left. His theories resonate with progressives, who champion the idea of a single political party ideocracy (hello California and most major American cities) and a centralized state, where unacceptable thoughts and ideas (conservatism) are suppressed. Senator Warren's language on corporate reform and purpose is, perhaps, most similar to Gentile's view on what industry needs to do. In her view, business needs to be kept in line, and it exists to serve all workers and the common good—or else!

Gentile's writings are deep and complex, but when boiled down to the essentials, fascism is pretty simple to understand. It's socialism plus nationalism. The modern left's vision of national identity is just that—identity. The Left's identity is to live in a colorless, genderless, uber-tolerant, conformist, borderless, and egalitarian society, free from the oppressive patriarchy. It is socialism with a unique American twist—a globalist American twist that sees the final transition of our society from what was an honor culture then a virtue culture and finally to a victimhood culture.

Hitler chose cultural and ethnic solidarity, rather than class solidarity, as the identified oppressed class the Germans needed to unify around. He envisioned his Nazi comrades uniting to create a more functional socialist society, in a struggle of proletarian Germany against capitalist England—and later, capitalist America—and against those misguided communists in Moscow. Jews, by virtue of being the merchant class, not of German blood and widely thought of in Germany as being dangerously sympathetic to communism, paid a severe price.

NAMES TO KNOW: BENITO MUSSOLINI

Mussolini was a charismatic magazine journalist, turned politician, who was quite fond of Marx, calling him "the greatest of all theorists of socialism." He was a humanist and socialist who studied the works of Kant, Marx, Engels and Bakunin. Both he and Gentile felt orthodox Marxism was outdated and needed tweaked to be implemented and sustainable. They felt the Italian Socialist Party lacked courage and vision, so they reasoned that, rather than the proletariat leading the revolution, they saw the revolutionary leadership as being reserved for charismatic types from any class, who could motivate the people. He was a popular and important member of the Italian Socialist Party but fell out of favor with his fellow leftists when he advocated Italy's entry into World War I. To him, the socialists did not seem to care about Italians. They only seemed to care about the labor movement. Why couldn't they care about both? Mussolini was driven by a desire to unify Italy and recapture portions of northern Italy that were part of the Austro-Hungarian Empire. He also felt parts of Slovenia and Croatia, as well as portions of France, should be annexed into Italy.

Mussolini was the champion who turned Gentile's words into action, as they implemented the National Fascist Party that ruled Italy between World War I and World War II. His slogan was "all is in the state, and nothing human exists or has value outside the state." Socialism is Marxist and so is fascism. Mussolini and Gentile thought they had a winning combination, and they did for more than 20 years. Hitler was a proclaimed socialist, and his National Socialist Party adopted most aspects of Gentile's philosophy. Obviously, Mussolini's and Hitler's regimes failed, and Gentile faded into obscurity, but his brand of socialism didn't.

Names to know: Francisco Franco

Francisco Franco (1892-1975), was a wealthy Spaniard with a reputation for bravery and attention to detail. He rose through the army ranks and by age 33 he was the youngest general in Europe. About 60,000 to 100,000 Italians and Germans fought with Franco in a rebellion against a left-wing government, in what is known as the Spanish Civil War (1936–39). The war wasn't left versus right; it was left (communist) versus left (fascist). The Spanish Republic—leftists and anarchists with the backing of the U.S.S.R.—fought and lost a patriotic rebellion by nationalists supported by Italy and Germany. The Leftists in power portrayed their struggle as freedom versus tyranny, while Franco's fascists portrayed their struggle as Christian civilization versus the reds. Needing additional political support to keep the communists from recapturing any strength, Franco, who was a leftist himself, formed an alliance with right-wing groups who were also opposed to the communists. The age old enemy of my enemy idea. The Leftists relied on students, labor unions, and intellectuals for support. Spanish fascists relied on Catholics, the middle class, and land owners for support. They prevailed, and Franco stayed in power for decades. Not many Americans know about the Spanish Civil War, even though it is considered by many historians as the first conflict of the Second World War. The relevance for today is in recognizing that the same groups who supported the republic's leftist regime—students, labor unions, and intellectuals—are the same groups we're seeing today in the progressive base.

As D'Souza says, leftists can't openly acknowledge what fascism really is, because to do so would undermine their false narrative, which is the permanent association of fascism with the American far right. Progressives know that acknowledging this lie would be political suicide, so they shout over anyone who may question this. Their goal, of course, is to portray socialism as being OK and fascism as a radical right-wing ideology (i.e., not OK). The irony is that the modern American left, perhaps even unknowingly, prefers a fascist state but wants the public to think of their system in more politically palatable, non-Nazi terms, like democratic socialism or something.

Conservatism wants small government so that individual liberties can flourish. Libertarians, who are a small but influential element in American conservatism, want even smaller government with little to no government intervention in our daily lives. The Left wants the opposite—to place the resources of the individual and industry in the service of a big centralized state bureaucracy. To be far right-wing cannot entail a system of government control, because the extreme far right is technically an ungovernable anarchy that is controlled (if there is such a thing) by individualism.

Fascism is not anarchist. It's the exact opposite, highly structured and tightly controlled, where labor and industry work arm-in-arm toward a social goal. To paraphrase D'Souza, to call fascism far right is absolute disingenuous nonsense, because it's actually a far left-wing ideology based on control. Again, to acknowledge Gentile or any kinship between socialism and Nazism is dangerous to the Left, because to acknowledge fascism correctly would require an acknowledgment of how close it truly aligns with the philosophies of the American left. The American left's storm troopers—antifa—are, in fact, a self-described anti-fascist organization that's actually doing the bidding of what they don't even realize is an American fascist ideology. And, through confusion, ignorance, or otherwise, they are fighting another small fascist element (the neo-Nazis) in America. President Eisenhower and President Reagan would get a kick out of it: Leftists attacking other leftists.

On June 26, 2019 NYC Mayor Bill de Blasio said the following at a Democratic Presidential Debate as transcribed by the Washington Post. "But let me tell you, what we're hearing here already in the first round of questions is that battle for the heart and soul of our party. I want to make it clear. This is supposed to be the party of working people. Yes, we're supposed to be for a 70 percent tax rate on the wealthy. Yes, we're supposed to be for free college, free public college, for our young people. We are supposed to break up big corporations when they're not serving our democracy."

Focus on the last sentence for a moment. Sounds like a harmless and typical liberal talking point, right? So, why is this a big deal? As far as I know, de Blasio is the first person who has openly quoted Gentile. De Blasio's comment, that corporate America needs to serve our democracy (i.e., our nation), sounds innocuous until you think it through. His quote is directly out of Gentile's playbook.

A conservative would never say what de Blasio said, because the notion that business serves the public, rather than investors, is un-American. Yes, business must adhere to the rule of law. But the purpose of business, industry, and commerce is not to build our military might (as the fascists wanted) or eradicate poverty (as the socialists wanted) or serve Big Brother (as the communists wanted). Business's raison d'etre is to make money for the investors.

What Exactly Is Antifa?

> "Those who permit themselves to be deceived into lending their aid toward the triumph of communism will be the first to fall victims of this error."

—Pope Pius XI, Atheistic communism, 1937.

Antifa, or anti-fascists, are a violent American left-wing group that can be best described as the anonymous and masked storm troopers of the modern American Marxist movement. Its existence can be traced to the 1999 World Trade Organization (WTO) meeting in Seattle, and possibly earlier, but really got started about 10 years ago. It has large followings in and strong ties to left-leaning cities on the West Coast, namely Portland, Seattle, and the Bay Area.

In classical Marxism, the oppressed class is always at war against the oppressive aspects of society. In the eyes of antifa, the oppressed class they fight for is a mix of political, racial, and lower socioeconomic individuals, who play the proletariat protagonists and who have been marginalized by white, conservative, and Christian capitalists, who naturally play the antagonist villains—the oppressors. Antifa believes the right wing is out to get them—to oppress them and hurt them. So, in taking a page out of Hegel's playbook, they are actively trying to destroy what they find as illegitimate. Conservative speech is anti-Marxist speech, and, therefore, in their view, deserves preemptive strikes. Antifa views their behavior as being justifiable self-defense, even if they strike first. This is consistent with the teachings of Russian anarchist Sergey Nechayev (1847-82), who believed in violent revolution by any means necessary.

Antifa is a violent domestic terrorist group. They automatically associate all conservative speech as not just hate speech but violence, physical violence, that needs to be met with retaliatory violence. Antifa doesn't think twice about destroying property because, ready? There is no such thing as violence against property, like cars and storefront windows. Antifa often sees personal property as manifestations of wealth and specifically, inequality, so somehow acting out like a bunch of hooligans is OK. Violence against the Right is justifiable in their world, because only evil people would vote conservative, and therefore evil people need to be crushed.

Antifa is a decentralized group that takes clues from various anarchist agitators, while waving banners for organizations like Satanic Portland. On a day where there might be a rally attended by some horrible people— Christians, capitalists, and old white people – they are whipped into

104

a frenzy by an anarchist mob, don their masks and commit mayhem. With any luck, only the people and property representing the patriarchy get harmed. These creeps, who feel good about having purpose in their lives by damaging symbols of capitalism, hegemony (flag waving, freedom of assembly, and full-time jobs), privilege, and patriarchy, all in one place and on one day, are emboldened by weirdos like Former Vice-President Joe Biden, who praise them as courageous Americans.

There is another key aspect of antifa that needs to be explained. In traditional American society, there is little if any difference between morality and legality. I can't think of anything that is moral that isn't legal, and I can't think of too many things that are legal but immoral, outside of certain vices. Antifa doesn't see it that way. They see protected speech, speech that would be seen by everyone as perfectly legal, as unacceptable and therefore immoral, and they have adopted sort of a Nazi Brown Shirt, Italian Black Shirt or an Iranian Revolutionary Council mentality to decide, themselves, what is moral (acceptable) and what isn't. Being pro-life, against open borders, or in support of stronger borders are immoral positions, as far as the Leftists go, and are evil and worthy of a violent response.

Traditional conservative views on things such as sex, drugs, theft, vandalism, and matters related to loitering or protest (including anarchy and dissent), and so on and so forth, are viewed by the Left as mean-spirited, authoritarian, draconian, or fascist, rather than valid or sensible. The Leftists cast those who hold those views as right-wing, old-fashioned and out of touch, which invokes images of Nazism and racism, and that is what they want.

Chapter 6

CULTURAL MARXISM: THE MARRIAGE OF MARX AND FREUD

FROM THE TIME OF THE FIRST INTERNATIONAL until World War I, Marxism generally took the form of labor parties in the U.S. and in Europe. Leading up to World War I, hardliners held out hope that either the inevitable "Great War" or class-based revolutions would finally bring about the international socialist utopia they dreamed of. To their disappointment, World War I failed to unite workers of the world who instead chose their flag over their class. Leftist intellectuals were perplexed as to why German welders would rather fight and kill French welders as part of a German army rather than fight German bankers or factory owners as part of a worker's army. Simply put, they neglected to factor how strong peoples ties were to culture, language and religion.

Shortly after the war, leftist revolutions occurred in Russia and Italy but the first effort failed in Germany. Later they succeeded in Germany and Spain. By the 1930's many leftists in the west were startled by the unwelcomed development in socialism's evolution: Workers were not uniting across borders according to class, but were instead uniting within their own national borders by culture. This brand of socialism is called fascism. The idea that the oppressors weren't the rich but instead the outsiders and the traitors. The intelligentsia was blindsided. They found fascism an affront to Karl Marx's legacy as it was too focused on a cultural hegemony that centered on language, customs and traditions along with national borders and flexing of military might. To them the Bolshevik model was the closest thing to, and only acceptable option for, orthodox Marxism and now this populist version was hijacking the movement. For a while it looked like it was going to sweep through Europe. To stop it enough people needed to be convinced it was bad. Bad enough to fight another world war over.

Fascism occurred when too many of the wrong people hear the wrong message (pride in one's culture) and there was genuine fear on the part of orthodox Marxists that populist socialism could spring up anywhere. Intellectuals were focused on fascism but they never lost sight of the bigger goal which was the toppling of capitalism. They reasoned that whether the enemy was fascism or capitalism in order to change a culture a series of events would have to occur. By changing how people communicate you can change how people learn, and through manipulation and influence on how and what people learn and how people perceive their environment you've established a prerequisite to changing behavior in a society. If enough people's behavior could be changed then a culture could change. Killing a nation's cultural identity would not happen through force. Permanent and transformational change requires psychological warfare.

The idea of military officers running a socialist country was at odds with Marxist orthodoxy which said that labor leaders are supposed to run a country with intelligentsia in the white towers of academia – the scientists, the philosophers and writers–providing policy guidance and the press being the medium to inform the people. As a sidebar, one reason why the media hates President Trump is that he has removed both academia and the press from policy and messaging roles they have traditionally enjoyed under all previous presidents, and especially under President Obama. As the 1930's arrived orthodox Marxists, who saw themselves as more intellectual and philosophical than their fascist brethren, wanted revolutionary minded people to pursue the Russian model. They worried that every leftist revolution from then on would take a brutish and populist fascist form rather than the more enlightened and intellectual Leninist/Trotskyist form. Rather than rely on a worker's revolution in Western Europe that could never come, or, just as bad, could lead to fascism, what if it was, instead, a carefully orchestrated and bloodless destruction of a nation's culture, concocted by the intelligentsia which, in time, leads to the oppressed taking power?

This period in the early 1930's marked the beginning of an American cultural revolution. It wasn't fought with force but with fear, confusion and misinformation. It marked the moment the forces of academia, the arts, the sciences and the media joined hands to start chipping away at American Exceptionalism. This marked the time when the humanists, the psychologists, the atheists, the skeptics, the doubters, the agitators, the misfits, the outcasts and the malcontents, drunk on Marxist promises, decided to wage war on America. The American cultural revolution, using a countercultural phenomenon known as Cultural Marxism, did not begin in the 1960s as many people believe. It began in the 1930's.

Marxists like Antonio Gramsci (1891–1937) and Herbert Marcuse (1898–1979) saw that a cultural revolution, led by indoctrination in higher education, the arts, and media, would weaken society, thus eventually leading to a political revolution. This explains why the Leftists tolerate petty crime, promiscuity, homosexuality, transgenderism, abortion, pornography, same-sex marriage, and anything that eats away at the Christian values in our culture. They really have no choice. To affect a bloodless Marxist revolution the norms and values of an entire culture first need to be dismantled.

Families have always been the base economic and structural unit of our society. Strong families make for strong people attending strong churches, who create strong and sustainable communities. Weak or non-existent families weaken our base economic unit and our churches. When people don't go to church, they go to a different type of church. The church of materialism and Satanism, which manifests as Marxism. FDR made a big push to transform America, and President Eisenhower pushed back. President Johnson made a big push, and President Reagan pushed back. President Obama made another huge push, and President Trump is pushing back. The election of Secretary Clinton would have likely put us on a faster path to a European socialist platform than we would have liked. Enough people saw this and stopped it. But for how long?

CULTURAL MARXISM

Leftists take their identity politics very seriously, but when conservatives hear about 71 genders or just about anything that relates to political correctness or PC, they either laugh, roll their eyes or ignore it. But PC is deadly serious, to not just leftist activists, the media, and academia but left-leaning people across America as well, who simply want to erase the Christian heteronormality of our hegemony. Cultural Marxism is the process of bringing political correctness into mainstream thought and it's been actively pursued by the Left in America since at least the early 1930's. Cultural Marxism is real and is not a right-wing conspiracy theory as the Leftists would like you to believe, it's very real and pervasive.

For the reader it might be helpful to explain what the phrases "right-wing conspiracy" and "right-wing talking points" means as it plays into the psychology behind the acceptance of Cultural Marxism, of which identity politics is a big part. It's a leftist deflection technique to draw attention away from an uncomfortable subject or inconvenient facts by discouraging a deeper dive. It's a classic gaslighting method to discredit a theory or set of facts by suggesting, you don't know what you're talking about, you're crazy, or that's so stupid it's unworthy of further comment. If you point out false narratives, ridicule or otherwise shine a negative light on leftist schemes they get on the defensive quickly. The phrase right-wing talking point can be translated as: "This is annoying, but something we can manage". Right-Wing conspiracy theory is when they're beyond annoyed and they're worried. It's a dog whistle usually attached to a more serious threat. Generally if you hear this phrase that means they're worried that you're onto them or that you're trying to recast the narrative in a more accurate manner.

Cultural Marxism takes many forms, but it almost always touches on feelings and thoughts revolving around personal and interpersonal relationships. It's used to capitalize on emotions and manipulates one's perception of how someone fits into society, into work, into relationships, into their community. Here's an example of how it's happening today. If a famous or popular person gets what is called canceled in Generation Y and Z parlance, this is a form of Cultural Marxism. To be canceled is to receive a modern day scarlet letter from the Left. The cancel culture is intended to describe a coordinated movement to silence unpopular opinions expressed by someone. Usually the target is a famous person with a lot to lose, but it could be directed at anyone. For the first time in American history, people are afraid of using certain words or crossing certain lines, for fear of being shamed, ridiculed, or ostracized. Conservatives need to understand the genesis of it and how it is directly out of the Marxist playbook. Did you ever wonder where it came from and when it started?

Surprisingly, political correctness didn't arise out of the 1960s, when Civil Rights and a culture of victimhood was entering the public consciousness, while people were also first becoming sensitive to pejorative labels and stereotypes associated with minorities, women, and gays. It dates back to the Frankfurt School—a Marxist think tank—around World War I. Prior to World War I, Marxism was seen as more theoretical than practical, and the neo-Marxists, who were carrying the torch for Karl Marx, were writers and college professors, not gun-carrying revolutionaries. At the time, they knew the classic economic model of Marxism was not enough to overthrow governments. They concluded that for a revolution to succeed, people needed to think beyond paychecks and governance and think about just how rotten the culture they lived in really was at that time. Gentile saw an opportunity to shape Marxism in nationalistic terms, but in most of Western Europe, something more was needed—a psychological aspect, a cultural aspect. Adding this cultural aspect of Marxism was the birth of political correctness.

Economic Marxism preaches that all of history can be explained by the ownership and means of production. Cultural Marxism is the notion that history can (also) be explained by power, specifically illegitimately obtained power, by and over groups based on race, sex, sexual orientation, religion, and so on and so forth. For more than a century, the neo-Marxists blended identities into additional classes of marginalized groups, so they could neatly fit into the Marxist model of oppressed classes. Whereas, Marx saw the proletariat as the oppressed class, the Cultural Marxists saw all marginalized groups as part of a broader class of protagonist victims (i.e., oppressed) and those who would oppose such marginalized groups (racists, misogynists, etc.) as part of the evil bourgeoisie, or oppressive class. Because Marxism defines itself as a revolutionary battle between good and evil, it's only natural that all oppressed people – be they women, minorities (race, ethnicity, and religion), and gays – were automatically classified as "good" and those who sought to preserve the patriarchy and hegemony – namely, white, straight, conservative males – as the oppressive bad guys. Over time, the new proletariat (i.e., the oppressed), aka the good people, would, therefore, fight the bad people to establish more equitable power structures. This explains why, in America today, the rich aren't vilified, unless they are conservative. It is a big reason why conservatives have such contempt for latter day Marxists in America. They have chosen to steer away from inapplicable third world economic theories to a very real and threatening method of cultural destruction.

The theory behind it was brilliant. If you add up enough left-leaning women, immature students, immigrants, minorities, and gays, you could end up with more than 50 percent of the electorate. And, if manipulated properly, the Leftists could prevail in local, state, and federal elections. Inclusivity is not the goal. Tribal group selectivity is the aim and pandering to tribal fears is the method of choice. And, if you only need 50 percent, plus one, to believe the patriarchy and hegemony is out to get them, this assemblage of terrified tribal groups is a clever way to use identity politics to manipulate and win an election. Remember, this idea of political correctness and identity politics as a path to power is not new. The Frankfurt School figured this out 100 years ago.

Because everything is portrayed as a battle against oppression, Marxists feel the fight is ongoing and very personalized. And, rather than fight individually, group battles need to be fought at the ballot box, in the state and federal legislatures, and in the courthouse. These groups are formed through identity. Furthermore, because few of them believe in an afterlife, there is an urgency for all political gains to be achieved while they are on this earth so as to fulfill a want of purpose. One needs to understand that, for many leftists, the nation was founded on falsehoods and, therefore, is illegitimate. They believe fights can and should be picked, and hard-fought battles can be won. And, if so, the outcomes will be codified in law. The Left's biggest wins over the past 75 years have not been achieved through legislative action but through the courts. Marxists don't see government and activist courts as counter to our Founding Father's ideals and vision, but rather as agents to provide employment or to redress grievances or perhaps turn their agenda item into law.

For Cultural Marxists, it's less about economics and more about decon-struction. That is, destruction of norms, beliefs, and attitudes that makes up the hegemony of a society and may have been in place for centuries, with the sole purpose of overturning power structures. It's important to point out that Karl Marx had issues with authority and power, and he wanted to destroy those structures. He disliked anybody and anything that had any moral, political, or economic control over him. What better way to get back at the power structure than to change the meaning of key texts that serve as pillars of society. And, to that end, the cultural Marxists took aim at literature. They would purport that the Bible is nothing more than a playbook for the suppression of race, religion, and gender. Or, the Declaration of Independence is a blueprint for racism. If enough people can be (wrongly) convinced that the written history of the West was nothing more than relentless oppression, the next thing to do is reinsert new meanings to bring Western culture down.

When communists took power in Russia, in 1917, the Marxists in London, Paris, and Frankfurt were optimistic that it could spread to other Western nations, but it didn't. A socialist version of Marxism, called fascism, was adopted in Italy, Germany, and Spain. But, the most extreme version of Marxism—that second state (communism) where private interests and capitalism didn't exist—simply didn't take root. Orthodox Marxists were still smarting from the failure of the Great War – World War I – to unite the workers of the world. Coupled with this, a new brand of socialism was spreading across Europe that they did not expect. Something needed to be done to expand the reach of the orthodox brand.

To remedy this, two key Marxist theorists—an Italian named Antonio Gramsci and a Hungarian Jew named Georg Lukacs (1885-1971)—got to work. Gramsci theorized that the proletariat would never see their true class interests reached, until they were "free" from Western cul-ture. By this, he meant Christianity. Whereas Marx openly advocated for all-out war against Christianity, Gramsci saw hope in systematically chipping away at, not just religion but, all aspects of culture that stand in the way of a Marxist revolution. Lukacs theorized that the great obstacle to the creation of the perfect Marxist state was Western civilization itself. Felix Weil provided the financial backing to establish an institute to advance this nonsense.

Gramsci saw "pop culture" as a manifestation of the struggle of subordinate groups – the oppressed–facing off against the dominant groups – the oppressors–that preferred "high culture". Today, rich and poor enjoy the arts, but at the time pop culture was not mainstream. It was radical, risqué and only engaged in by people on the margins of society. It was jazz clubs in Harlem or nude art in Paris. Gramsci believed that blurring the distinction between pop culture and high culture would eventually empower the marginalized and promote tolerance. Attacking pop culture would be to attack the oppressed; therefore, a good leftist like Gramsci decided it was better to blur the distinction by chipping away at the cultural values the upper class held. This was the first step in post-modernism which is skepticism or rejection of a culture's grand narrative.

Lukacs was considered the father of Western Marxism and felt the path to power was the destruction of the oppressive classes thru shamelessly tearing down cultural norms. In 1919, Lukacs was named the Deputy Commissar for Culture in Hungary, and the first thing he did was introduce sex education. It was shocking and extremely controversial, but it served a purpose—an attempt to normalize, through government sanction, an otherwise taboo topic.

In 1923, the son of an Argentine-German millionaire named Felix Weil became one of the first wealthy members of the bourgeoisie class to openly support the Marxist cause since Engels. Weil studied political science at the University of Frankfurt – later renamed Goethe University

Frankfurt–and experienced the failed German Communist Revolution of 1918-19. He graduated a couple years later feeling the Marxist movement was too divided. He helped host a successful leftist summit and afterward sought to bring the brightest leftists together under a unified vision he and like-minded leftists had for the future of socialism, so he founded an institute in Frankfurt to serve as a Marxist think tank. Through Weil's efforts to finally get the key Marxist theorists on the same page, cultural Marxism and political correctness were born. At the time of its founding, the institute was known as the "Institute of Marxism," but there was concern among them that it wouldn't be such a great idea to be so open about it, and instead it was named the Institute for Social Research and later became known simply as the Frankfurt School.

Naturally, Jews like Weil were marginalized in Germany so it's not surprising that he wanted to populate his institute with trustworthy fellow Jews who shared his vision. The first director of the Frankfurt School was an Austrian economist named Carl Grunberg (1841-1940). His goal was to have Marxism thought of as a scientific methodology, rather than just a philosophical, economic or political theory. The goal of course was to have the intelligentsia accept Marxism in psychological or sociological terms.

The second director, Max Horkheimer, one of the founders of critical theory, took over the Frankfurt School in 1929. He expanded Marxism's appeal in academia through due to the emerging acceptance of "science" in the Leftist movement by embracing the teachings of men like Sigmund Freud and marrying it with Marxist thought he and his cohorts cleverly brought psychology into political science. Gaslighting, a form of psychological manipulation, became a useful tool to sow doubts and change perceptions of how Americans recollect the past and understand the present. Horkheimer's agenda was not initially embraced. He was considered such a renegade in the Marxist movement that even Lenin and Stalin rejected the brand of critical theory-based Marxism at the Frankfurt School as too radical.

Latter-day university programs in feminist studies, African-American studies, Latino studies, and gay studies are rooted in Horkheimer's critical theory, which at its core was more than studying the merits of a field. It was also to criticize socioeconomic structure of the oppressive class's impact on the oppressed. Horkheimer's theories and the Frankfurt School's agenda was catnip for progressive humanities departments at American universities back in the 1930's and Columbia University welcomed their diaspora when Hitler took power. He believed that empowering workers disrupted culture in a positive way by introducing behavioral changes that erode confidence in the status quo and could be a bulwark against fascism which was socialism within the existing culture. His logic went like this: By uniting socialism and culture in Germany meant that there would be those who would be left out of power structures due to their rejection of that culture. Leninism provided political and economic equality through the destruction of the dominant culture. Because fascism provided socialism within the context of the existing cultural hegemony, any economic and intellectual power that was once held by people not 100% committed to the German cause was suddenly and permanently lost. Consequently, the members of the Frankfurt School had a political and personal crisis on their hands. Fascism was replacing the Soviet communism system as the dominant socialist movement in Europe and, worse, the fascists were coming for those who were sympathetic to Russia.

The Frankfurt School taught that the Christian capitalistic order the West lived in created a Freudian condition, where people are unknowingly repressed. Critical theory preached that the Christian structures that repressed individuals—heteronormality or patriarchy for example—deserved the most destructive criticism possible. When you hear feminists complain that society is out to get women, it is a criticism out of the critical theory playbook from as far back as the 1920s and 30s, not the 1960s. Horkheimer taught at Columbia until 1940 at which point he decided he could do more damage by moving to Hollywood.

Their critical theory modus operandi was, basically, complain, complain, complain and yet not offer ideas or answers that Western democracies could study, let alone implement. When pressed for details, their response was, "We'll tell you the answer only after you supplant capitalists with Marxists." Their logic was that Americans, or the British, probably couldn't stomach a society as the Marxists envisioned it, so rather than tell them what it would be like, they would make vague promises of an idyllic utopian society. This explains why American cities, trapped in a perpetual death spiral of leftist mayors and city councils, can't solve the problems they promised to address. They're great at complaining and spending money but bad at solutions.

NAMES TO KNOW: HERBERT MARCUSE

Herbert Marcuse added another dimension in the 1930s that was central to political correctness, which was a sexual element and, more specifically, sexual liberation and gender roles. Marcuse held that masculinity and femininity were not differences defined by God and those traditional roles for men and women in the workplace and in the bedroom were not essential to sexuality and gender identity. These were, instead, constructs of the Christian world order and were therefore deemed by Marxist theorists as repressive.

What was the Frankfurt School up to besides critical theory? When the Nazi's came to power in 1933, they shut down the institute. Its members fled to New York City and took up residency at Columbia University, where the institute was located in exile. Now, rather than writing in German and pondering the German political and culture scene, they shifted their focus to a criticism of American culture, which was a society even more fundamentally Christian than anything in Europe. In a bit of fascinating irony, the Frankfurt scholars desperately needed America patriotism to defeat fascism, but at the same time they were plotting for the destruction of American culture.

A target of the Cultural Marxists at the Frankfurt School was the environment. Whereas, the Bible maintains that the Earth was created for the use and enjoyment of man, and that man is above nature, the neo-Marxists had some emerging ideas that deviated from Marxist orthodoxy. Whereas, Marx saw factory work as noble and necessary, Horkheimer was alarmed at man's "manipulative dominating attitude toward nature" and felt human sensual happiness was tied to quality of life. By the mid-1930s, the environment was suddenly central to the Frankfurt School's leftist philosophy.

How did all of this end up on American college campuses? The reason was the ideologues at the Frankfurt School were, to a man, Jewish, and they needed to escape Nazi Germany and land at institutions of higher learning where they could continue their research, and as writers and researchers, political pamphlets don't make money and newspapers can go out of business, while elite colleges certainly don't. Columbia with its strong psychology department, coupled with New York's huge Jewish population and the fact that Columbia was one of the first American universities, along with Harvard and the University of Chicago, to award tenure to professors beginning in 1900 made a lot of sense. Was there something about the, "Us versus them," dynamic that drew their intellectual focus? How and why did leftism appeal to so many Jewish intellectuals, and why was Marx, an ethnic Jew, so obsessed with the oppressor versus oppressed dialectic? Was it a calling? Perhaps Marxist teachings carried more weight with Jewish intellectuals or resonated with a historically discriminated group, like the Jewish community.

When World War II came, Horkheimer and fellow critical theorist, Theodor Adorno, moved to Hollywood. Adorno fled Germany in 1934 and taught at Oxford for three years before departing for Princeton and later UC Berkeley. Unlike the others, he felt art, rather than reason, was the key to human emancipation. Adorno and Horkheimer co-wrote a book called Dialectics of Enlightenment, where they suggested pop culture was a factory that produced goods (movies, theater, music, radio, etc.) and proposed they are used to manipulate mass society into passivity. Consumption of these products can influence people of all socio-economic classes. This work by respected Marxist theorists proved out what an underground leftist culture in Hollywood had long believed— people could be manipulated culturally and politically through the arts. This was certainly not unnoticed by conservatives and communist influence in Hollywood led to the Red Scare after World War II.

After World War II, Adorno migrated back to Frankfurt, and the Cultural Marxism, or political correctness, laid low during the McCarthy Era between 1948 and '55. Then along came Marcuse's Eros and Civilization, written in 1955 at the end of the Red Scare and shortly before the subsequent rise of the student rebellion and Civil Rights movement of the 1960s. Marcuse, straying more and more away from class struggle, probably because he knew the American middle class would never knowingly accept socialism, was fully onboard with the Cultural Marxism train. Class happiness, and identity, rather than class economic status was the focus of leftist intellectuals in America. Now in his mid-60s, Marcuse saw a chance to finally make the Frankfurt School's countercultural theories based on sex, drugs, and rock and roll the basis of the new and more Marx-leaning left in America.

Marcuse wanted to influence and change culture not study it and he had written Eros and Civilization 10 years earlier ahead of its time, but it didn't receive much attention until the 60s, when it became sort of the new leftist Bible on how to feel good. He argues, as the Frankfurt School had for decades, that the capitalistic order gave rise to a repression that Freud would have described in his works—an individual with a bunch of issues and anxieties, because his or her sexual instincts are repressed. From this, came the sexual liberation: freedom to do your own thing, and if it feels right, do it!

Unlike past esoteric Marxist work, he chose to simplify the terminology and not make it too deep. He coined the popular term "Make love, not war!" and urged people to explore new ideas and do what they liked (i.e., smoke pot) rather than what they needed to do (i.e., stay off the drugs, go to class, work, or war) in order to create a world of sexual freedom and play and devoid of work or obligation.

The key takeaway here is that cultural Marxism is real and lives on in the enforcement of political correctness. The Left is seeking to expand it to include thoughts they don't like and not just actions they object to.

TOLERANCE AND IDENTITY POLITICS ON COLLEGE CAMPUSES

Marcuse saw a need for what he called a "liberating tolerance" on college campuses, which wasn't the tolerance of all opinions; it was the intolerance for anything coming from the Right and tolerance for anything coming from the Left. Marcuse felt tolerance was false because it allowed for the acceptance of everyone's opinion, including those on the Right. Since what is tolerable and what isn't, particularly on college campuses, is defined by the Left, his liberating tolerance theory fit into their thought process and was accepted as the only true form of tolerance. True tolerance was seen as the only acceptable brand of tolerance allowed on college campuses, and was accepted by the intelligentsia as the enlightened ability to identify and reject intolerant (i.e. oppressive) opinions. Again, tolerance to them is therefore intolerance of conservative viewpoints.

This concept prevails on college campuses today, even private ones. Anything that attacks the political correctness that Marcuse and the Frankfurt School worked for decades to promote in American culture and on American college campuses is met with firm resistance. Since most historians, political scientists, and philosophers are, by virtue of looking at their paychecks, liberals who lecture at college campuses, it's no surprise they are all influenced by the irresponsible, feel-good nature of what Marcuse was preaching.

Scott Greer wrote a fascinating book in 2017 called No Campus for White Men. He argued that the campus radicalism of the 1960's is far different from today. Greer explained that the activists of the 1960's wanted more freedom of speech available to them, but sadly todays activists want less of it. They see freedom of speech as allowing a platform for conservative thinking which is seen as oppressive.

According to Greer, to the activists on college campuses today the two most important things they claim they're seeking are equality and diversity. Regrettably identity politics causes people to believe rewards should come based on what we claim to be rather than what we have accomplished. Jobs, housing and other opportunities should be set aside for each tribe regardless of merit and policy actions that favor tribes over merit should be prioritized. They somehow believe this will solve the equality problem. The diversity issue is really peculiar. What they certainly don't want is unity for all people because by definition that would mean reaching accords with conservatives and perhaps unwanted compromises with other identity-driven tribes. Diversity to them doesn't mean having different people of different races, different creeds and different opinions around. It means everyone except the oppressive class. In practice it means creating a safe space for their ideological crusades with fewer white conservative Christians around.

THE LOCUS OF CONTROL

It's not easy to succeed in life without a lot of hard work, and the world can be a big scary place if you allow it to be. One of the horrible gifts humanistic psychology gave us was convincing many impressionable Americans that they were thinking about the world all wrong. Psychologists began to study human behavior in the context not of what you can control but how others control you. Psychologists realized there was money to be made telling people it's someone else's fault, but it wasn't just psychologists who were in on it.

Educators began to study how curriculums and classroom settings rather than study habits and parental commitment shaped our minds. Sociologists began studying how our institutions were shaping our thoughts and behaviors. Planners began to think of how the built environment negatively affected people's lives. Lawyers, activists and economists began to see crime and poverty as a result of capitalist failings and racism rather than the personal failings of the individuals. The Catholic Church even went through a controversial and radical transformation (1962-65) that allowed individuals more flexibility in how they carried out their faith in response to social, political, technological and economic factors.

Until the mid-twentieth century one's successes and failures were always seen as the result of an individual's choices. This pivot, which now called for everyone to focus on the external rather than internal factors helped end the virtue culture that prevailed in America and signaled the beginning of the victimhood culture we live in today.

As Emily Ekins explained while writing for the Cato Institute one of the key differences between the Left and the Right is how they view something called personal agency, which is the degree to which we feel we're in control of our lives. It revolves around a concept in psychology called locus of control. The Left has an external locus and low degree of personal agency, and the Right has an internal locus and high degree of personal agency. Conservatives believe individuals have responsibility for, and control over, their own personal situations, and through their internal "agency" can control situations and manufacture results through individual initiative, hard work, education and ambition. Liberals on the other hand believe people's situations are not controlled by their own agency but determined by external factors such as racism, an unfair capitalist system or unequal educational opportunities.

These completely different perspectives of how much control an individual can have in their own lives explain why there are such different conclusions drawn by the Left and Right on how our government should address public policy matters. It also explains why the Left is so freaked out about global warming, corporations too big to fail or nuclear war and the Right isn't. What makes this divide difficult to bridge is the sincere belief by today's Left that the external forces that control their lives and cause stress are in fact oppressive forces that are controlled by conservatives such as industry, banking, the church and the patriarchy (i.e. the oppressors). Since everything they care about from lifestyles to public policies about can be traced to Marxist ideals the oppressed (the Left) believes that the only way to better manage, if not eliminate, these external threats is to remove the oppressors (the conservatives) from power.

MIND VERSUS FEELINGS

Marxism was embraced by many psychologists and social scientists because of its ties to emotions and Freudian needs of self-fulfillment in the midst of sexual frustration. The Frankfurt School was the first to bring the teachings of Marx and Freud together, and with it was born Cultural Marxism—the desire for everyone to go through their day without risk of being exposed to dissenting views or insulted or offended, whether directly or indirectly. Capitalism, on the other hand, relies on empirical facts and logic, as well as common sense.

Marxism is feelings based on appeals to things that make us feel good, rather than things that make sense. My brain says eat donuts, pizza and ice cream three times a day, because it tastes good. My mind uses logic and says it's irresponsible to do so.

A great way to characterize the difference between feelings and the mind is in the context of ice cream. Just the thought of ice cream makes you happy. You smile and feel good even before taking a lick, thinking about how great the ice cream is going to taste, but your mind tells you it's not good for you, so you pass. Letting poor people through our borders "feels good," because we somehow feel like we are helping those poor migrants. Our mind, on the other hand, knows that our borders lack the proper immigration, security, and documentation controls to absorb documented aliens, let alone the endless number of immigrants arriving every day. Letting them in feels good. Keeping them out makes more sense.

Because Marxism relies on emotions to trigger anger or tug at heartstrings, it thereby encourages personal feelings to cloud one's judgment. Obviously, empathy or compassion should play a role in how decisions are made, but without logic also being applied to it, there is no sensibility.

THE PRESS AND FAKE NEWS

Traditional liberalism is not Marxism, but I wonder how many honest-to-goodness liberals actually exist in America today. Liberals and conservatives will agree that an objective, unbiased, and ethical press is essential to a functioning and civil democracy. However, the media has lurched so far to the Left over the past few decades that it's not always objective or fair, and sometimes it doesn't tell the truth. Sometimes it advances false narratives and lies. Sometimes it advances an agenda. As educator and writer, Dennis Prager likes to say, "Truth is a liberal value, and it is a conservative value, but it is not a Leftist value."

Marx, despite fancying himself as a philosopher, did not place any value in truth, ethics, or virtue. In his mind, truth was telling it like he saw it, or as he'd prefer it. In fact, he proclaimed, "It is the first duty of the press to undermine the foundations of the existing political system." He was like Machiavelli—the end justifies the means. Marx did a lot of thinking, drinking, and idea sharing with like-minded anarchists, but there isn't much record of compromise in his extreme positions. To him, and the Leftists who followed him, lies and deceit are acceptable. He believed he was right, and if you would disagree—or even if you agreed—for all he cared, you could join him in hell.

Whereas, kindhearted inspirations, patriotic good news, and the Bible were the daily chicken soup for the soul, leftist dailies, like the New York Times and Washington Post, have become what commentator and author John Nolte calls "comfort food" for leftists. Big city newspapers are in the business of selling printed words. What sells is not what their readership needs (honest and unbiased reporting) but what it wants (soothing daily messages that President Trump is evil and his days are numbered). They take their clues from a professional and cultural elite bent on globalism and diversity yet is surprisingly homogenous – white, urban, educated and liberal.

There was a time when newspapermen were interested in accuracy and printing the truth. Local newspapermen, like policemen, firemen, preachers, and teachers, were trusted pillars of society. That was when reporters, if they even had college degrees, majored in history or English or maybe classical literature. Over time, as news moved from reporting to opinions, editorials, and columns, and as the available platforms in the industry grew, schools began offering professional degrees in communications or journalism. Many received minors in one form of identity studies or another. But how did these schools, and more specifically these students, become dominated by Marxist thought? They were able to attract leftist faculty, who were groomed on Cultural Marxism and unquestionably supported by like-minded leftist administrations. Under the guise of free speech and advancement of knowledge they allowed leftist professors to indoctrinate their students. A battle cry for the Left in the 1960's was, "If you want to change the world become a teacher or a writer." Ultimately these forces weeded out the nonconformists in the teaching ranks to where today nearly all humanities professors are liberal if not far-left leaning.

For hundreds of years the European press had seen itself as a separate "fourth estate" in society. The three main estates or realms were the church, the aristocracy and the commoners, but the press decided that they would invent a special class for themselves, hence the fourth estate. In the U.S., although there was no church or aristocracy, governing hierarchies still existed. The American press has always seen itself as having an oversized role in society similar to their European counterparts but as an unofficial fourth branch of government. They saw their role as a counter balance to legislative and executive power, and certainly during the presidency of Donald Trump, but not traditionally, a counter to the judicial branch too.

Most conservatives are annoyed at the power the press has bestowed upon themselves. To them the press is an activist and partisan mouthpiece for the Democratic Party and absolutely not unbiased. The Left on the other hand sees the press as an unbiased pillar of democracy and essential to holding the powerful accountable. President Trump's disdain for the press as evidenced through him bypassing them in his direct communication to the people thereby allowing him to protect the timing, authenticity and accuracy of his messaging. Accuracy in this case meaning unfiltered and untranslated. A president regularly questioning their role and motives, was long overdue, and was unheard of until the age of Donald Trump. His open rejection of the press being the fourth pillar of democracy largely explains the adversarial relationship the media has with President Trump.

An irony in the age of President Trump is that the Leftists have long been complaining about the illegitimate power bestowed upon the oppressors in the patriarchy and hegemony having been achieved through nefarious or questionable means. Illegitimate power, they claim, is wrong and outdated and is only used to oppress. However, when President Trump calls out the illegitimate power the press has bestowed upon themselves the media kicks and screams. In their view any power, illegitimately obtained or not, is good if it helps fight the oppressors.

As I noted earlier, Marxism poses a bigger threat to our society than illegitimacy, drugs, gangs, immigration, or government programs ineptitude. Global warming, income inequality, and social justice are not the biggest issues, although the Leftists would certainly want you to think differently. These three issues are manufactured distractions, created by Marxists, to tap into emotions (i.e., fears) about existential threats, unwanted moral judgment, and perceived unfairness caused by white patriarchy. Schools advance the narrative to young people and the press has played a huge role in advancing the Leftist narrative with adults. Thoughts and actions that run counter to that agenda were once reported as part of the balance people expected in reporting. Now, it is downplayed, ignored, or even shamed. An irony is that the Leftists are all about freedom of thought, freedom of expression, freedom of the press, and freedom speech, except when the Right thinks, acts or speaks. Controlling or shouting down differing views, particularly as part of a gaslighting maneuver, is a classic Marxist stunt. When you here a leftist say, "you don't know what you're talking about", or "that's not how it was", be very suspicious. It's very possible they're trying to take you on a gaslighting trip.

It's no secret that newsrooms are full of people who honestly believe that America needs to be broken down and replaced by a socialist, colorless, genderless, and atheist regime that resents the enemies of the Left, which includes families, capitalists, churches, gun owners, and homeowners.

I've known several newspaper reporters and editors in my lifetime. They're good people who are trying to make a living. I've noticed that the people who write for news organizations were usually not the big men on campus, or the popular kids or the starting quarterbacks on their high school football teams. More than likely, they were the kids who wrote for the student paper and/or the yearbook. And, there is nothing wrong with that. They were often the observers who documented results, collected data, and pondered the results. Since tomorrow's news story is always unknown, they needed to be quick studies and know a little bit about a lot of different things, which is one of the hallmarks of a good local reporter. However, they are the sports reporters, not the players. They are the geeky, fantasy football players and not the personable gamblers. They wrote the review of the school play and didn't perform in it. They were probably the outsiders who watched and wished they were part of the in-crowd but were left with no option but to write about their feelings. Doers write autobiographies. People who are watchers write biographies about what the doers did.

With few exceptions, most writers (be it novelists or newsmen) make a very modest living, and many hold idealistic thoughts of somehow, someday getting their big scoop that will change the world. Or, perhaps, they'll get that big break and publish the next great American novel or maybe land an interview that leads to a spot on CNN. Conservatives watch TV and read newspapers too. But, why such a left-leaning slant? It's believed that more than 90 percent of political contributions by journalists went to Democratic candidates in 2016. Few professions benefit from transformative cultural change like the news industry does, and I wonder if any profession harbors as much fantasyland daydreaming about, and envy toward, those who have financially succeeded due to the foundational hegemony found in America. They will never be the multi-million-dollar athlete or multi-million-dollar CEO or the handsome movie star.

Compounding this is that many news organizations have policies in place to uphold unbiased journalistic integrity. That sounds fine and dandy, but many in the media see their roles as public servants—as if they have a God-given duty to speak out—so they carelessly cross back and forth between their jobs as objective reporters and their own personal biases. Then, get this, when they rant on their personal blogs and get caught, they claim that what they write on their free time is personal speech and independent of their news reporting. Yet, when a conservative says something unpopular during their downtime, it gets reported about, not as private, after hours speech, but as their regular day-to-day political agenda. These are the people who critique a game, a movie, or speech but never coach, produce, or deliver it. These are the people who watch movies, not the ones who make them. They are sad, angry, or frustrated about their lack of skills, looks, athleticism, work ethic, or lot in life, and often wrongly blame capitalism for their poor life choices or oppression for their underachievement. They speak of equality (as in opportunity), but what they want instead is egalitarianism (equal outcomes). I once heard a writer lament that a pro athlete or actor should make no more and no less than a newsman under the weird (certainly Marxist) notion that they all appeal to people's desire for two or three hours of daily entertainment. In other words, if you spend two hours watching a movie or a professional ballgame or reading the Sunday paper, it's still two hours. Ergo, all media types should make $10 million per year, like a pro athlete or actor.

According to political commentator Greg Steinbrecher, there is subtle but pervasive bias that can be seen in this old trope: when a conservative does something bad, the story focuses on the conservative's deeds, but when a liberal makes a mistake, the story becomes the conservative reaction to it. But, why the fake news? Why do they hate President Trump? They don't rip him when he makes a mistake. They rip him for everything. There are a number of theories for this, ranging from misunderstanding the circumstances to being defensive, because they were never previously questioned about their integrity or accuracy, to simply wanting conservatives, and President Trump in particular, to look bad. It's comical when you hear them fall back on the old, "Our job is to hold the powerful accountable." No, it isn't. Your job is to report news, not make news. It's likely political, given how Marx and his disciples felt about the media's purpose and the Leftist leanings in the newsroom. So, we end up with a case where almost all of President Trump's achievements or comments are spun in a negative light, no matter how positive the achievements may have been. I understand that many reporters are naturally skeptical and assume the worst, but this president gets no benefit of the doubt.

Many conservatives simply acknowledge that the mainstream media is just pandering to its readership/viewership base. Author and political commentator John Nolte described the business model of The New York Times as nothing more than providing, "Comfort food for leftists." These writers, reporters, and editorial board members are the outsiders who want to be the newsmakers themselves or want to reshape society to their liking or, like Marx, want to tear it down. They can't win the game of life, but they want to improve their lot, so the Leftist theory in play here is that the system needs to change, not them; the patriarchy needs to change, not them; the hegemony needs to be turned 180 degrees, not them; and the capitalist model needs to change, not them.

The capitalist way is not so hard. It can work for one and all. Everyone can make a great career in one field or another. Instead, they want a nonpartisan third party (government) to redistribute resources and change the laws, policies, rules, or paradigm to change the outcomes. Because writers are mostly post-modernists at heart and view themselves not as documentarians but as change agents, the news media finds and prints stories, trends, and issues that are useful toward their leftist agenda. They do not just report on these matters but go beyond reporting news to making news, by creating or otherwise influencing stories, to advance their agenda. Facts be damned.

Their utopian world of egalitarianism will only occur if the Marxists prevail. They pounce on nuggets—often lies—that confirm their bias and break down what they see as the privileged class: the modern bourgeoisie, the oppressors. They generally ignore stories that portray leftists in a bad light, because they need the Left to succeed to improve their lot. They leap to judgment when someone on the Right is perceived to have committed a wrong but wait for the facts and "won't race to judgment" when someone on the Left does the same. They seek reinforcements of their leftist cultural orthodoxies and pounce upon words, sound bites, and other particulars that punish their enemies, namely conservatives. Confirmation bias is a major problem in the media.

The point here is that Marxism has always appealed to outsiders, outcasts, the envious, and the underachieving, rather than the successful and well-adjusted capitalists, because that is the whole premise of Marxism. It's the promise that the marginalized will rise up, challenge the patriarchy, change the hegemony, and rewrite the rules. Peddling lies can advance political agendas and even help one's lot in life. Writers are observers and not doers and are not paid much. Their lot stands to improve if cultural and economic norms about what is deemed valuable and important are overturned. In this age, where a tweet is worth money to a writer and a "like" of that tweet by a reader worth even more, why not be inflammatory? The rise of President Trump has, thankfully, smoked out the progressive/Marxist agenda in the media. Whereas, in the past, people may have assumed the press was moderate and, perhaps, only a few news organizations openly leftist, now they've all been exposed for what they are in just a few years. Never underestimate the temptation on the part of the media to shame or falsely accuse someone on the Right for political purposes. It happens every single day.

Marxists attack pillars of society, because they cannot win the economic debate. The Left is waging a cold war on many fronts, including attacks on social norms that define our cultural and economic institutions, gender, religion, sexuality, class, and national identity, as well as our children and elderly. Whereas, in the past, political opposition from either party would focus on social and economic matters that affected everyone—crime, the economy, transportation, energy costs, unemployment or war. However, today the political dialogue is focused not on fixing problems but tearing down the structural foundation of the American civilization in order to remake them in a Marxist image. These pillars are the backbone of our society, the foundations for our laws, and the fabric that binds us together as Americans. These pillars have been built over centuries and defend us against Marxism and are described pejoratively by the Left as part of the hegemony, patriarchy, male toxicity, and heteronormality that, in their agenda, must be broken down for the good of the country. The tip here is that, if you hear someone using those terms in their complaints about society, chances are, they are Marxists.

Chapter 7

POST-WORLD WAR II GLOBALISM AND THE NEW PROGRESSIVES

THE PROGRESSIVES AT THE TURN OF THE TWEN-
tieth century were basically activists in the Democratic and Republican
parties, whose primary objective was initially to rid politics of corruption. But scope-creep set in and their objectives expanded. Since progressivism at the time was closely tied to Christian morality, the agenda
shifted to include compassion for the poor. Soon, big government was
thought of by the early progressives, as it is today, as the key to ensuring
oversight of everything in society from industry to poverty programs,
housing, immigration, education, policing, banking and voting. Social
progressives took up health issues including a desire for prohibition. In
time, they were instrumental in implementing an income tax, women's
suffrage, direct election of senators, and the Eighteenth Amendment–
Prohibition. It didn't take long for left-leaning politicians to realize
that people who were dependent on government for welfare, jobs and
housing could be depended on to vote for progressive candidates.

Interestingly, the progressives did not initially align themselves with the
Socialist Party of America as they felt our capitalist-Christian nation

was just fine and only needed some oversight. The SPA was founded in 1901 and had its best showings in the 1912 and 1920 general elections, garnering more than 900,000 votes. By the 1920's the bi-partisan experiment of progressivism had passed and people who trusted big government and desired structural change in society migrated to the far-left as Conservative ideals were seen as outdated and Marxist ideals were seen as, well, progressive or forward thinking.

Franklin Delano Roosevelt (FDR) capitalized on leftist intellectual sentiment for equality and labor's desire for jobs programs during the Great Depression to win four presidential elections. Socialists won two seats at the congressional level and saw their candidates become mayor four times in Milwaukee between 1910 and 1956. (I chalk that up to the not-so-coincidental ethnic German demographic.) The socialists stopped running presidential candidates after 1956, because nobody would vote for them, and they eventually changed their name to Social Democrats USA, and a splinter group eventually became the Democratic Socialists of America (DSA). The DSA claims that it is a political and activist organization and not a political party; however, they describe themselves as today's progressives. Senator Sanders, as well as congresswomen AOC, and Tlaib are members of the DSA.

Basically, there have been different iterations of progressive thought over the past 120 years, and by the 1920s, Republicans left the fold, and progressive thought became a part of the Democratic and socialist agenda. At the turn of the 20th century, the Social Gospel movement was the primary school of progressive thought. This was an intellectual approach that liberal activists of the era took, to apply Christian values to social problems, most notably alcoholism, poverty, crime, unclean air and water, education, and war. LBJ and his parents were believers in the Social Gospel approach to progressivism, which sought to transform the narrative around social problems that affected only certain sectors of America into moral problems that could rally conservatives. By the

1960s, liberals began to view Social Gospel and the New Deal as unsuccessful, because neither went far enough in attacking capitalism more vigorously, nor did they help blacks, women, and gays achieve equality.

From that point, progressivism took a hard turn left, and it has now hijacked the Democratic Party. Traditionally the DSA has had to reluctantly partner with the Democrats under the old saying, "The enemy of my enemy is my friend." Since the DSA is not a party—they see establishing themselves a third party as a disaster waiting to happen —they have aligned themselves with the Democrat's opposition to the Republicans. Senator Sanders is a DSA member, who runs as an independent but caucuses with Democrats.

Despite what you read in the news or hear on TV, progressivism is not a spin-off of classical liberalism; it is the antithesis of classical liberalism. Liberalism lost many of its conservative and moderate voices in the 1970s, as conservative Democrats rejected what was then a hard turn left and flocked to the Republican Party. These people joined what was a "neoconservative" or neocon movement within the Republican Party, which was the softer, gentler party Bush 41 spoke about. Many of these people are more pejoratively described by the modern Right as "RINOs"—Republicans in name only—for their interventionist foreign policy. They prefer strong anti-Soviet and pro-Israel positions and yet favor colossal government spending, particularly on defense and international relations, as well as deficit spending rather than austerity measures, pro-immigration, a mixed economy, and rescue packages, along with ever more tolerant views on social policies.

Interestingly, backlash against Bush 43's confusing neocon policies by moderate and independent whites—and frustration with never-ending wars in the Middle East—helped lead to the election of President Obama in 2008. Republicans realized that neocon policies and Libertarian policies favored by the Koch brothers may not be the way to ever regaining legislative or executive control. Conservative backlash included the subsequent rise of the reactionary Tea Party Movement in 2009 that led to Republicans taking control of the House of Representatives and nearly the Senate in 2010. The early dismissal of neocons from the 2016 Republican primary field was evidence that the Tea Party still existed.

In hindsight, the people who left the Democratic Party in the 1970s, because they couldn't stand the increasingly liberal policies of people like Ted Kennedy, Walter Mondale and Jimmy Carter—and radicals like presidential hopefuls Lyndon LaRouche and Jerry Brown—were the same people who, ironically, 30 years later, because of failed moderate-leaning neocon policies, led to the 2008 election of a far more left-of-center candidate in President Obama. It took a grass-roots effort between 2010 and 2016 to mitigate what could have been an even worse Obama presidency and prevent four more years of it with Hillary Clinton.

THE UNITED NATIONS AND MARX

Moses Hess was the one who taught Marx that socialism was inseparable from internationalism. This is why socialists are bent on globalism, no borders, international accords like the Paris Agreement, international organizations like the United Nations, international events like the Olympics and the World Cup, and so on and so forth. Marxists founded the International Workingmen's Association in 1864. Internationalism is a big thing to the Leftists.

The Marxists, then as they do today, believed the proletariat has no fatherland—only a fraternal kinship with other proletariats across the world. How do you peacefully unite such disparate nations? You can't. It requires domination, the eradication of boundaries, and enforcement of a single-party system, lest someone goes off the reservation. Who could pull this off? In the 1850s, nobody could, but someday, someone as strong and determined as a Greek god could. Marx kept a bust of the Greek god Zeus in his study for a symbolic reason: Zeus took Europe captive, just as Marx fantasized about doing himself. Is it, therefore, any surprise that Zeus is a leftist role model? Dominate, change, and control. Yikes!

It's important to reiterate that the Left needs globalism, and, ideally, a borderless world, because there can't be places for economic, political or religious asylum that can harbor capitalists, or the religious, who are seeking refuge from the Leftist agenda. The Left needs whatever capitalists are still standing to pay taxes and be subject to whatever regulation Big Brother can approve.

Marxists have always been drawn to the notion of a powerful force being able to hold the world captive; it just never ever works, but does that stop them? No. Is it any surprise, given the one-worlder's agenda, that the only religious or mythical figure in the lobby of the UN building in New York is, ready, a bust of Zeus? Why not Jesus? Or, notable earthly leaders like Lincoln, Gandhi, Churchill, or FDR? Why Zeus? Because he is the symbol of one-worldism. The Marxist vision for a single-government, new world order. It's as simple as that.

ANIMAL FARM AND THE UNHEEDED WARNINGS ABOUT THE SOVIET'S BRAND OF SOCIALISM

During World War II most Brits and Americans considered the U.S.S.R. as an ally for their role in the allies' victory over the Axis Powers. Leftist intellectuals were tickled that there was a certain acceptance of socialism as an equal player on the world stage with capitalism. Up until World War II most leftist intellectuals in the west felt the Soviet model was the best Marxist option out there particularly when compared to fascism. In the intelligentsia's world pro-communist literature was acceptable and pro-fascist literature was not. Then, one of their own spoke up.

British author George Orwell was a committed socialist and didn't care for either of the prevailing European models – Russian communism or German, Italian and Spanish fascism. He felt there were plenty of people who were against fascism but nobody was recognizing the ills of Stalinism so he decided to write a polemic essay on the failures of the Soviet system using an allegorical method and called it Animal Farm.

Animal Farm was the story of a countryside property owned by a debt-ridden, inattentive and alcoholic farmer. Some animals, namely the pigs, symbolized key players in the Bolshevik Revolution, while other animals represented other elements of the Russian population. Old Major was Marx, Napoleon was Stalin, Snowball was Trotsky and the young pig killed by Napoleon was Bukharin. The dogs were the security forces while the sheep and horses, who didn't understand what was going on, were the compliant and conformist masses.

Orwell was not subtle and caught hell for writing it. During the war anti-Soviet literature was frowned upon by the British government and absolutely not condoned by the intelligentsia. Despite completing the book in February 1944 it took Orwell over a year and a half to find a publisher willing to stand up to leftist pressure. Months after VE Day it was finally published and today it remains a polarizing work as just it was then. Orthodox Marxists find it offensive, but the CIA has a different opinion and bought the film rights to the book in the early 1950's as the Second Red Scare arrived. The battle between conservative and leftist messaging was now in full swing.

THE SECOND RED SCARE AND THE RISE OF CONSERVATISM

Immediately after World War II, most Americans considered the U.S.S.R. an ally for their role in the defeat of Germany, and the Soviets were awarded with a permanent seat on the United Nations Security

Council. However, distrust of the Reds grew, and American attitudes quickly changed.

In 1947, President Harry S. Truman issued the Loyalty Order in response to fears Soviet agents were infiltrating every government across the globe. It required that all federal employees be evaluated to determine if they were loyal to the U.S. government or not. President Truman's action initially alarmed people on both sides of the aisle. Republicans and Libertarians, who valued personal liberties and Democrats, who wanted freedom to associate with whatever political party or organization they chose were uneasy. But, generally, it was seen as necessary given the behavior the communists were exhibiting in the years after World War II.

Between 1945 and 1949, the Soviets created satellite states in East Germany, Bulgaria, Hungary, Poland, Czechoslovakia, Romania and Albania to build a protective wall around their nation, and by 1949 had successfully tested a nuclear bomb. That same year, a four-year civil war between Soviet backed Mao Zedong and the American and Japanese backed Kuomintang (KMT) ended, with Mao prevailing and establishing the People's Republic of China (PRC). The First Indochina War (1946-54) drew the U.S., China and the Soviets into what started as a local insurgency by the Leftist Việt Minh, led by Hồ Chí Minh, against the French. The U.S. provided naval, air force and CIA assistance on behalf of the French. From 1950-53, the Korean Conflict occurred. By 1955, the French had left South Vietnam for the Americans to manage and the Second Indochina War, more commonly called the Vietnam War, began. In 1953, a socialist uprising began in Cuba and by New Year's Day 1959, a leftist government was just 90 miles off the Florida coast. Communism was spreading in Europe, Asia and Latin America and something urgently needed to be done to prevent leftist sympathizers from making any headway in the U.S.

UNION MEMBERSHIP

In Economic Marxism, the working class was the oppressed group. As the industrial revolution spread from Europe to the United States and Canada, so did union membership. In the 1930s, several laws were enacted to protect the rights of workers in America and after World War II, union membership, as a percentage of the workforce, grew until it peaked at 35% in 1954. But America was becoming more conservative. A Republican congress passed the Taft-Hartley Act in 1947 that restricted union power and although no longer enforced, it kicked any communists out of top union positions. America never had a strong leftist tradition and the 1950's marked a turning point. Membership declined from 35% in 1954 to 20.1% in 1983 and it's now at 10.3%. Globalization, automation, environmental regulation and labor costs played factors. The U.S. has the 5th lowest union membership rates out of 36 nations studied by the Organization for Economic Co-Operation and Development (OECD). Unions, who supported Socialist candidates in the early part of the 20th century, and later FDR and Truman, began to lose the narrative of the Democratic Party to people in academia, intellectual elites, the arts and the media. Today, the only growth in the union movement is in the public sector.

WHAT THE MARXISTS MISUNDERSTAND ABOUT PATRIOTISM AND NATIONALISM

The 1950s are seen as an extremely patriotic time in American History and since the Left hates nationalism, patriotism, flag waving and the America First ideals of that era, they look at it with a certain amount of contempt. Attacks on patriotism are not a new thing. As you've concluded by now, nineteenth century Germany had no shortage of strange characters. Wilhelm Marr (1818-1904), a part-time writer, anarchist, politician, humanist and revolutionary, who carried Feuerbach's Essence of Christianity with him during his travels, wrote a book titled, Secret

Societies of Switzerland, in 1846, which documented the happenings with humanist clubs. In it, he encouraged stirring hatred and contempt and waging a war "Against all prevailing ideas of religion, of the state, of country, of patriotism." There's no indication that Marr ever met Marx but, perhaps, due to the similar spelling of their names, their quotes are sometimes misattributed. But, there's no doubt Marr was a leftist who had issues with patriotism. Later, after being repudiated by fellow socialists for being too extreme, he pulled a 180 and abandoned his Jewish faith, became an anti-Semite and nationalist and predicted an inevitable battle between Germans and Jews that Hitler later took keen interest in. Who are these people?

Whether your name was Marr or Marx, the Leftists have always had issues with nationalism and patriotism. Nationalism means different things to the Right and Left. Patriotism is also misunderstood. A lot of people see them as interchangeable words. Whereas, the Right views prideful America in a fairly simple and straightforward context—proud patriotism emanating up from the people as seen in the love and devotion to one's country and our great flag—the Left sees this as Nazi-like nationalism and, by association, has a negative connotation—a conscious placement of one's country and culture above all others. The simpleton logic train is that patriotism is embarrassingly disrespectful to members of any oppressed class, and it really feels Nazi-like; therefore, patriots are fascists!

What the Left tends to get wrong is that nationalism is a top-down phenomenon, where the government advocates or encourages behavior that's in the national best interest. Nationalism was the narrative Mussolini and Hitler used to motivate labor and industry to get on the same page. It's the federal government telling the people, "This is the way to think if you are a good citizen." A great example is Chinese, North Korean or Soviet-era edicts, military parades, and their anti-West propaganda. It's the state telling people why they should be glad to live where they do. It's the state telling parents, "We'll teach and raise your children better than you."

Patriotism, on the other hand, is more of a ground-up action where people express pride in who we are as a people (the land of the free and the home of the brave), where they live (one nation under God), what their country stands for (life, liberty, and the pursuit of happiness), and what it means to them (freedom and opportunity). The government does not need to tell patriots these things. The federal government has never told the American people, "Be glad you live here." Patriotism does not come from the state. It's passed on from parents to children. Religion does not come from the state. It's passed on from parents to children. Love of baseball, football, hunting and fishing does not come from the state. It's passed on from parents to children. Unlike those communist examples above, they don't need to be told that their country is great, because they already know it.

There hasn't been such a thing as "white nationalism" in the U.S. since the days of the Confederacy, and that lasted a whole four years. It simply doesn't exist and hasn't for over 150 years. This deliberate blending of the two, nationalism and patriotism, plays perfectly into the racist/white supremacy narrative being pushed by the Left in America. To them, patriotism is an embarrassing fondness for America's founding (i.e., slavery) and an unnecessary chest beating (by deplorables in the flyover states who vote red) that endorses and perpetuates white patriarchy, to the detriment of oppressed groups, like immigrants from the Middle East or Central America.

Nationalism across the globe is good, when it encourages a commitment to the essential spirit of a country. The best examples are tourism and every four years when the Olympics come around. Nationalism by a country's leadership, and not patriotism, drives the local tourism industry. This type of nationalism can put a spotlight on a country's unique economy, its culture, its sports teams, its natural beauty, and so on and so forth. On the contrary, nationalism can be bad when it deviates from things like sports, food or tourism and manifests itself in the devotion to wars, dictators or personality cults, who are up to no good. Racism (including ethic and religious divisions) exists in every nation, to one degree or another, but the Left only wants to equate nationalism with white racism and, specifically, white supremacy. Conservatives do not identify nationalism with white nationalism, but the Left wants Americans to believe otherwise. This erroneous association is a construct of the Left, because Hitler tied top-down nationalism to legislatively-mandated racism, and the Left wants to tie conservatism to racist, white nationalism.

One thing that torques the Left is how nations were able to advance moral thought, country-by-country, as lands were explored, and populations expanded. When man first appeared on Earth, there were just families and tribes and neighboring tribes and maybe some hostile neighboring tribes, but there were no nations. The development of nations in the Western hemisphere, in particular, but Japan as well, allowed people to identify with something beyond their family and tribe. It allowed laws to be debated and enforced for the benefit of groups larger than the tribe. It was a major reason some nations grew, morally and intellectually, faster than others. There are many reasons why the Hutus murdered more than one million Tutsis in Rwanda in 1994, including a clear lack of national identity that could have bound those two tribes into something bigger. It's unknown if the existence of a national identity would have prevented some or all of the genocide in Rwanda, but the absence of it certainly didn't help.

IF PROGRESSIVISM IS MARXISM, IS LIBERALISM MARXISM TOO?

The short answer is, no. Comedian Dennis Miller once said, "Liberalism is like a nude beach – it sounds good until you get there." If that's the case, what would he say about Marxism? As the '60s approached, many leftist intellectuals began to think that the liberal idealism our country was founded on didn't lean leftward enough. Moderates on both the left and the right felt that classical liberalism promotes freedom and individual rights and liberties. The pillars of freedom are the rule of law (contrasted with the rule of men) and private property, andclassical liberalism promotes free enterprise (people voluntarily engaging in financial transactions) and a severely limited government. The term laissez faire is often used to describe the free-market economics of classical liberalism.

Liberalism in the eighteenth century meant a movement away from monarchies and theocracy and more toward elected governments, led by educated individuals and an economy run by businessmen and not kings. They were children of the Enlightenment and were liberating themselves from the whims of a king or a bishop. Sounds noble, doesn't it? Liberalism in the 19th and first half of the twentieth century in America referred to a Whiggish ideal of inevitable social and idealistic progress, along with a measured movement away from classical Christian fundamentalism and toward a more enlightened and scientific way of thinking. Liberalism from World War II and into twenty-first-century America remains rooted in a science-based skepticism.

Through the twentieth century in America, there were essentially five types of American Democrats: (1) southern conservatives, who voted democratic out of a distrust of northern Republicans; (2) educated suburban moderates; (3) blue collar workers, who preferred strong unions and ample government spending and who usually vote blue, despite holding conservative views on guns, gay rights, and immigration; (4) urban dwellers, including the elites; and (5) a radical Marxist element, who vote Democrat, due to no viable socialist avenue. In 2020, the first one is virtually gone, the third is transitioning in its socioeconomic composition from rust-belt whites to Latinos, and the last one is growing. JFK was a traditional American liberal, as was LBJ and Jimmy Carter. Except for the radical leftists, the Democrats, for most of the 20th century, were pro-American, pro-military, pro-Christian, pro-second amendment, and pro-law and order. This is changing. Thanks to the progressives, the American left is lurching further and further leftward, to the point where a strong military, the church, and police are no longer trusted pillars of society.

Although they took on social issues, such as civil rights and the environment, liberals of the twentieth century did not address too many capitalistic aspects of American life, instead preferring a "mixed economy," whereby the government played a significant, but not dominant, role in the national economy. Beginning in the Civil Rights era, the southern conservatives abandoned the Democratic Party as Cultural Marxism moved it too far left, leaving two factions: (1) Moderates and liberals, who believed in addressing social ills like poverty, housing, and health care. (2) A growing and more radical wing believed the liberals weren't doing enough to address more subjective concepts, like racism or nebulous concepts like social, economic and environmental injustice and their presence began to show on the national stage in the 1960s.

The more radical Democrats that emerged after World War II, and certainly after the Red Scare, did not abandon the Democratic Party, but believed that the keys to bringing change to America were for them to become activists, teachers, and writers. Most college-educated liberal boomers alive today embrace Cultural Marxism but reject—to various degrees—economic Marxism. The boomers liked the cultural aspects of Marxism, like freedom to fornicate and smoke weed and not be hassled about it by parents, pastors and police, but disliked the economic constraint of not being free to make a lot of money. Today's young people take cultural Marxism for granted and seek more of the economic and governance aspects of Marxism. They would view the boomers as conservative.

THE MARXIST HIJACKING OF AMERICAN LIBERALISM

The high point of American liberalism came in the mid-1960s, with the accomplishments of LBJ. President Johnson had several signature achievements during his tenure, including the enactment of many of his Great Society programs. LBJ's agenda centered on civil rights, education, and poverty, the adoption of Medicare, the breakdown of segregation, and a growth in activism (war, environment, social policy, etc.).

Post–World War II liberals, coming of age in the 50s and 60s, did not feel their parents' New Deal programs went far enough. They felt FDR's New Deal was too nationalistic (how ironic in today's political climate—a Democrat with nationalistic views) and, despite the adoption of Keynesian economic theory, was still focused on the preservation of capitalism, wealth, equity, and private property ownership. Gradually, liberal intellectuals crafted a new vision for achieving economic and social justice.

The mainstream liberalism of the early '60s contained no real hint of radicalism, no clear inclination to revive New Deal era crusades against concentrated economic power, and no intention to fan class passions or redistribute wealth or restructure existing institutions. Internationally, the liberal worldview was strongly anti-communist. It aimed to defend the free world, to encourage economic growth at home, and to ensure that the resulting plenty was fairly distributed. Their agenda—much influenced by Keynesian economic theory—envisioned massive public expenditure that would speed economic growth, thus providing the public resources to fund larger welfare, housing, health, and educational programs.

America was the wealthiest and most successful democracy in the world, but not all liberals were content. Many saw the Kennedy administration as falling short in tackling society's issues. They wondered how a country so wealthy could have so many poor people. Marxists recognized the disenchantment certain liberals saw with the social programs that began in the mid-'60s and, by the late '60s and early '70s, advocated a much more radical and militant approach to social economic change.

The "New Left" Movement of the '60s was exactly what leftists like Marcuse wanted—a group of young politically involved activists, who advocated for social issues (civil rights, abortion rights, drug law reform, etc.) and withdrawal from an anti-communist war (Vietnam), rather than traditional Marxist positions on labor and socioeconomic class.

NAMES TO KNOW: MICHAEL HARRINGTON

Activist, writer and atheist named Michael Harrington (1928–89) founded and chaired the new Democratic Socialists of America in 1973 and is considered one of the founding fathers of the modern left in America. A lifelong leftist, he was already on J. Edgar Hoover's watch list as a "dangerous character" by his mid-20s. His 1962 book, The Other America, was a rant about how an indifferent America wasn't noticing pervasive poverty, right in front of its own eyes. It was light on facts and heavy on anecdotes, personal observations from his days working in a Manhattan soup kitchen, and his emotional calls for action, that tugged at the heartstrings. Someone gave a copy to JFK, and next thing you know, it became tied to the War on Poverty that he and LBJ pursued.

Harrington was a Marx apologist. As the Eastern Bloc crumbled in the late 1980s, he seemed surprisingly perplexed as to why Marxism wasn't working and blamed it on authoritarianism. I guess he struggled to understand how large state organizations could be so dysfunctional that some people ate, while others starved. Despite this, Harrington really wanted the Soviet Union to remain Marxist. Rather than admit the Leninist-Stalinist model failed, he doubled down and claimed Marxism could work, if just given the right chance and under the right circumstances. He actually advocated for keeping the Soviet Union intact, as if he, somehow, knew better than the hundreds of millions of people who wanted it to disintegrate.

This is classic leftist thought that you see in the leadership of many large, one-party American cities today. No matter how bad things are, just trust us and stick to the program. It might be bad and getting worse, but if you vote conservative, vote for freedom, vote for liberty, vote for capitalism, or wish for smaller government, it will be worse than worse.

Harrington died in July of 1989. He did not live to see the collapse of the Berlin Wall, just a few months later, in November or the lowering of the hammer and sickle flag from the Kremlin on Christmas Day, 1991. I'm sure those events would have brought a tear to his eye, and considering his zealotry, calls from him to never give up the dream!

NAMES TO KNOW: SAUL ALINSKY

Another founding father of modern American Marxist strategy is a man named Saul Alinsky (1909–72). Although fellow leftist, Abbie Hoffman, is better known, due to his highly visible public appearances, Alinsky was the behind-the-scenes architect who shaped much of '50s and '60s Marxism in America. He was essentially the brains behind the '60s white radicalism, and although he died in 1972, three latter-day presidential candidates have referenced his brand of leftist activism— Barrack Obama, Bernie Sanders, and Hillary Clinton.

Alinsky was a writer, lecturer, and community activist, who was highly influential with college students and blacks in the '50s and '60s. He was, for all intents and purposes, a radical and an anarchist, who claimed to be neither a capitalist nor a Marxist; however, the ideas he spewed and methods he encouraged were clearly out of the Karl Marx playbook. He recognized that Americans, during the Cold War, were not ready to embrace Soviet-styled Marxism, so he cast his ideas in more acceptable terms familiar to Americans: Democratic (i.e., the best of America) and socialist (i.e. the best of Europe). What he really meant was socialism, being implemented gradually through Democratic means. He was the one who coined the term Democratic Socialist—Senator Sander's and AOC's platform.

Unless you were alive in the '60s or followed President Obama's platform closely in the mid- to late-'00s few people in America today would recognize the name Saul Alinsky, but he is a demigod for the Left. One of Alinsky's more controversial methods was the advice he gave anarchists to find a way to be deemed a dangerous enemy in the eyes of the establishment, in order to gain credibility. His writings are a must-read for aspiring leftists, as they outline various anarchist tactics and Marxist tenants. Alinsky believed that the Left needed to fight on two fronts—political and cultural—and follow Lenin's playbook, which was to use culture to your advantage and find a way to shape a dystopian society of "useful idiots." If Lenin's ideas were executed properly, these useful idiots would be dependent on the state for every aspect of their lives.

Lenin and Alinsky believed this dependency would transform people's lives into one that needed the government for everything, and if the population needed the government to eat, it ensured that the population could no longer risk voting for another party. Because the useful idiots needed the government for food, housing, and healthcare and being unarmed and without options, they could not risk revolting, lest they wanted their lives turned upside down. They became useful to the state.

Alinsky wrote that control of a population—necessary to create what he called a Lenin-like social state—requires coordinated disruption and upheaval in eight sectors of society. These include healthcare, poverty, debt, gun control, welfare, education, religion, and class warfare. Alinsky advocated government control of health care; increased poverty rates (counterintuitive, but necessary to create dependency and force higher taxes on the wealthy); extreme Keynesian tax-and-spend policies;, confiscation of guns from private citizens; increased welfare rolls to control income, health, and housing; taking control of education, from spending to access to what students read; removal of God from government, schools, and the workplace; and finally dividing people into two classes: a large underclass, who will eagerly support confiscatory taxes placed on a (shrinking) minority—the wealthy.

MARXISTS AND WOMANHOOD

Because Marxism is designed to appeal to the oppressed class, you cannot paint a complete picture of its reach into American culture, without talking about womanhood and, specifically, feminism. I've known strong and principled women, who vote conservative and others, who vote liberal, and I'm well aware it's a statistical fact that more women vote liberal than conservative. Also, married women are predominantly conservative and single women are predominantly liberal. Feminists are almost universally progressive, which, again, is not liberal.

Like everything these days, it's pretty easy to figure out what's happening, if you examine it through the Marxist lens. All you need to do is substitute male-dominated patriarchy for capitalism and the template is identical: an oppressed group, being put down by an oppressor.

Although one could argue that feminists have existed for thousands of years, its forever home is linked to the Marxism principles born in Victorian England. Many women of that era understood and accepted that there were defined roles for men and women in the home and in society, and others resented this ideal. The barriers to employment, education and politics drove a small but determined band of activists and they found allies on the Left, who saw gender and not just socioeconomic class as fitting into the oppressor-oppressed dichotomy. At first, the campaign focused on abolition of slavery and working conditions for the poor in general. Eventually, it grew to include women's suffrage and other gender inequalities. Early western feminists found allies in Marx and Engels, who believed women were the equals of men at the dawn of human history, with little physiological or biological differentiation. (Sounds just like a Marxist to deny Christian beliefs, in differences between men and women). The Marxists felt that, rather than biology, it was feminine obligations (child birth) and the creation of social structures that evolved over time and forced them to be submissive. Classic Marxism—all of history is one group oppressing another.

It's worth noting that Engels was opposed to marriage, on the grounds that state and church-sanctioned marriage was oppressive. Therefore, feminists maintain that those who accept traditional gender roles should just die off physically. In their view, traditional female roles are submissive and the demise of women, who choose this life, can't come fast enough. To the Leftists, choosing that role is an illegitimate calling, in an unequal arrangement, which is preventing them from being a complete being. In their view, to serve the family is an oppressive choice they shouldn't make. To make matters worse, they shouldn't be raising children. Some harbor the notion that in order to raise children who value equality, they must be removed from families and raised communally.

Engels felt monogamy was oppressive, because it allowed men to control their children and pass the property down to their heirs. Apparently, polygamous men or philanderers, like his buddy Marx, controlling children from multiple women was not oppressive??? Engels suggested that private property needs to be abolished, because it leads to slave ownership and the submission of women, which are, of course, forms of oppression. Therefore, in Engels' eyes, if you were married and owned property, you, therefore, are by definition, oppressing your women and your slaves.

Whereas, capitalists in the nineteenth century were willing to employ women to meet production demands, the concept of empowerment and equality for any low skilled employee, let alone women, was initially unheard of at all. Marxism was the driver behind workplace empowerment, through the support of labor unions and the advocacy of a sexless workplace, where all workers dressed alike and had numbers, rather than names on their uniforms. Marxists knew a woman may not be able to hammer as hard or as fast as a man, nor be able to carry as much weight across the factory floor, but they showed up for work and didn't drink, gamble or get in fights, on or off the job. Early feminists believed a working woman was a productive woman, who didn't need a man for survival. Working women set good and sometimes embarrassing – but necessary–examples for lazy men and best of all, they'd pay union dues, party dues and taxes! Over time, the social stigmas of delayed marriage, illegitimacy, higher education and making a career outside the home waned, as did the concept of welfare as a tool to aid underclass women. Just as being female, single and employed was once frowned upon, so was welfare, until the government became an acceptable provider for single mothers, instead of men.

Hardline Marxism is at work here. The Leftists want women to work, because besides liberating them from men and children and, therefore, working means they are paying taxes for programs. It means they are putting society ahead of the family. If they are at home, they are not producing and not paying into government programs. Stay at home moms are, in the eyes of modern American Marxists, net takers and not net givers. These takers should die off, as feminists insist. Their contributions to their husbands, children, extended family, church and social clubs take away energy that could be invested in political agendas.

See, deep down, Marxists hold different views than Americans do on what it means to be a woman and when you stop and think about it, radical feminists have adopted Marxist views on womanhood. Marx believed in equality between the sexes, but equality also meant the value women could add to the factory floor and their value in tax revenue contributions.

As a conservative man, it's particularly challenging to discuss the distinction between womanhood and feminism, because to those on the Left, there is little to no distinction; therefore, commentary on feminism is not correctly seen as commentary on Marxism, but rather incorrectly taken as an attack on womanhood. By way of quick background the first wave of feminism came about with the progressive movement in the late 1800's. It tended to focus on voting, workplace safety and civil rights. By the 1960's and 70's it was about sexual liberation and workplace behavior including pay and sexual discrimination. Today it is about changing men's annoying behavior that can't be modified through legislation.

People wonder what the world would be like if woman's liberation prevailed as the dominant cultural norm and someone who has studied this has an idea. What could a world of no-strings-attached relationships and without the burdens of marriage and child care that could come in the way of career futures look like? Bonnie Noonan, a professor at Xavier University in New Orleans, and writer of two books on women in science fiction, suggested in her 2015 book titled, Gender in Science Fiction Films 1964-1979: A Critical Study, that woman's liberation, and not technology, is at the root of the utopian-dystopia of the year 2274 that is depicted in the classic 1976 movie Logan's Run.

To be clear, conservatives understand equality of the sexes. We know there is nothing wrong with being a woman. There is nothing wrong with a woman choosing to go to college, either part time or full time, or not at all. Or, working part time or full time, or not at all. There is nothing wrong with a man staying home and caring for children while his wife works. There is nothing wrong with a woman being paid more than a man. There is nothing wrong with a woman being a man's boss. There is nothing wrong with a woman choosing to tend to elderly parents or to a husband or children (or all of the above) or choose to be, or not to be, estranged from her family and/or not to marry at all. Also, unless you're a Marxist, there is nothing wrong with a woman volunteering her free time at her church.

Each of those options sound like the types of lifestyle choices modern day feminists would insist upon. Options are good, right? Choice is good, right? Not if you're a Marxist. To them, women should be free to make their own choices, unless of course they make choices the feminists don't like. Choice means making the appropriate decision a good leftist would make. Marxists speak of choice (in the context of school, employment and marriage, not abortion), but in reality, it's not a choice to work, stay home or go to school, or a combination thereof. They want women to work, and, more accurately, they need women to work. But, why exactly? Is it to help a woman realizing her full potential, provide aspirational goals to young girls or achieve personal or professional fulfillment? Is it to provide a second household income or prove that women can do what men can do? Not necessarily. The feminist view on employment is straight out of the Marxist playbook. They want to be equal with men and the way to be equal is to engage in an activity – such as full-time work—that hinders, if not eliminates, family and child-bearing obligations, which they claim is an, if not the, advantage men have over women in the workplace. Only when they have deprived men of this advantage, can they be equal. To them, forsaking traditional feminine roles needs to be done, first and foremost, out of spiteful disdain for the patriarchy. Besides, good Leftists instinctively know tribute to the state and their tribe is more important than tribute to the family.

Have you ever wondered why the voices of four leftist freshmen congressmen known as The Squad are so outsized? Normally, young people elected to the U.S. House of Representatives for the first time yield little power or influence, and are rarely so outspoken, but not AOC (D-NY), Omar (D-MN), Ayanna Pressley (D-MA) and Tlaib (D-MI). The reason for this relates to a controversial theory associated with feminism that has emerged over the past 20 years and it's worth discussing, because of its Marxist ties to oppression. It's called intersectionality and it arose out of dissatisfaction by some in the feminist movement, who felt the movement was only concerned about gender equality and not race, sexual orientation and socioeconomic class equality.

Think of intersectionality as a layering of discrimination, like the building of a sandwich or a birthday cake. Each layer would represent an identity threshold, which carries increasingly more weight. By virtue of being a woman that constitutes one layer of discrimination an individual has to live with. A woman of color would therefore have two layers. An immigrant woman of color would have three layers. An immigrant woman of color, who is a lesbian, would make four layers, and if that woman is also a Muslim, it would make five layers. In the Leftist mindset, layers are therefore levels of credibility – the more the better. In the case of The Squad, you have four women of color and two whom are Muslim and one of whom is an immigrant. Mind you, there is nothing wrong with anybody voicing their opinion. Everyone's voice counts equally. The Marxist element here is the hypocritical insistence that the voices of some people, because of their gender and the color of their skin, matter more than others. To them, some people are just more equal than others.

At the end of the day, is using sexism as a resentful tool to anger people productive? Is creating a culture of victimhood (the oppressed class) really empowering? Or, is it really just an excuse to fight the oppressive class for the sake of fighting them (because that's what Marxists do)? The right for a woman to make choices on education, employment and family is understood; however, one cannot write a book about Marxism in America without pointing out that female empowerment does not require blind adherence to militant feminist positions on concepts such as the workplace, marriage and family. Workplace success is great and holistic, and balance in one's life is desirable, but it's wrong to suggest patriarchy, or childbearing and caring for the nuclear or extended family automatically interferes with this.

Earlier I mentioned how society was once an honor culture then a virtue culture, but today we've devolved into a victim culture. But is it a victim culture or is it actually a Marxist versus anti-Marxist culture? One of the ironies of the Leftist movement is that they are trying to use the constitution to legislate anti-Marxist behavior out of America by casting any and all conservative positions as racist, sexist, homophobic or xenophobic (i.e. oppressive), yet traditional conservative-Christian views are the basis of the same constitution the Left wants to use to tear down those views.

WHY LEFTISTS HATE JEWISH (AND AMERICAN) NATIONALISM

Marx rejected nationalism, because in his view, as noted in The Communist Manifesto, "A working man has no country." The idea that there could be an enclave, where the elite could live in a walled-off and fortified capitalist or religious exile was unacceptable; therefore, in Marxist orthodoxy, nationalism, with its borders, walls and army defending its hegemony is a non-starter for progressives. Dating back to Hess and Marx's time, the Left's attacks on religion are not just limited to Christianity but to Judaism as well and, in particular, conservative Judaism and, specifically, nationalists who live in Israel. Muslims tend to get a pass from the radical Left, because they are viewed as a cultural, racial, and religious minority in Europe and America. The Left has long since concluded that white America hates Muslims, so they got invited to join the oppressed club, whether they wanted to or not.

To most American Christians, religious morality, along with ethical, business, and political morality are the same. Our Constitution flowed from fundamental Christian values, and this a big reason why leftists see our constitution as a pesky impediment to the implementation of their agenda. Many leftists believe the world's future is secular and borderless and no place in America has this ever been as alive and well as New York City. The Big Apple was, for decades, the epicenter of the Frankfurt School's leftist agenda, and remains the spiritual home of Marxism in America and not because if it's location or it's institutions but because of the people who live there. Rural Americans are very homogenous and don't see disparity in economic standing or differences in religion or skin color as often as those in large cities. Urban dwellers tend to be better educated, more diverse and more amenable to a secular and globalist perspective.

No city in America represents that way of life more than New York City where an estimated 176 languages are spoken in the homes of school children and there exists an extraordinarily high degree of what World Religion Report calls "Post-Christianity".—New York City being the home of approximately 1.1 million Jews—the largest Jewish community outside of Israel—is clearly globalist leaning. Leftism has always appealed more to New Yorkers than anyone else in America. Anti-Marxist candidate Donald Trump only secured 9.8% of the Manhattan vote in 2016 including a whopping 7.5% in the People's Republic of the Upper West Side where Columbia University is located. As a consequence of decades of the Left's influence in New York, and contempt for anti-Marxists like

President Trump most American Jews are neither conservative nor supporters of the Israeli state.

While Christians would agree that decisions consistent with Christian-based ethics trumps decisions made based on race, culture, and ethnicity, when it comes to judging actions, American leftists see it slightly different: secular ethics trumps religious or cultural convictions. An example of this is the pro-Palestinian leanings of news outlets, like the New York Times, Los Angeles Times, and Washington Post. Their anti-nationalist views are in line with the secular – and left-leaning – ethical values the Left prefers to have about the Palestinian question, compared to the more conservative religious and moral values that might be held by Jews in Israel.

Add to this, the Leftist concept of one-worldism, where nationhood is frowned upon and borderless multiculturalism is encouraged, and it's little wonder why many American Jews hate borders and hate nationalism and, therefore, have disdain for border advocates like President Trump and Benjamin Netanyahu. Ethical values get turned into action and many New Yorkers support the anti-Israel Boycott, Divest, and Sanction, or BDS, movement. The New York Times knows its readership's anti-conservative and secular preferences and, therefore, has no issue with commentary that disparages President Trump and Netanyahu.

CULTURAL MARXISM: WORDS WITH NEW MEANINGS

Ever since Marcuse and the Frankfurt School got their hands on our cultural norms, generally accepted concepts Americans took for granted took on entirely different meanings. What was considered normal thinking and responsible commentary is now some version of hate speech directed at an oppressed class. Dissenting opinion is considered hateful or unconstitutional.

All societies limit some speech in some way or another and usually it's linked to imminent and dangerous behavior. In the U.S. for example speech is protected unless it incited panic such as screaming "fire" in a theatre. In Europe even truthful speech can be illegal if it hurts someone's feelings. For example, in Austria it is illegal to say anything, even if it's truthful or impossible to prove or disprove, if it makes a Muslim sad.

Let's explore some other examples. A Marxist scheme once described pejoratively in the West as one-worldism and intended to depict the eradication of capitalist havens, the reestablishment of a new cultural hegemony, and the formation of a single socialist order, was rebranded into the softer sounding, friendlier, and more environmentally conscience term globalism. Make America Great Again was mocked, because in the Left's eyes, America was never great to begin with. In the Leftist mindset it's inconceivable that anyone would promote making America great when it would be much more essential – and rewarding – to make the world great. Marcuse and his Cultural Marxist gang got to work redefining terms under the thinking that if you can change words you can change thoughts and if you can change thoughts you can change behaviors.

Over time common words and phrases to describe things were erased and new, less offensive and less hateful words started to take their place. Christianity, rather than a moral compass and a path to salvation, became "oppression." Illegal immigrants became asylum seekers. Capitalism became exploitation. Criminals on trial and prisoners in jail became "justice-involved persons." Making a salary you're proud of is now income inequality. Satanism, materialism, humanism, Darwinism and Freudism went from the fringe anti-Christian notions they are, to constitutionally protected and widely accepted views. Drug usage went from a moral weakness to a personal freedom. Vagrancy and panhandling became homelessness. Children went from joyous family assets to financial liabilities. Abortion became a woman's choice, then, bafflingly, reproductive rights (even though reproduction happened at conception many months prior). President's Day is now February Recess, and Columbus Day is now Indigenous People's Day.

Sexual proclivities became normalized aspects of human sexuality. Promiscuity went from a sin to a liberating lifestyle. Like drug usage, homosexuality went from a morally deficient behavior one chooses to engage in, to a lifestyle, and then to a genetic predisposition and an identity. Genders went from two to 71 and counting, if you ask Facebook. Pornography went from filth and dirt to indecency, then to adult material, and finally to erotica. Questioning whether a trans woman can—let alone should—be eligible for taxpayer abortions is not allowable, because such common-sense thoughts are now hateful. Homelessness rather than an individual accountability issue, became was rebranded "housing challenged" suggesting that the homeless were victims of capitalist factors.

Seasonal weather patterns became global warming, but when that didn't explain polar vortexes, it became climate change, and when that didn't alarm enough people, it became climate emergency. During the 2019 football game between Harvard and Yale, protesters gave it an even newer name, in what must be an odd appeal to constitutionally minded Americans: "Climate injustice." White guilt became privilege awareness. Questioning any leftist logic or behavior is now considered assault. Vandalism of private property is now OK because storefront windows are a manifestation of wealth and throwing a brick through it is a statement against income inequality—and besides, there was no harm done because, ready, windows aren't people. Anarchists are now "courageous Americans," as Joe Biden calls antifa, while those that used to be described as patriotic are now called right-wing provocateurs. Leftism is now "the resistance," as if we're living out a certain space opera, in real time. Lower taxes became gifts to the rich. Voter ID laws and efforts to remove people who died decades ago from voter rolls became voter suppression. Ferreting out a deceptive or dangerous scheme went from honorable and meritorious to a right-wing conspiracy theory.

Even some very touchy matters of race are trying to be recast into a new narrative. National borders became racist barriers, invented by white nationalists, to preserve the patriarchy and hegemony. George Washington and Thomas Jefferson became privileged slave owners. Neither Erickson, Columbus, de Avilés, Raleigh, the American Revolutionaries, nor the Native Americans gave birth to America—the slaves did, back in 1619, if you ask the New York Times. Betsy Ross's flag became a symbol of state-sponsored slavery. The Pledge of Allegiance became a xenophobic expression of patriarchy. This is Cultural Marxism at work.

THE FRANKFURT SCHOOL AND ONE-WORLDISM

Despite the contention and wishful thinking of many in academia, one-worldism wasn't an American political theory that was conceived and died in the mid-20th century, during the red scare. It was a concept first conceived by Kant and endorsed by Hegel and Marx, then refined by German neo-Marxists from the Frankfurt School living in exile from Hitler and working at Columbia University. One-worldism is still alive today, although it's more commonly called globalism. You can see it manifest itself in countless ways but thankfully American's have been slow to adopt it. The metric system and soccer are two staples of insufferable internationalism that have enjoyed only limited penetration America. The World Health Organization, the United Nations and even the Olympics are not as important to American's as they are to citizens of other countries.

Please note that other Marxists who fled fascist Italy and Germany in the early '30s ended up at their own "university in exile," known then as the "New School of Social Research" (now known as The New School), and, like Columbia, it is also located in Manhattan. But, Columbia seemed to be the epicenter of leftist American thought. Nonetheless, between The New School and Columbia, you had two separate groups working at two separate Manhattan schools, but on a similar mission: To import Marxism to America. They were Germans, living and working in exile within a safe democracy, far from the turmoil in continental Europe. Sounds familiar doesn't it? The New School's own website tells you everything you need to know about political, and, specifically, left-leaning political activism on college campuses: "The New School was founded a century ago in New York City by a small group of prominent American intellectuals and educators who were frustrated by the intellectual timidity of traditional colleges."

Let's be clear, one-worldism is a German Marxist concept that happened to get conjured up at Columbia because the theorists were running for their lives from Hitler and needed a safe space and found it on the Upper West Side. (Yes, Columbia is technically in an adjacent neighborhood called Morningside Heights, but many people consider the area from 110th to 125th Streets where Columbia lies as part of the Upper West Side.) The Left runs with the fact that since many of the globalist's theories were drafted at Columbia on American soil, it should be considered an American concept, as if that somehow Americanizes it or otherwise bestows some legitimacy to it. Globalism is a Marxist thing. It's a European thing. It's a Columbia University and Frankfurt School thing. It's not an American thing.

The one-world fantasy for the last 175 years has been to create a single, borderless Marxist utopia—no borders, no walls, and no place for the capitalist elite to escape. No more passports will be needed, as we're all citizens of the world. It would obviously be, by default, borderless (hence the one-world part), because if everyone lived in one single country, there would be no borders with another country, right?

This new world would have a single set of norms, based on typical socialist economic and political policies, a heavy dose of Cultural Marxism, and, get this, human rights. As everyone knows, socialism and human rights mix like oil and water. The vision of Marcuse and others was to make New York City—where Columbia and the New School are located—the new epicenter of leftist thought, just in case Hitler took over Europe. Taking what Marx, Darwin, and Freud taught and giving it a refreshing FDR-like American liberalism twist appealed to many American intellectuals, who would support Senator Sanders if they were alive today.

Cultural Marxism + the New Deal + a bit of capitalism to pay for everything = Utopia.

Many American leftists residing in the ivory towers of academia between the two World Wars embraced a socialist-centered economic policy, including a Brit named John Maynard Keynes (1883–1946), who was a lecturer at The New School and is known as the Left's "Patron Saint of Economics". Given the groundwork the Frankfurt School laid at Columbia from 1930 through World War II (along with the influential exiles and foreigners working at The New School), it should, therefore, be no surprise that the United Nations Headquarters (UN) is in New York City. Many conservatives today, as they did in the late '40s, question the purpose and need for the UN. Whereas, many on the Left have always seen the UN as the template for an overarching, socialist-governing order. Its Manhattan location had less to do with NYC being the financial capital of the world and the largest city in the U.S., and more to do with the fact that in the late '40s, NYC was the intellectual epicenter of one-worldism.

One-worldism did not go unnoticed by American conservatives, and this is what got Senator Joe McCarthy (R-Wisconsin) so torqued in the late '40s, through the mid-'50s. His campaign to rid America of the growing threats of cultural Marxism, the un-American concept of a single leftist world order, and organizations such as the ACLU was largely led by FBI Director J. Edgar Hoover. Their objectives were not the issue. It was their tactics. Their efforts put an unwanted negative spotlight on the three pillars of Marxism in America—the arts, academia, and the media. Because the populations of those industries were primarily left-leaning, and indeed many were outted as committed Marxists, the Left needed to find a way fight back, so the American public would be sympathetic to them, rather than condemn.

And, to that end, they employed a standard Cultural Marxist tactic, which was to use the media to change the public's perception. They were very clever. They chose not to say that Marxism was good (which would never have worked during the Cold War), but instead cast McCarthy's accusations and draconian methods against American citizens as unconstitutional. Attacking the constitutionality of normal American conservative thought became increasingly common through the '50s and '60s, as a way to undermine conservative agendas and American values, without ever hinting of their Marxist intents. An element the Left had infiltrated—television news—was the tool they used to tear down McCarthy and his Red Scare.

Legislators, at the time, felt the American public needed to see these hearings to fully understand what was at stake, and, rather than just providing congressional transcripts, TV was the chosen medium. However, McCarthy, being the face of the anti-Marxist resistance, miscalculated how Americans would view him and his tactics. His guilty-until-proven-innocent mantra didn't resonate with an America that felt our leaders should be held to a higher standard and were above totalitarian interrogation techniques. McCarthy and the FBIs draconian methods were pounced on by an opportunistic left-leaning media. In the end, McCarthy's verbal sparring with an American military officer on live TV wasn't a good look for his cause. But, by then, television, and the news media as a whole, had successfully shaped the public's perception of him as being angry, obsessive, untrustworthy, and accusatory.

GLOBALISM AND WHY THE MARXISTS WANT IT—BADLY

One-worldism, which was exposed during the McCarthy era as a Marxist plot for a globalist, borderless world, is now labeled as globalism and is a renewed leftist scheme that will never be accepted by normal Americans, because it flies in the face of something called American Exceptionalism—an understanding that the U.S. is different and more special than any other country. The term was actually coined by Josef Stalin, as far back as 1929, to describe how America was essentially immune to certain elements of Marxist theory. This has not deterred the Leftists. They want America to be seen as equal, and certainly not superior, to Europe, where views on guns, homosexuality, immigration, and public assistance, among other things, are far more progressive.

Most Americans will rightfully state that we are different from, and better than, any European nation. This conflicts with Karl Marx's belief that each society needs to be egalitarian and politically equal, as part of a borderless world (one-worldism), to eradicate any capitalist republic, where the wealthy could exile themselves. Make no mistake about it, globalism, or one-worldism as it was known in the years after World War II, is not about tariff-free international commerce and convenient passport-less travel. That's the pretext to fool people into supporting it. It's about creating a single worldwide Orwellian (leftist) government.

Only a leftist would think of us as global citizens, living in a multicultural society, populated by immigrants. We are one nation under God, populated by settlers who normally buy into the notion of American Exceptionalism the day they arrive at our ports. We are Americans, and this is the United States of America—the best country in the world for many reasons. As President Trump says, "A country without borders is not a country," and the targeted deterioration of our customs and principals will always be viewed as un-American and morally wrong.

Chapter 8

PRESIDENT TRUMP AND ELECTION DAY 2016

WITH 2016 BRINGING A SHOCKING, WATERSHED event, that ushered Trump into the presidency, there's been a terrifying prospect, since that fateful day, that has consumed the progressives: Leftism, and the vision of the future that Obamaism had promised, had not only been exposed, but rejected. And progress–a word that means overthrowing the patriarchy in the grand march towards a leftist utopia– had been stopped. With Republicans then holding the trifecta–the presidency, along with senate and house control– it dawned on them that maybe 2015 and the first half of 2016 was the best it was ever going to get for Leftists in America. President Trump, and his hated followers from fly-over country, were cast as enemies of the revolution and their war on America took a sudden and more radical turn. President Trump must be removed from office, now, at any cost.

What's happened since 2016 is that President Trump's populist rhetoric has effectively peeled back the skin of the onion that once disguised the dark blue hues of some Democrats—and the media—and as each layer is removed, it's uncovered their actual numbers and true intent. President Trump's unpredictable and unorthodox methods have smoked out elements in Washington, DC; Hollywood; and the media as Marxists, not liberals, as these actors would like you to believe. Senators Warren, Kristen Gillibrand, Cory Booker, and Kamala Harris, along with at least 50 Congress members exposed themselves (if they hadn't already) as Marxists, through their endorsement of the preposterous Green New Deal, as well as their rejection of President Trump and every policy he has endorsed.

Although he ran as one, President Trump is not a Republican—at least not in the traditional sense—just as President Barack Obama, or Senator Sanders are not typical Democrats. President Trump does not adhere to traditional Republican orthodoxy and this is why there are so-called "Never Trumpers" in the Republican Party. Although President Obama was more left-leaning than any president since FDR, it could be argued that he had more in common on immigration, global warming, and the Middle East with President George W. Bush (Bush 43) than President Trump and either President Bush (41 or 43) do. So, it's no surprise that President Trump rejected every one of the Bushes, just as he did President Obama. The feeling was undoubtedly mutual.

Trump is nearly impossible to describe, because there hasn't ever been a politician like him holding national office. He's an American populist who preaches traditional American values that emphasize conservative views that focus on values such as freedom, liberty, and sovereignty. President Trump's views can swing between traditional American conservatism (crime), libertarianism (low taxes/low regulation/small government), confederalist (state's rights) and populist (pro-blue collar worker) positions. There's enough consistency on the Constitution to call him an originalist and an upholder of the ideals set forth by our founding fathers that constitute our American ethos—sort of a collection of ideals rooted in freedom, liberty, patriotism, capitalism, Christianity, and nationhood. And, with that image, one can say he looks and feels like a Republican. Yet, on the other hand, he caves on many border and budget issues, is not anti-LGBTQ (which annoys many in his Christian base), and is certainly not a deficit hawk, as federal spending is skyrocketing. These examples alone demonstrate that many of his positions are not those of a conventional Republican.

According to author and commentator Charlie Kirk, "What (President Trump's) arguing for is revitalization of the nation-state and restoration of sovereignty ... President Donald Trump stands affront of history to actually change the course of America back towards the protection of sovereignty." President Trump's world view is a rejection of globalism, a belief in protectionist nationalism for the U.S. (and Israel), and a strong military defense but military non-intervention. He rightfully holds our most trustworthy allies in high regard—Israel, Japan, the U.K., and Australia, while holding European – and Canadian–leftism, radical Islam, and rule breakers in contempt. He sees the European Union (EU) as contemptibly soft and his tactical approach with bold leaders and rogue nations is refreshing to conservatives but disconcerting to liberals. He has learned that as president, as it was when he was a business mogul, there are rules, exceptions to rules, and loopholes, but coming across the border illegally is not "finding a loophole"—it's breaking a rule. We have reached a point where pointing out illegal behavior is demonized. Neo-reactionaries, paleoconservatives, libertarians, and many conservatives embrace his pro-Christian, U.S. first, and anti-globalist agenda, which is 180 degrees from what the Left—and the international community— had become accustomed to under President Obama.

Obama-ism had become, as the Left believed when November 2016 approached, the starting point for the way America was going to be for the next 40 years or more. Secretary Hillary Clinton was the anointed successor and destined to bring eight (or maybe 40 or 80) years of increasing and irreversible leftism to America. However, along comes President Trump, and it's not just his rejection of President Obama and all the leftism his adoring followers were committed to maintaining. It's 63 million deplorable Americans joining President Trump in rejecting the prior eight years of Leftism and saying, "That's enough!" And, Secretary Clinton didn't have a concession speech planned. The Left was in shock. Oh, my God, they thought. Suddenly the world is coming to an end.

President Trump's alleged undermining of President Obama's signature achievements has been conveniently misunderstood and weaponized by the Left as proof that President Trump and his supporters are racists and climate-change deniers. Reactionary deviation from the things President Obama and his collaborators, like U.S. Attorney General Eric Holder, held near and dear, like globalism; an activist judiciary; softness on crime, drugs, and school discipline; and high regulation were seen as not only extremely troubling but existential threats by the Left. "Make America Great Again" is not a call to go back to the days of Jim Crow; it's a call to erase Marxism in America.

What was a bit surprising, was to see the "Never Trumpers" movement not give up on that, either. You would have thought Republicans would put away their differences and support their president, but that hasn't happened. This camp is/was full of the neocons like President George H. W. Bush (Bush 41), President Bush (43), Jeb Bush, Former Secretary of State Colin Powell, Former National Security Advisor John Bolton and Vice President Cheney, and RINOs like Former Ohio Governor John Kasich, United States Senator Lisa Murkowski of Alaska, Former United State Senator Jeff Flake of Arizona, Former Presidential Candidate Joe Walsh and Former California Governor Arnold Schwarzenegger—the latter-day Rockefeller Republicans. They were seen as establishment Republicans and their unwillingness to support a Republican president fed into the media's narrative that President Trump isn't a trustworthy Republican but something else—something evil and someone unhinged, a loose cannon, someone unworthy to carry the banner of conservatism, and someone unworthy of the highest office in the land. But, perhaps, most worrisome of all: What if President Trump isn't an anomaly?

What if a sleeping giant has been awakened? What if President Trump accurately represents the sentiments of American conservatives?

The reality is that President Trump is the most dangerous type of politician to the DC establishment. One with nothing to gain and no urgency to build consensus or make friends. President Trump is neither a fascist nor a white nationalist and his open rejection of Marxism and it's one-worldism, his acknowledgement of conservative Christianity, his verbal position on border security and obvious—and thorough—embrace of capitalism are sore spots for the Left, as well as an embarrassment to the globalist neocons and RINOs who had made up the Republican Party for the past 30 years. The truth is, only a Marxist would oppose the advancement of American populist views, and every day more and more of them in the political, media, and academic arena are getting smoked out.

American Political Parties

Most American's probably couldn't name more than a half dozen political parties in the U.S. Republican, Democratic, Libertarian and Green Party probably come to mind first. But, there are at least 61 political parties active in this country and an astonishing 31 individuals received at least one vote for president in 2016, including four who ran on a communist or Trotskyist platform, including Gloria La Riva, who received 74,392 votes – 66,101 from California. The 61 parties span the entire spectrum, but what might surprise people are the number that are from left of center to full ultra-leftist.

My analysis of the current landscape yields the following tally: Ultra-left and Far-Left, 30; Left, 4; Center-Left, 11; Centrist, 2; Center-Right, 6; Right, 4; Far-Right, 3; and Ultra-Right, 1. You may be asking why there aren't more politicians from the far-left in congress today, given that there are 30 far-left political parties in America. Well, there are. Author and political activist Trevor Loudon identified 50 members of the House of Representatives in the 116th congress with ties to groups like Communist Party USA (CPUSA), Democratic Socialists of America, Socialist Party USA and the like, yet they all run as Democrats, with the exception of Senator Sanders, who self identifies as an Independent, but "Caucuses with Democrats". Let this stat sink in for a moment: 50 of the 232, or more than one-fifth of, Democrats in the House have ties to far-left political organizations.

Parties such as the Peace and Freedom Party (based in Oakland, with 90,000 members in California), Party for Socialism and Liberalism (San Francisco), Socialist Workers Party (Manhattan), World Workers Party (Manhattan), Socialist Equality Party (Detroit), Freedom Socialist Party (Seattle) or the anti-capitalist Green Party – based in Washington D.C., with membership of about 250,000 – are where leftist politicians like Senator Sanders, Senator Warren or AOC should take up residence. The far-left platforms of those parties line up much closer with these politician's ideological positions than the Democratic Party. But, running as a 3rd party candidate is an unelectable proposition, so voters are led to believe they are Democrats or at least anti-Republicans, as is the case with Senator Sanders.

By way of comparison, the Constitution Party, with its paleoconservative leanings and approximately 105,000 members, leans further to the right than the Republican Party and would thus be the largest far-right party. Of course, because the Constitution Party is anti-Marxist and considered the philosophical home of the Tea Party, it has been identified by the radical Southern Poverty Law Center as a hate group. Remember, to the Leftists, if you are not part of their revolution you are evil, and if you hate taxes they hate you.

WHAT THE MEDIA GETS WRONG ABOUT PRESIDENT TRUMP

Columnist Mark Davis points out to those who bother paying attention that President Trump does not target his opponents or their agenda by race, but rather than by the positions they take in opposition to his agenda. The media, of course, never takes notice of that nuance. They pounce on President Trump's tweets, because they are generally anti-Marxist and, therefore, they are, by definition, coming from a place of oppression and, therefore, are hateful and racist.

According to writer and commentator John C. Goodman, President Trump can't truly be classified as a conservative or Republican. According to Goodman, President Trump is not an economic conservative, is unwilling to rein in government spending or debt, is for entitlement spending (at least as far as Medicare or Social Security goes), and seemingly does not want to oppose labor, is OK with gay marriage, and is OK with not going to church.

President Trump ran as a Republican, and has enjoyed for the most part Republican support in Congress, but he is a Populist. This irks people like Senators Sanders and Warren, who see themselves as the true Populists. While President Trump's positions are in line with traditional values that are certainly popular with most Americans, in the Left's mind, in Senator Warren's mind, President Trump's populism is translated as things deplorables like. As for President Trump, populism mean everyone who holds American values near and dear, both rich and poor. As for Senators Sanders and Warren, populism means population, which means the masses, which can mean the huddled masses—the immigrants, the poor, the non-elite, and the rank-and-file working class laborers of the nation, which are exactly the type of oppressed classes with which the Left wants their Marxist message to resonate.

Chapter 9

PRESIDENT TRUMP AND HIS ANTI-MARXIST AGENDA

BEFORE I CAN EXPLAIN HOW PRESIDENT TRUMP IS an anti-Marxist it's important to understand what Authoritarianism, Totalitarianism and fascism are so that it's clear that he is none of the three. Authoritarians want strong centralized federal power and limited civil liberties. They often want to enact single-party or militarized states to ensure their continued tenure. President Trump wants neither. Leftists in the media and academia tend to define authoritarians as those who systematically eliminate checks and balances to their power and they point to two things he's done as examples of authoritarianism in action. These are the reduction in the amount of influence academia, the intelligentsia and the scientists have played in policy making, and the denial of the press as the unofficial fourth branch of government. These two players – the intelligentsia and the media–have had traditionally strong roles in leftist movements and were key players in the Obama administration. Trump's justifiable downgrading of their roles from activists under Obama to observers under Trump is seen as an open and aggressive attack on two of democracy's critical checks and balances.

Totalitarianism would be the authority to use government resources any way necessary to regulate what is acceptable in public and private life. Leftists go out of their way to find connections between President Trump and some of the world's most notorious totalitarian dictators. College professors, well versed in history and political science textbooks, tend to misinterpret President Trump's populism as being similar to the populism that led to the rise of authoritarian dictators and Hugo Chavez in Venezuela. Chavez saw himself as the people's true champion and viewed opponents as enemies. He delegitimized dissenting points of view which polarized society but in doing so made his supporters more fervent. The Left of course says, aha, Donald Trump is pulling that one right out of Chavez's playbook and only an authoritarian would use another authoritarian's playbook.

Rather than offering an unbiased analysis of why President Trump distrusts the deep state, the unfair media or the agenda driven scientific community the Left proceeds to enumerate how often he is offensively mean and dismissive to those groups. Pointing this out at every turn is intended to make the President appear to be behaving like any evil dictator would – consolidating power by eliminating checks and balances. In the bizarre world the media, academia, and the Leftist elites live in populism isn't helping the American workers, rather it's nothing more than an authoritarianism power play directly out of Chavez's playbook to eliminate or discredit any and all checks on his power. As noted earlier, the media sees themselves as the fourth branch of government. An indispensible element of our democracy. President Trump, like most conservatives, sees the media as a vehicle to help Democrats frame social and political issues as they see fit.

Conservatives and anti-Marxists want government out of our lives and we absolutely don't want a bunch of military officers from the pentagon running government agencies. Nor do we want to see police officers on every corner, like in Italy circa 1930, or thought police monitoring our Internet usage. If President Trump was really a dictator, he would never allow the continued political interference in his personal life or the attacks on his agenda. If he really had authoritarian powers, politicians like Senators John McCain and Mitt Romney would be afraid to vote against him. It's beyond time for the Left to get over this.

Marxism had two enemies in the 19th and 20th centuries—religion (any theological dogma that puts God before the state), and capitalism (private profit and the exploitation of the underclass). Now it has three: Religion, capitalism and the conservative populist movements in America and Europe. President Trump is deemed evil, because he's a threat to Marxism. Simple as that. He's the candidate that would have terrified Alinsky, which explains why Alinsky's disciples – President Obama, Senator Sanders, and Secretary Clinton – are so disturbed by President Trump's election. Activists like Alinsky like to win their cold war battles in courts and through legislative compromise. A liberal Supreme Court and a willingness by President Nixon to negotiate on environmental issues were battles leftists won in the '60s and '70s. President Trump's judicial nominations and disregard for conventional beltway negotiations and bi-partisanship has thrown the Left an unexpected curveball. President Trump is not President Nixon, and those who are familiar with Alinsky would know how disturbed he'd be with President Trump in the White House.

Cultural Marxists have been attacking religion and the American way since the '30s. Leftists have been attacking the perceived evils of capitalism since the 1800s. Since 2016, leftists in America have taken to demonizing President Trump and President Trump supporters as racists and criminals, who are out of touch with Americans. The most comical one is when they call them fascists, which is ridiculous. The last thing President Trump or any American wants is a big, highly-regulated bureaucracy run by a bunch of career military officers. Running the Pentagon, OK, I can see it. Running the Treasury, or any other department, absolutely not.

President Trump is, as far as I know, the first American president who actively chose to look inward to smoke out Marxists and expose them for what they are. Previous presidents dealt with external Marxist forces (President Truman and President Eisenhower with North Korea and the Soviets, and President Kennedy with the Soviets, LBJ and President Nixon with China and Vietnam, President Reagan with the Cold War, etc.) The Red Scare of the late '40s and into the '50s was led by certain congressmen and the FBI, not by President Eisenhower. The American Left was never agitated by a president the way President Trump is doing it to them, almost daily. The Left detests President Trump, because he is placing a relentless and unwanted negative spotlight on their agenda. The agenda Secretary Clinton had promised to continue.

There is one thing the Lenin-Stalin Marxists and Americans had in common—a war against socialist (Nazi) Germany. Antifa and their apologists shy away from the words national socialism, and instead reference the old fascist trope as a confusing diversion. The Marxist intent is to portray President Trump as an enemy that both the Left and reasonable, perhaps moderate, awakened or privilege-aware members of the Right. Antifa dates back to around 1979, but nobody ever heard of it until the dawn of the President Trump era. It stands for anti-fascism. The antifa crazies fancy themselves as fighting a moral war against a latter-day Hitler, but who are the real enemies? Who are the real fascists in our midst? Antifa are the violent street thugs of Marxism. American conservatives, even the paleoconservatives, are not Hitler and far from national socialists (Nazis) or any fascist ideology. It's comical.

The Antifa movement employs typical Marxist name calling tactics, because it makes for easy to identify labels that Americans can grasp. The logic train goes like this:

President Trump = racist = white supremacist = KKK =
white nationalism = Nazis = white nationalism = KKK =
white supremacist = racist = President Trump.

Bigot, racist, misogynist, and so on and so forth are all names antifa throws around daily, because in the antifa mind, these are insults that conveniently represent the things the Leftists hate, which are prideful exclusivity (American Exceptionalism), capitalism, patriotism, and Christianity. These are antithetical to Marxist conformism, wealth redistribution, egalitarianism, godlessness, and borderlessness. Trumpism—a brand of American populism—is not even in the same sector as fascism. It's more closely tied with the low tax/small government/state rights philosophies of confederalism and libertarianism, which are a full 180 degrees from fascism.

However, political science realities present inconvenient truths for intellectuals working in the ivory tower of academia or at the New York Times, and these nuances are far too complex for millennials to grasp. Everyone hates Nazis, because they're so easy to hate. Hollywood convinced the last of any doubters to hate them. Therefore, the narrative is simplified to present the oppressive class (white, conservative Christians) as possessing and, by extension being equal to, the traits of those evil Nazis. The progressives have posited that since fascists were angry, white, and mean, and killed Jews and other ethnic minorities, and the KKK is angry, white, and mean, and killed an ethnic minority (blacks), and since most southerners vote conservative, and most KKK members were southerners, therefore, all conservatives are, by definition, fascists. After all, it was those darn fascist rubes who voted President Trump into power. Good grief.

Chapter 10

MARX'S ILLEGITIMATE CHILD: FASCISM

FANS OF THE CLASSIC GODFATHER MOVIE TRILOGY will remember that Sonny Corleone had an illegitimate son named Vincenzo Mancini. For decades "Vincent" was someone who the family knew of, and he worked in a business similar to the family's, but due to various circumstances, including opportune timing, Vincent became the patriarch of the Corleone crime family. (Spoiler alert: At least for a while until he was killed in Part IV which Coppola needs to finish.) Fascism is something the socialists like to distance themselves from, but due to circumstances in the 1903's fascism stepped in to become the dominant socialist entity in Europe. It's a period in the socialist time-line that they'd prefer that you remember differently. Frankly socialists would prefer that you not know that Vincent was indeed a Corleone, and if you dare say this they'll scream that you're crazy and he is really Al Capone's son.

Since 1932 the Left has been lying about fascism by calling it right wing and describing it as something other than what it is – Marxist. It's sort of like telling everyone a tiger is really a German shepherd, because it has fur, a tail, four legs and bites. Leftists have an inconvenient truth on their hands – Vincent is regrettably one of them. Therefore, they had no choice but to gaslight this so you remember the details differently. The gameplan was straightforward: Convince a confused America that Vincent Mancini was Al Capone's child and he's really, really bad. Fascists are deservedly one of the greatest cinematic and literary villains of the twentieth century and that's through no small effort by a collection of leftist interests that has a huge stake in this. It worked. American's have no idea what fascism is but they hate it because the media, books, movies and television told you so, and what better way to demonize someone than to say he's one of those evil fascists.

Since the day Donald Trump declared his candidacy for president they've sought to equate President Trump with nationalism and, specifically, white nationalism. In their view, Trumpism is synonymous with white nationalism, white supremacy and white racism, and when you couple that with a nonsensical belief that President Trump and his followers must believe the same things as those Nazis did 80 years ago, you end up with the false narrative about President Trump and his deplorable followers we have today. Therefore, President Trump and his supporters, by the Left's simpleton logic, are neo-Nazis.

Hitler, being the most obvious and universally accepted example of white racist nationalism, is the poster child for everything American liberals hate, and if the views of a conservative politician can be tied— even dubiously—to Hitler, all the better. The irony was the mutual admiration society Mussolini and Hitler had with FDR in the early to mid-'30s, before CPUSA began their disinformation campaign. FDR's fascination with fascism is an inconvenient truth that you probably never heard until today.

Fascism is socialism, and here comes the inconvenient truth, leftists want to portray President Trump as a racist Nazi, which he isn't, and fascism as a conservative or Republican thing, which it's not, and here's the rub, my Marxist friends: Nazism refers to the German National Socialist

Workers Party. Yes. It was socialist, and Hitler claimed his whole platform for National Socialism was based on Marx. Hitler declared himself a socialist. Germany was a socialist country when Hitler ruled. There is no mistake about it.

This is a problem for the Leftists, because they want you to believe socialists are only loving, tolerant globalists and multiculturalists who hate borders and walls, and Hitler and his party were intolerant racists who were Nazis, not socialists (as if Nazi meant something other than Hitler's socialist party), and they liked borders and walls, like President Trump does, and since President Trump believes a country without borders is no country, he must be a Nazi.

If the average American, leaning toward Senator Sanders or AOC understood that Hitler was a socialist that would be a problem for the American Left, wouldn't it? The Left has been suggesting, wrongly, since 1932, that Hitler was some sort of right-wing phenomenom, a Republican, like President Harding, President Coolidge, Senator Goldwater or President Reagan. But, the inconvenient reality is that Hitler was, like every other twentieth-century Marxist leader, a murderous, socialist dictator. Liberals, going back as far as FDR and Winston Churchill, only want you to know Hitler as a murderous dictator, so they, and latter-day progressives, use terms that redirect you from national socialism to alternative and more useful (i.e., derogatory) terms like fascist, intolerant, totalitarian, authoritarian, dictator, white nationalist, or racist. Leftists in the media and academia believe as long as Americans unknowingly consider the terms fascist and Nazi to mean right-wing racism, rather than left-wing socialism with borders, they are winning the information war.

Fascism's Left-Wing Positions

The National Socialists, aka the Nazis, aka the fascists, had nothing in common with Trumpism and vice-versa, but the Nazis have a lot in common with the modern far left. And, I wonder why? Gee, they were socialists! The Nazis preached class warfare, agitating the working class to resist "exploitation" by capitalists, particularly Jewish capitalists, of course. Their programs called for the nationalization of education, health care, transportation, and other major industries. Nazi's wanted a big government with lots of regulation, policies and controls. They wanted colleges and the media to endorse and reinforce their views, because, hello! Nazism is a leftist single-party ideocracy, like China and California and most major American cities. They wanted an unarmed compliant population. The Nazis did not tolerate any dissenting views, just like today's Left. They instituted, and vigorously enforced, a strict gun-control regimen. They encouraged pornography, illegitimacy and the burning of books advocating or promoting religion, and they denounced Christians as right-wing fanatics. Does this sound familiar? Darn right. Sounds like a description of the modern American left.

This was Hitler's vision for Germany, and a popular myth persists, one perpetuated by devious, but otherwise intelligent people on the Left, that the Nazis were right-wing extremists when they were actually left-wing extremists. American leftists like to connect conservatives with Nazis, because it feels logical. Whites in Germany who want to discriminate against or enslave or maybe kill people who don't look like them sounds like the Confederacy in the Antebellum South. You need to remember that racism is bad, but the thought of it sells, and the association between the Nazis and rural, white, fly-over America sounds plausible. Their logic train goes this way: Nazis were mean, sexist and racist white men just like President Trump, and therefore President Trump and his supporters are fascists. Good grief. Nazi Germany was socialist, fascist and leftist. There is no doubt of this. President Trump is as far ideologically from the Marxists as any American politician I can think of since Pat Buchanan and President Reagan, possibly even Senator Goldwater.

To suggest that President Trump or President Trump's followers are Nazis is a ridiculous and disingenuous lie. This is part of the nuance and complexity that leftists don't want to engage in, because they, themselves, invented the lie in 1932 and they can't openly disavow it. If you counter their narrative they shout you down. The Left wants to appeal to emotion centered on resentment of Christian values, the meritocracy and the American hegemony they see as the hallmarks of conservative America. This deceitful narrative about President Trump somehow being a closeted fascist confuses even intelligent people and biases and complicates a broader political issue of today, which is: Can we have a serious debate about unity in a post-racist world when President Trump, and his followers are wrongly—and relentlessly—being identified as Nazis?

Leftists desperately don't want Americans to associate Senators Sanders and Warren, or AOC and her Squad, with Hitler. They don't want people understanding fascism as the brand of Marxism that it is. They don't want people knowing who Gentile was and why he invented fascism to be the most practical way to implement Marxist policies. They want to associate fascism with reactionary American conservatism that values order, ethics and predictability, but which is instead portrayed as a draconian and outdated faith-based system that resists change and denies science. They want to appeal to the unthinking sheep and associate President Trump with Hitler, because too many Americans view Hitler as a white nationalist racist, rather than the Leftist dictator, with white nationalist racist positions that he was—as if leftists could never ever be racists.

ANTIFA IN THE AGE OF PRESIDENT TRUMP

Notwithstanding some extremists who call themselves neo-Nazis for the shock value, the Left wants you to believe these individuals actually thought this through and that white America somehow "knows" Nazism is right-wing conservatism. Most Americans are too smart for that. Nazism is leftist, not right wing, and those individuals who wear tattoos of swastikas are simply trying to shock and offend people. Do you really think people who live in rural America want big government? Of course not.

What really hampers constructive dialogue is how disingenuous the Left can be on this. As an example, organizations like antifa actually believe Nazism is right wing and an affront to leftism, and they fight back on some self-righteous crusade to rid the earth of right-wing extremism. But, let's think it through for a moment. The Leftist agitators (antifa) are fighting against those they consider racists (the American Nazi Party), who possibly unknowingly label themselves as leftists (Nazis). But, at the same time, the antifa agitators unknowingly misidentify their fellow leftists (Nazis) as right wing, even though at the end of the day, antifa and the Nazis are both left wing. Therefore, the irony in all this is that antifa is actually a fascist-leaning organization (left wing) doing a reactionary right-wing thing that President Eisenhower or President Reagan would be proud about, by striking back at fellow left-wing radicals (Nazis).

THE SOCIAL DEMOCRATS AND FASCISM

Rather than admit fascism was a strain of Marxism that went wrong, they strongly claim it was conservatism in Italy and Germany that went wrong. Leftists really, really want you to believe fascism is a far-right position that white conservative America is not only sympathetic to, but secretly aspires to. That's asinine. It's actually a leftist ideology that more than 250,000 Americans died in Europe fighting. American conservatives do not want authoritarianism. We do not want hierarchies, and where they do exist they are limited in power and based on merit. Conservatives want no president in office for 12 years, let alone a dictator. Progressives try to tell you that Hitler couldn't possibly be a socialist, because he wanted hierarchies and inequality and they say this with a straight face, while they ignore the rigid social, cultural and economic hierarchies that exist in China – a country with far greater income and political inequality than the U.S. Hitler and Mussolini openly claimed they were socialists, while both believed socialism was the wave of the future, and both strove to appeal to a growing leftist population, dissatisfied with orthodox communism and eager for a uniform nationalist identity. Frankly, if Hitler proudly said he was a socialist I'll ignore the misinformation supplied by CPUSA and take him at his word.

Leftists try to discredit this obvious fact: Socialism is statism/collectivism and Nazism was statist/collectivist, while latter day "Democratic Socialism" is statist/collectivist. They fight this truth by claiming the Germans really didn't hold traditional socialist views that Senators Sanders and Warren, and their cohorts hold near and dear, which is obviously untrue, because fascists were for universal/free health care, gun control, strong secular public education, a strong blue-collar middle class, free and abundant public transportation, government oversight of private industry, and so on and so forth. Or, how about this one: The Nazis were inherently mean, like President Trump—and people who like President Trump must, therefore, be mean too—and socialists aren't mean, so it's not only impossible that Nazis could have been socialists, but perfectly possible that President Trump supporters are Nazis. Orwellian doublespeak if you ask me.

The point I'm trying to drive home here is that Hitler and Nazism are bad. And, despite leftist contentions, bad politics exists on the Left side of the aisle, and Hitler was a prime example. Simply put, the Nazis were on the left side of the political spectrum, not the right. Senators Sanders and Warren, and The Squad's leftist policies (education, transportation, healthcare, etc.), just like Hitler's, were out of the Marxist playbook. I'm not implying Senator Sanders or AOC would be the next Hitler, but latter-day American socialism is statist, one-party minded, anti-Christian, conformist, intolerant of dissenting opinion, and collectivist, just like we saw in every failed leftist nation over the past 100 years. There is no doubt of this. The Nazis were socialists, and socialists are, by definition, Marxists. And, Marxism is un-American, anti-Christian, and bad. If you want to talk about the prospects of totalitarianism in America, Senator Sanders, not President Trump, has some explaining to do.

The Left neglects to recognize that Nazi fascists sought what the American left currently wants—unity of thought, control of media and academia (and the Left has full control over both!), as well as dismissal of Christian-based values and morality, strong centralized planning, tight regulation on industry and commerce, and a state influence (if not control) over labor and business in the economy. The Left controls the media, and it has for decades. All President Trump is trying to do is counter the lies and slanted narrative, by reaching out directly to the people and bypassing the traditional media. He's not controlling the media; he's avoiding it.

> "There is nothing more beautiful in the world than to bite one's enemies."

—Vladimir Lenin

WHY AMERICAN CONSERVATIVES ARE NOT FASCIST

Unlike fascists, President Trump, his administration, and his supporters do not seek, or envision a fundamental change in our political or economic systems. Fascists do. Yes, President Trump wants to protect the existing systems from reckless left-leaning change, and "Make America Great Again" implies the eradication of Marxism from our nation. But, otherwise, President Trump does not want change to the status quo. President Trump wants to "Make America Great Again" by placing a renewed focus on traditional constitutional, economic, and moral values that every American can flourish under. Everyone knows conservatives are not seeking to put leftists in jail, but the feeling is not mutual. Silencing enemies is a leftist thing, not a conservative thing. Fascists are imperialists and seek interventionist foreign policies. As everyone knows, President Trump is an isolationist who does not want to intervene in foreign affairs or global policies. In fact, he does not want to sit at the head of a world order like the neocons (President Bushes) or globalists (President Obama) did.

Fascism conflicts with conservative principles rooted in family, church, social standing (i.e., are you an upright citizen or living in a criminal underworld?), and respect for personal and real property. A transition to fascism happens when citizens go from enjoying rights to being participants in group think and ceremonies of conformity. Conservatism seeks personal liberties without government mandates and regulation. In fact, conservatives do not want government mandates, and I have no idea why the Left doesn't get this. The further you move to the right, the less the government plays a role, to the point that the farthest, or the far right, has no government at all – just you, your family and your church, minding your own business. So, when the ridiculous antifa movement says the far right is fascist, it's so stupid it shouldn't warrant a response. But, their lies are so persistent, and you have to remind yourself what Hitler and the Frankfurt School said: "If you tell a lie enough times it becomes truth." Fascism is more government, more rules, more regulation, and more control of thoughts and actions. So, to suggest that fascism is anything other than far left is to not even understand what leftism is.

What the Left gets wrong about fascism is a misunderstanding, perhaps a deliberate misunderstanding of fascism, and, in particular, Hitler's brand of Marxism—National Socialism. The Left gets caught up in a few aspects of fascism that appear to indicate to the uninformed that it's a right-wing philosophy. It seems reactionary, sexist, and racist – as if sexism and racism are solely the purview of the Right–and therefore something white conservatives in flyover states might like. Added to this is an exaltation of nationhood, which plays into perceptions the modern left has with patriotic, flag-waving American conservatives. Remember that fascism is socialism with borders.

Few Americans understand how the fascist system worked with industry, but one can look to communist China's corporatism to see how that works. Essentially, the state gives direction to all industries on how and where to perform, under the theory that central planning and government control are all for the common good. Business leaders have no choice but to be Communist Party members and comply with these directives. In return, the government guarantees certain demand and prohibits competing private interests from interfering in that particular industry sector. The Nazi economic system was much like this, with big government telling industry that they have to join the Nazi Party and do things their way or else. To suggest that this is what President Trump wants is nonsense. But Will, Wikipedia and my college professor both say fascism is right wing. Are you saying they're wrong? Yes, in this case they are wrong, and it's by design. As Dinesh d'Souza points out, the intelligentsia cannot risk having anyone associate fascism with leftism, because it would undermine their false narrative. It's ironic that they hate Hitler but use one of his tactics daily. As Hitler once said, "If you tell a big enough lie, and tell it enough, it will be believed."

Chapter 11

PROGRESSIVISM TODAY—
GOVERNANCE AND CONTROL

"We have to use any ruse, dodge, trick, cunning, unlawful
method, concealment, and veiling of the truth."

—Vladimir Lenin

PROGRESSIVES TODAY ARE NOT TALKING ABOUT
economic growth or prosperity. They really have no answer to what the
economy has produced under President Trump, so they instead focus
on nebulous concepts that will never be solved, no matter how much
money is thrown at them, as well as collectivist and redistributive policies that will do nothing but restrict the economy. Coupled with this are
social policies and regulatory structures designed to ensure the financial
and ideological support of intellectual and business elites. The theory
is that corporate elites benefitting from a globalist economy, but who
lean socially liberal, will trade their support on environmental and social
issues, in exchange for protections from the Leftist power structure of
their economic interests.

Marxists believe America is rich and has the resources to not only fix all the world's problems but simultaneously have money left over to still flourish as a society. Conservatives, of course, believe the government only has an obligation to protect the rights of people to life, liberty, and the pursuit of happiness and not the obligation to solve humanity's woes.

Polls show that about four in 10 Americans having a favorable impression of socialism and the base of support are primarily younger, immigrant, urban, and blue collar. Of those four, almost half, 47 percent, would vote for a socialist candidate for president, meaning about 19 percent of Americans would vote for a Marxist. Yikes. Thankfully, most of the people who vote are older and smarter—almost two out of three Americans say decisions on the economy should be left up to a capitalist-free market. If you vote progressive, you are voting Marxist.

Throughout this book, you have learned how, when, and why socialism started, how Karl Marx took the concept and turned it from an theoretical idea to a compelling political and economic philosophy, how neo-Marxists modified it (fascism/Leninism) for practical implementation purposes, how clever marketing and messaging could advance the agenda of transforming capitalist and Christian cultures into Marxist and atheist ones (Gramsci), and later, how it all got re-branded into a psychology and sociology project (the Frankfurt School), bent on creating a countercultural movement based on false information and political correctness.

The following are a series of examples of what we've learned about Marxism and how it manifests itself today. The goal would be to help the reader see through the lies, deceptions, and false promises of the Marxists to better grasp what the progressives are up to today and how their agenda hurts America. Before diving into it, it's critical that one important concept be explained.

WE ARE A CONSTITUTIONAL REPUBLIC—FOREVER

America is not a true democracy; it's a constitutional republic and is not a land of immigrants, but rather a land of settlers who founded the nation ex nihilo. For a few hundred years, the premise was that social pressure from family, neighbors, your county sheriff, and your church congregation kept people in line with the settler's vision of a morally upright society, which was rooted firmly in Christian values. For centuries, social norms ensured effectively everyone was morally responsible for their behavior. The Marxists reject traditional theological doctrine and have advocated a paradigm shift in personal accountability and moral responsibility from the individual to the state, placing accountability solely at the feet of the powerful. The oppressors are defined as the powerful and vice versa. When you hear people on CNN or MSNBC talking about "holding the powerful accountable," this is a Marxist dog whistle, meaning holding conservatives and their hegemony and patriarchy accountable.

BIG GOVERNMENT

Marxism is all about control. It creates a society dependent on government programs and handouts through entitlement and social program expansion. The message to the masses is clear: "Government knows best." Beware when you hear leftists speak of needing to pump resources (a code word for taxes) into "underrepresented and underserved" communities. This is a dog whistle code to tug on heartstrings to gain the citizenry's empathy and, more importantly, the citizen's permission to implement tax-and-spend policies to address wasteful programs in the name of social justice. Remember, Alinsky's idea was to implement socialism through the population's consent (democracy).

191

MARXISTS NEED TO SHOW THEIR BADGES AND CREDENTIALS

A tenet of Marxism is to proudly show your uniform and display your rank on your person as part of your employment, which ties to your party status. Pride isn't a sense of satisfaction you have in your profession, but whether you proudly become card-carrying members of the Marxist party. Workers of the world, unite! This has manifested itself in signage and mandates as to who is acceptable and who isn't. This is strange for a party that professes tolerance, but tolerance is accepting different shades of blue and not dissenting opinion. Few people wear uniforms to their jobs these days, but Marxists have other ways to "Show their true colors." "We don't serve Republicans" or "Republicans are not welcome!" on restaurant doors or storefront windows are examples of being card carriers. But, now, we find a mayor of a large city proclaiming that Republicans may not be welcome in cities anymore! In 2019, New York City Mayor Bill de Blasio proudly stated this about President Trump's future, "And when his presidency is over, really soon, he will not be welcome back in New York City."

THE CONTRASTING HIERARCHY OF PRIORITIES BETWEEN THE LEFT AND RIGHT

The Left and Right both see humans as needing a hierarchy of responsibilities to give everyone guidance and predictability as they go through life. However, the list each side would come up with is different, and this explains how and why the Left is more receptive to the globalist agenda and Marxist authoritarianism. Conservatives see this hierarchy in this order: Oneself, family, church, community, nation, and then to global mankind. (If asked, the Left would insert race between family and church in describing the Right's priorities.) The Right sees the protection of oneself as primary, the family as the core structural unit in society, morality flowing from the church, and the nation as different from government. Conservatives typically do not see themselves as responsible for solving an issue overseas. Poverty, genocide, and AIDS in Africa, for example, are for churches and governments to address, not idealistic warriors on American college campuses.

The hierarchy of the Left would go something like this: Oneself, government, mankind, and finally, family. Church would probably not appear on this list. Marxists see each individual as a soldier (oneself) in service to the government, and collectively they are bent on a globalist crusade against various existential threats facing mankind that are above the family, church, or community, such as poverty, global warming, and so on and so forth. They place their idealism above family or community, because they are self-righteous and could care less what Dad or Dad's pastor thinks of their position on social justice or LGBTQ rights. In leftist theory, the church is a fantasy—the opium of the people as Marx described it—that does nothing but perpetuate what they see as an outdated, sexist, and classist order, standing in the way of their egalitarian, totalitarian utopia.

This de-prioritization of family and church is by design. Morality flowing from the state needed to be seen as more virtuous and purposeful than morality flowing from one's parents or church, and this was a major part of Marx's social deconstruction campaign. Marx saw families as passing along conservative religious views that hindered an individual's capacity for achievement and, of course, would hinder the advancement of his ideology. This is something the cultural Marxists capitalized on.

THE JUSTICE DEMOCRATS, AKA "THE SQUAD"

Leading up to the 2016 election, a new group emerged on the Left calling themselves "Justice Democrats," and they aligned themselves with Senator Sanders over Secretary Clinton. The "Justice Democrats" purported to try and rid politics of the perception of corruption, particularly from corporate special interests that funnel money into elections through political action committees (PACs). This was a major issue of Senators Sanders and Warren; however, the faces of the so-called "Justice Democrats" have moved from old and white to young and brown. These are known in conservative circles as the "Four Horsewomen of the Apocalypse: Congresswomen Omar, Pressley, Tlaib, and AOC." Outspoken and unapologetic, they are not just the faces of the new socialist left, but the faces of the Democratic Party heading into the 2020 general election, much to the chagrin of House Speaker Nancy Pelosi, Senator Chuck Schumer and the Democratic establishment.

The "Justice Democrat's" platform is not really rooted in the elimination of corruption, but rather to create a new party within a party that could be a landing spot for the increasingly left-lurching agenda items to be synchronized into a new leftist agenda for America. These include the Green New Deal, an increase in minimum wage, federal job guarantees, the legalization of drugs, free college, forgiveness of student loan debt, universal health care, gun control/elimination, abolition of Immigration and Customs Enforcement (ICE) and, of course, higher taxes to pay for all this.

Why the American Marxists love China

China has fascinated the intelligentsia in the West for decades. For many of them China has a few warts here and there, but it's beautiful and mysterious and its brand of Marxism is the type of utopia (I'd call it dystopia) they'd like to see in America. California times fifty. A single-party ideocracy with a dominant party that cannot be questioned let alone voted out of power. (Yes, there are a handful of other small parties permitted to exist in China with a grand total of about 1 million members, but they really only serve to pay lip service to political diversity. In fact as a condition of their existence they can't hold power over the CCP.

The Chinese Communist Party – the CCP–rules the land with an iron fist despite making up only about 6% of the population.)

Some of the other things they love about it is that they use "trust scores" and other forms of surveillance to exert immense control over thoughts and behaviors. It's a great way to keep those deplorables in fly-over country in line! It's a land where equality is supposed to be assured, but a handful are clearly more equal than others. A globalist-minded country that abandoned the outdated command-based economic strategies of Mao Zedong and replaced them with a socialist market economy which means the elite can get rich and have their mansions and other privileges like travel so long as they swear allegiance to the CCP and the unique value they add to the state is deemed essential.

To conservatives, China is leftist fantasyland where private gun owner-ship is generally illegal, religion is not tolerated, the elite can get ahead but the deplorables can't, the branches of government are all perma-nently leftist, media's messaging is in complete alignment with the gov-ernment's, and Marxist hardliners can swiftly, and with impunity, crush dissenting opinion. President Trump is the first American president to openly challenge China and the globalist world order the conservatives have such disdain for, and the Left is really bothered by this.

SOCIAL DEMOCRACY AND DEMOCRATIC SOCIALISM ARE MARXISM

In 2019, as more and more candidates declared for the 2020 election, you heard the terms socialist and socialism linked either before or after the word democracy. The roots of social democracy, or democratic socialism, go back to German writer and philosopher Ferdinand Lassalle (1825–1864). Whereas, Marx and Engels envisioned a world where, ultimately, the state wasn't necessary after the violent revolutionary transition from capitalism to socialism to communism was complete, Lassalle believed the state—with the right people elected and appointed, of course—should persevere in a peaceful transition to socialism, because it could be the source to perpetually help the working class. The idea was that the proletariat might not be able to take care of themselves in the ultimate communist society Marx envisioned, but they probably could if a socialist government took hold and built a society full of programs and safety nets. In their model, a transition to communism wasn't wanted or needed. This is the basis of European-style socialism that exists today.

Of course, the working class first needed a political party that could champion their cause and most importantly get elected. Over time labor parties emerged across Europe to try to make socialism a reality. Like many leftists in the 19th century, social democrats didn't agree with every single thing Marx said. They all had slightly different ideas of how big and how homogenous the working and middle classes would be, and some social democrats even saw a purpose in keeping the bourgeoisie around; but, they were all united in their goal of taking power away from the church, the aristocracy, and the capitalists and putting that power into the hands of the working people.

You may have also heard more and more legislators in Washington, DC use the term "social democrat" to describe themselves and/or democratic socialism to describe their views. President Wilson and FDR were Democrats, but they implemented programs that could be described as Democratic socialism. (Remember, Mussolini said FDR was a fascist!) Congresswomen AOC and Tlaib are members of both the Democratic Socialists of America and "Justice Democrats"—both socialist organizations—dedicated to weakening the power of capitalists and strengthening the power of working people. Whether you call it democratic socialism or social democracy, they are Marxist concepts that openly want to transform the economy to their liking—from capitalism to socialism.

Democratic socialism was referenced by Alinsky in the '60s, and it kind of vanished until it was adopted by people like Senator Sanders and Congresswoman AOC. Alinsky and the other leftists knew many Americans might be intrigued and possibly confused (in a good way) by those terms. The thinking being that most Americans wrongly believe we are a democracy, and being social creatures, the will of the people for the good of the people should prevail. We are actually a constitutional republic that uses representative democracy.

The term democracy in the Alinsky-Sanders worldview is thereby weaponized by the Left to invoke feelings that every vote should count, and every voice must be heard, and every individual must have a voice. The elimination of the Electoral College is but one example. True democracy would paralyze America, because decisions wouldn't be made until every opinion—no matter how crazy or misguided—was vetted. "Social democracy" is not democracy in action, but socialism that is incrementally implemented by the consent of the people. Unspoken democratic consent would be through the ballot box. If enough voters endorse enough of the Left's candidates, then their transformational agenda could be advanced.

Remember, a borderless, globalist world with socialism at its head is the aim. Is anyone surprised that the Senator Sanders–led Progressive International movement is an attempt to unite all the democratic socialists from around the world under one globalist umbrella?

Make no mistake about it, socialism is Marxism, and socialism can indeed be totalitarian. Socialism leads to communism—a more drastic stage. Socialism appeals to millennials. It sounds fun and friendly, as in "let's be social." Or "let's solve our problems as a society through collective action." If we're social and friendly with everyone in the world, there won't be war or hate or crime or famine or poverty, right? Europe is a fun place, and they have socialism. World War II was the last war that may ever be fought on European soil, and everyone there seems happy with socialism running their lives. Therefore, it must be working, right?

The Marxists are keenly aware of the contempt conservatives have for their views. If you're not tolerant and social like they are or socially conscious like they are, you are therefore a closed-minded racist or bigot. You are a hater who stands for the king (the patriarchy), rather than the common folk, and those people are evil. It follows, then, that evil people are immoral, greedy, and morally bankrupt, and people like that irresponsibly plot for the apocalypse. According to the Marxists, President Trump is a moment away from launching the nukes or appointing conservative judges or enacting regulatory reform, because people who are against Marxism are, by definition, plotting for the apocalypse! Since he can, and likely will, launch nuclear weapons at any moment or appoint conservative judges or sign off on regulatory reform, it's full blown crisis time! Conservative cartoonist Henry Payne has a mock, liberal newspaper where the snarky headline changes, but the daily weather report in the upper right margin always reads: Cloudy with a chance of apocalypse. That's how the Left has come to view the world under President Trump. Today could be the day the world ends.

Socialism is the mother of communism and fascism, and these are Marxist ideologies. Don't let anyone ever tell you that socialism isn't Marxist. It is. They are all big cats, remember? "Democratic socialism," or whatever Senator Sanders or Congresswoman AOC call it, is a red herring designed to fool otherwise patriotic Americans into accepting, adopting, and preparing for increasingly leftist agendas, disguised as socially and globally responsible policies. When somebody defines himself or herself as a democratic socialist, don't be fooled. They are Marxists, who want you think they are nothing more than liberal Democrats being "socially conscious." Call them out.

WHY DO MARXISTS LIKE TO CHANGE THE RULES?

Marxists are, by definition, at war with American values and American institutions, particularly ones that they feel obstruct their agenda. They don't like fair institutions that have existed for decades, if not centuries, and ignorantly reject the grand narrative of why our economic and political system is the best in the world. In an effort to rewrite the rules to help ensure their team wins, they propose things like stuffing the Supreme Court, rewriting how the Electoral College works, or changing qualification requirements to prohibit certain candidates from appearing on a ballot, as we've seen discussed in California.

As to the Supreme Court of the United States (SCOTUS) stuffing, it's interesting to look back at a very liberal majority that controlled the Warren court from 1953–1969 and apparently to the Left back then, nine justices was just fine. But, when the ideology of the court balances or shifts more to the right, the Left wants to counter this by creating avenues to appoint more liberals to the court. You never heard conservative legislators discuss, let alone demand, SCOTUS stuffing as an insurance policy during the Obama or Clinton presidencies. Conservative legislators often complained that the Warren court "legislated from the bench" in deciding many landmark aspects of the civil rights agenda (Brown, Miranda, etc.), but SCOTUS stuffing was not discussed. President Eisenhower selected a liberal justice (Warren) in '53. President Nixon selected a liberal in Blackmun. President Bush 41 selected a moderate who turned out to be a reliably liberal justice in David Souter. Do you think conservatives hold out hope that the next democratic president with a SCOTUS seat to fill will return the honor? Heck no.

President Clinton and President Obama did not return the favor and instead, each selected two liberals. Elections have consequences, and the fact that President Trump, and not Secretary Clinton, was allowed to select two new members to the SCOTUS is unacceptable to the Left.

So, the obvious conclusion is that nine justices are fine with the Left, so long as they render opinions in favor of the Left. President Trump has actually balanced the court, and most American moderates should appreciate that. The fact that the current Roberts court is balanced with four conservatives, four liberals, and a swing vote (Roberts himself) the Republicans consider too liberal and the Democrats consider too conservative seems to imply that the number of Supreme Court justices is appropriate.

The Left can't get over the elections of President Bush 43, let alone President Trump. They have cast the Electoral College system as some sort of white nationalist institution that disproportionately favors some states over others. This movement to eliminate the Electoral College as the system to elect the president of the United States fails to recognize, among other things, that the system was implemented to ensure states have adequate representation in an election. The Founding Fathers knew it would be unfair for a single city, with a narrow and homogenous list of local concerns, to be able to outvote an entire state, where a wider range of social, cultural, and economic interests are at stake.

The Left is seeking ways to try to avoid having President Trump appear on their 2020 ballot. The most blatant, unconstitutional stunt is demanding that any candidate release five years of tax returns. It's obvious that this paper-thin mandate is intended to block President Trump.

Past precedent isn't stopping the Left from trying to implement new rules to tip the scales in their favor. This is consistent with Marxist ideology that wants to rewrite the rules of the game to ensure perpetual reelection of their candidates and advancement of their agenda. In communist China, Soviet Russia, Nazi Germany, and modern-day Cuba and Venezuela, you can't run for national election without the ruling party's endorsement. And, you're not going to get the endorsement if you are not already Marxist, like the ruling party.

EVERYONE IS A SOLDIER IN THE LEFTIST ARMY

In traditional Marxist theory, every proletariat is a soldier in the never-ending war against the oppressors. I can't think of a better way to articulate this concept than through how environmental legislation can be hijacked by activists acting as soldiers in the Leftist army. I'm referring to the California Environmental Quality Act (CEQA). CEQA was adopted by the state legislature in 1970, a year after the National Environmental Quality Act (NEQA) was signed into law by President Nixon. The purpose of CEQA was to evaluate public construction projects in the context of their potential impact on the environment, but it was quickly interpreted to mean any project—public or private—that requires state or local public agency approval, such as residential development. Since its inception, it has been the single biggest obstacle to meeting housing and infrastructure needs for California's rising population. A problem with CEQA is that there is no state agency that administers it. Initially, it was assumed local agencies would make reasonable decisions, but when activists realized they could leverage CEQA to stop any and all projects, it became a tool for environmental and community activists bent on stopping housing.

The responsibility to ensure compliance was delegated to local agencies (city councils) that placed their trust in a handful of planners within their city-planning departments to shepherd projects through the CEQA process. Since it's impossible to rely on local planners to catch everything, there is a safety net the Leftists can count on. CEQA actually relies on left-leaning activists to serve as watchdogs, raise questions, and otherwise scrutinize development projects ostensibly on behalf of society. CEQA litigation, or the threat thereof, is considered a useful tool in the Leftist's toolbox, because it often results a windfall of exactions from a developer. In Leftist theory, everyone in California should be a concerned citizen, who is willing to invest time and resources in a unified stance against those rotten capitalists, and everyone should be an activist who speaks in opposition to projects at city council hearings or, better yet, hires lawyers from a CEQA litigation cottage industry to throw monkey wrenches into development schedules.

The method of administration for CEQA was a brilliant leftist tactic. By delegating CEQA to the local level and encouraging local citizen engagement, it allowed a citizen army to control the size and pace of development. In a state like California, with a massive supply side imbalance of housing, the activists have ironically inflicted pain on the capitalists in the form of delays and financial exactions—that are passed along to homeowners—and downsizing at the expense of affordable housing for the masses.

Another example of the citizen army concept is the idea of empowering ordinary citizens to issue parking tickets. It has been done in Malibu, California, to great success in the eyes of the city council, because it allows the police to focus on other priorities. Washington, DC is also considering implementing this program. In the world of monkey-see-monkey-do leftist public policy, this is a slippery slope. What could happen next? Why stop at parking tickets? Citizens could be incentivized to report transgressions by their neighbors to their comrades in arms for a financial reward. Basically, our society would devolve to activists on a citizen's arrest spree. Think this isn't happening? Think again.

WHY MARXISTS ARE SO FOCUSED ON GUN CONTROL

President JFK once said, "Today, we need a nation of minute men; citizens who are not only prepared to take up arms, but citizens who regard the preservation of freedom as a basic purpose of their daily life and who are willing to consciously work and sacrifice for that freedom." This country does not need policemen or national guardsmen on every corner. Nor do we want morality police on every corner. But, what we do need are responsible citizens on every street and every corner, willing to take a stand for our constitutional freedoms.

Gun ownership is a huge problem for Marxists and not because of gun violence. Gun violence and, in particular, mass killings is the pretext the Left uses to push for getting guns out of the hands of private citizens. Ending mass shootings sounds great, but the real reason why the Left wants guns more highly regulated if not eliminated lies in the answer to this simple question—who owns guns? To the Left guns need to be taken out of the hands of civilians just like what was done in Venezuela. The only way to prevent tyranny by leftist security forces is to have a citizenry that can match or exceed its firepower. It is impossible to undertake a successful leftist revolution in this country without significant gun control measures being enacted. That is highly unlikely, but that won't keep them from trying.

There is a correlation between gun ownership and political ideology. The nine states where more than 50 percent of adults own guns (Arkansas, North Dakota, South Dakota, Idaho, Mississippi, Alabama, Montana, Wyoming, and West Virginia) all voted for President Trump. The eight states where gun ownership is less than 20 percent (Hawaii, New Jersey, Rhode Island, Connecticut, New York, California, Massachusetts, and Illinois) all voted for Secretary Clinton. Nearly 50 percent of white conservative voters own guns, and 85 percent of gun owners say guns are part of their identity. In the eyes of conservatives and gun owners, the right to own a gun is viewed as a civil right. As for more numbers, 46 percent of rural residents own a gun, while 19 percent of urban residents do. And, 29 percent of gun owners own more than one firearm. Gun ownership in 2016 "Red States" was at 44.4 percent, while in "Blue States," it was at 27.3 percent.

To put the sheer volume of guns in America into context there are about 120,000 federal police officers (FBI, DEA, DHS, etc.) and about

765,000 sworn officers at the state and local level. That's approximately 885,000 police officers in America with a little more than 1 million guns in police service. American civilians outnumber local police about 350 to 1, and they own 393 million guns, which outnumbers guns in the hands of local police by almost 400 to 1. What about the military? Don't they have more guns than our citizens? No. Civilians outnumber active and reserve military personnel more than 150 to 1 and outgun them nearly 100 to 1. Marxists realize that conservative gun owners significantly outnumber local and state police and national peacekeepers. In order for their brand of the SS to take control of every block in America, guns need to be taken out of the hands of every civilian. The elimination of gun violence is the pretext. Control of the population is the actual aim. This possibility, no matter how remote, is why conservatives view the Second Amendment as a civil rights issue.

So, for the sake of discussion, if 50 percent of the 63 million President Trump voters own at least one gun, that's better than a 30 to 1 advantage. The reason why the population of Venezuela can't overthrow the Madura regime is because the Marxists made private gun ownership illegal. That was by design. The citizens will never win battles in the streets, even at a 30 to 1 personnel advantage, by throwing sticks and rocks against security forces that have machine guns.

The Left's problem with guns in America is the wrong people have them, and the wrong people have too many of them. To be clear, for the Left, guns are great as long as the police and police alone have them. I suppose the Leftist elites want their bodyguards to be able to have them too. Theoretically, the Left needs the police to outman conservative gun owners to ensure enforcement of their agenda, if and when their day arrives. In Venezuela, once the Marxists took over, one of the first things they did was take away the right to private gun ownership to disarm potential opponents and prevent an armed uprising. Then, they recruited thousands of Cuban immigrants with experience in state-sanctioned thuggery and armed them in an effort to create a national storm trooper network. Marxists need obedient storm troopers, and the Left's decades-long ties to local police unions has always created an intriguing hypothetical for conservatives, because it raises a conflict of interest: Would rank-and-file police officers, dedicated to strong unions, take orders from totalitarian masters to oppress a conservative uprising or side with the conservatives and liberal 2A advocates and uphold American principles? We're finding out in some counties in Virginia that the local police would lean towards the latter.

Although it certainly seems highly unlikely in our lifetimes, there does exist the possibility that a conservative movement may take armed action as part of a counter resistance to leftists and their gun confiscation policies. It's impossible to implement a full-blown leftist movement in this country (and maintain their control), if conservatives own guns and actively push back against Marxism and gun control. The firing mechanisms of the firearm, the magazine capacity, the types of guns, the background checks, and the intense media coverage of shootings is intended to make gun ownership seem unnecessary and bad. Therefore, the long game being played is a systematic chipping away at gun rights and a relentless narrative that only paranoids, crazies, murderers, or neo-Nazis own guns. (Remember, gun violence, and especially mass shootings, is actually useful to the Left, because it presents a convenient opportunity to paint all gun owners as evil or crazy.) The eradication of private gun ownership is a long-term goal, and it is real.

The point here is that gun control is not really about preventing school shootings. Yes, school shootings are horrible and preventable, but progressives aren't about to let any crisis go to waste. Remember, when a leftist uses a school or synagogue shooting as a reason for gun confiscation it's a pretext. Sadly, to them, this isn't about victims, in fact to the Left the more the better. It's about repealing the Second Amendment. It's about incrementally more restrictive regulations to create a post-firearm future, where citizens are ultimately disarmed and, therefore, cannot overthrow what the Left believes is an inevitability a post-capitalist, Marxist regime.

More Cops and Less Gun Access Do Not Reduce Murder

A common talking point on the Left is that fewer guns in the hands of fewer private citizens means fewer violent crimes and, therefore, safer communities. So, to them, background checks are nice, but don't go far enough. The narrative is that the elimination of assault rifles is a good start, as is the reduction in magazine size and the taxation of bullets, but there are still too many guns in the hands of too many people. The Marxist theory, as opposed to traditional America thought, but in alignment with their authoritarian objectives, is that a large and well-armed police force, rather than a largely well-armed private citizenry, is the best way to deter crime.

It's important to point out that conservatives, and liberals, want to deter crime and keep the peace. Educated urban leftists who live in the inner city and are otherwise gentrifying their neighborhoods want safe streets, safe transportation, and safe parks; and they count on large, well-funded and well-trained police forces to protect them. In the U.S., police are pillars of our society, but their numbers do not need to be large. In the Marxist world, they are large in number and an omnipresent part of our lives.

Societies have always adopted new or innovative methods to deter crime, with public executions being the most notorious. The more civil and effective form of deterring crime we have in our country derives from a Christian concept of community peacekeeping—neighbors respecting one another, keeping an eye on things, and employing an accessible and ethical police force being called upon, as needed.

Traditionally, crimes were considered embarrassing to the family of the criminal, and ideally crimes didn't happen, but when they did, they were dealt with swiftly. To most Americans, crime is seen as a matter of choice, spurred by lack of intelligence, judgment, maturity, self-control, and/or morality and is not a byproduct of racism, segregation, or poverty. Liberals, of course, see it differently. Crime, in their eyes, is an outgrowth of failings within society that need to be regulated, if not reformed. They believe people commit crimes because they are oppressed, and as our society "fails" in more and more aspects (income inequality, disinvestment, drug addiction, homelessness, etc.), the Marxist playbook is to throw more money and regulation at it. In the case of violent crime, the more police we have and the fewer guns we have becomes the simplest solution. Gun ownership in the hands of private citizens is a tremendous deterrent to crime. Generally, criminals have always shied away from homes and vehicles that have American flags and NRA stickers on the windows. Crime 101 teaches them to never walk into a bullet.

Here are some facts to consider: Based on nationwide FBI statistics, guns are involved in about two-thirds of all murders that were committed using a weapon, and with a few exceptions, there is not much variation in that ratio from state to state. Murders by gun happen in red states and in blue states. In the state with the lowest murder rate (Iowa), 58 percent involved guns. In Washington DC, where the murder rate is the highest, it's 75 percent. In California, where the most gun murders occur by raw numbers, it's 69 percent.

The nine states that have more than 50 percent of their adults as gun owners all voted for President Trump in 2016. These states (and their murder rate by guns per 100,000 people) include Arkansas (3.2), as well as North (0.6) and South Dakota (1.0), Idaho (0.8), Alaska (2.7), Montana (1.2), Wyoming (0.9), West Virginia (1.5), and Mississippi (4.0). All eight states that have less than 20 percent of their adults as gun owners voted for Secretary Clinton. These include: Hawaii (0.5), New

Jersey (2.8), Rhode Island (1.5), Connecticut (2.7), New York (2.7), Massachusetts (1.8), California (3.4), and Illinois (2.8). The point is that murders with guns occur fairly consistent from state to state, even those with low gun ownership and left-leaning populations.

In the states President Trump won in 2016, an average of 44.4 percent of the adults own guns. In the states Secretary Clinton won, it's 27.3 percent. States with the highest evangelical populations (West Virginia is 44.2 percent) own the most guns (West Virginia is 55.4 percent) and overwhelmingly voted for President Trump. States with the fewest evangelicals (California is 15.0 percent) own the least guns (California is 21.3 percent) and overwhelmingly voted for Secretary Clinton. Is there a correlation between gun ownership and conservative voting? Yes. Is there a correlation between murder rates and conservative voting? No.

Where liberal and moderate Democrats are willing to acknowledge a more moderate stance on gun ownership and see the importance of the Second Amendment, the Marxists are far more hardliners and want to confiscate all guns from private citizens—no matter how law abiding they are. However, when you look at real world examples, the evidence relative to gun violence and policing is eye opening. Take Houston and Chicago, for example. Each has comparable, although not exactly similar, demographic and socioeconomic conditions. For example in January 2020 Chicago's unemployment rate of 3.8% is only slightly about Houston's (4.1%). Where Chicago has more than 13,000 cops, Houston has about 5,000. Whereas there are no gun stores in Chicago, there are hundreds in Houston. Chicago's murder rate (24.1 per 100,000) is more than double that of Houston (11.5), and robberies are notably higher too. Marxists don't want you to focus on stats like this, because it flies in the face of their narrative that guns, and not people, commit crimes. The disparity in murders alone between Chicago and Houston is evidence that a combination of more cops and less private gun ownership does not deter violent crime.

THE STATES RIGHTS HYPOCRISY

Traditionally, leftists in America saw states' rights as something of an anachronistic phenomenon out of the confederate South. Most of the states' rights matters of interest to the Left, such as those associated with Jim Crow laws, have been eradicated due to civil rights legislation and the passage of time. Marxists detest local control because it allows for too much deviancy from secular policy goals. For example a city council with five practicing Christians is unlikely to advance or enforce leftist agenda's unless federal or state law forces them to do so. Leftists always championed the federalist approach, where federal laws and policies—mostly achieved through the courts or bold legislation such as the Civil Rights Act of 1964–trump all local laws, in all 50 states. However, federal laws aren't so great when they prohibit something the progressives enjoy, like marijuana or sanctuary cities. In these cases, states' rights are good, and local rights are really good. It's extremely selective. As noted previously, Marxists like federal laws, policies, rules and left-leaning circuit courts when they advance their agenda and dislike those aspects of federal policy that don't.

WHEN OPPORTUNITIES ARE REDEFINED AS "RIGHTS"

A common trope from the Left is that conservative values stifle opportunity. These values are portrayed as discriminatory and draconian and exclude people from opportunity. They neglect to recognize that every American child has an equal opportunity to go to school, for example, and has equal opportunity to live in any neighborhood they choose, so long as they can afford to live there. Unlike a time in the past, where restrictive covenants or other segregationist policies were in place, everyone has the opportunity to live in Newport Beach, Beverly Hills, or San Francisco. Earn enough money, and you can buy your way in, no questions asked. Marxists believe everyone should have not just the opportunity, but the right to live there, if they so choose. If a homeless

209

person wishes to live on the streets of Beverly Hills or in a park in Beverly Hills or at a storefront in San Francisco, that should be their right.

Related to this is education. Every child has an opportunity to go to a public school, but the Left believes every child has a right to an equal outcome, when it comes to test scores.

MARXISTS BELIEVE THAT BIG BROTHER KNOWS BEST

A fundamental belief of Marxism is the need to have government tell us what is right and wrong, what is good and what is bad. Righteous thoughts are defined and promulgated by the state, and, wrongful thought is shamed. For several hundred years in America, proper, moral and righteous thoughts and behavior came through norms passed from the family, church, and traditional social and community leaders. Marxism believes that individual thought and choice is a threat to their conformist ideology. If one believes in anything that is inconsistent with an inclusive conformist agenda, they are a threat. Therefore, Marxists use the courts and liberal state legislatures to legislate (i.e., beat) behavior out of people. If non-Marxists don't change their horrible conservative behavior voluntarily, we will enact laws to legislate that rotten behavior out of people. What this means, in simplest terms, is if you want to be a racist or sexist or xenophobe or homophobe, we will make it illegal to think, act, or behave in ways that encourage, support, or condone those thoughts or publish those opinions. Forget about outright discrimination. In a short time, it will be illegal to have discriminatory thoughts.

MARXISTS NEEDS IMMIGRANTS TO ACHIEVE GOVERNMENT CONTROL OF THE ECONOMY

For the past 50 years, the government's average spending as a percentage of the GDP has been about 37 percent. Expansion of entitlement programs and Keynesian economic policies pushed it to an all-time high of 43 percent under the Obama administration, but it declined to 38 percent during President Trump's first year in office ('17) and is expected to remain at around 38 percent through at least 2020. In the European Union, it's currently about 50 percent and as high as 56 percent (France). Would the U.S. ever spend that much? If allowed to, yes. Marxists believe the larger the role the government can play in the economy, the larger their regulatory influence and control over private markets and unwanted behavior can be. The Marxist theory, in play here, is that once the population becomes used to increased government spending, the people will be reluctant to push for austerity measures, even during an economic downturn. Cutbacks to government benefits and government employment are politically challenging. This is because many Americans quickly come to depend on them and believe government spending should be high, not only in downturns but also during good economic times.

California is a good example of how single-party public agencies can get addicted to tax-and-spend policies. In 1998, the population of the Golden State was 32.68 million and the budget was $58 billion. In 2020, the population is estimated to be 39.94 million and the budget will be $222 billion. Think about that. In a 22-year period, the population coincidently increased 22% or an average of one-percent, per year. The budget has increased an average of 17 percent, per year. California has the highest income taxes, highest sales taxes, highest vehicle license taxes and highest gas taxes in the nation and now the bureaucrats in Sacramento are launching an assault on property tax protections to try and grab even more money. California seemed to work just fine in 1998, when the budget was $1,775 per capita. Today it's $5,558 per capita. What gives?

Besides progressive programs like the bullet train boondoggle and weather-related initiatives, it's the unions and their generous contracts that are behind this. The governor has said that California's actions are designed to match its values. In other words, if the people like to see tax-and-spend policies, the state has no choice but to tax-and-spend. The last I checked, the state was sitting on $1.1 trillion in unfunded liabilities for state employee and teacher pensions. That's an average of about $83,000 per household. There was only one city in the entire state that had its public pension liability fully funded and the situation is spiraling out of control, despite a strong stock market. The concept of using austerity measures to address this is heresy to leftists.

Although poverty or unemployment will never be eliminated, in any country, ever, government spending is a favorite strategy by the Left to gain votes from classes of people who may stand to benefit from money, food, or job handouts. Leftists need economic immigrants to understand and appreciate the good that government programs can do for them, so that votes eventually ensue. Conservatives see the game here, but they're not complaining about it in the right way. This should not be only about crime or suppression of wages. It should be about Marxism.

Leftists see conservative pushback to immigration from Latin America as racist. Remember, if something can be examined in oppressive terms, it gets the Leftist's default label–racist. Conservatives, both Democrat and Republican appreciate traditional Latin American values on social issues, family, and faith. Americans should be having more children and going to church every week. The issue conservatives have, for the most part, is the appeal which strong central governments and authoritarianism has for too many Latin Americans. I can anticipate your comment – Cubans are conservative. True, to a degree. The Cuban-Americans who settled in Florida during the twentieth century generally had an anti-Castro/anti-communist slant and 78% voted for Reagan in 1980 and as many as 85% voted for Bush 41 in 1988. However, that dominance began to change by 1992 as Bush 41 slipped to an estimated 77%. Today, the second and third generations of Cuban immigrants in Florida remain more conservative than other Latinos but more left leaning than their ancestors. Cuban-Americans in Florida voted for Trump at a 54% rate compared to other Latinos across the state (26%) which was only slightly better than the estimated 47% Mit Romney received in 2012.

In 2004, the United Nations Development Program conducted a survey of 18,600 residents in 18 Latin American countries to get their opinions on a wide range of political and economic issues. They found that 55 percent of people said they would support an authoritarian government, if it resolved their economic problems. The survey also found that most people feel corruption in government is OK, if it leads to economic growth. That's not good.

Americans are aware of the region's historical problems with social struggles, poverty, and a weak middle class, caused by what the Left would say was oppression by colonial powers, coupled with capitalist exploitation. The fear conservatives have is a relentless influx of people, who are prone to either support or are used to big, corrupt, and authoritarian government as a means for their continued economic survival. This is a description of the conservative Democrats mentioned earlier –pro-family, pro-children, pro-church, and anti-gay marriage, but when push comes to shove on Election Day, the union knows best, so they vote blue.

So, to put a bow on this, most countries south of the United States have some level of experience with Marxism. Cuba is the most well-known country to be fully under Marxist rule, and there's the United Socialist Party in Venezuela that stands out. Central and South American leftists, fueled by immigrants from France, Spain, Germany, and Italy, and motivated in part by Lenin's animosity toward imperialism, held active and significant political power and influence during the 20th century—and into the twenty-first century in many cases—in Mexico, Nicaragua, Chile, Bolivia, Argentina, Paraguay, Uruguay Brazil, Ecuador, Guatemala, El Salvador, and Columbia, as well as Cuba and Venezuela mentioned earlier. In the 1920s, Marxist philosopher Jose Carlos

Mariategui, who founded the Socialist Party of Peru, felt socialism was right for his nation, because the Incas had implemented what he felt was a communist society. (Yes, there have been labor, socialist, and communist parties in America's past, but none have ever yielded any significant political power.)

WHY CHARITY MIGHT BE THE NEXT THING MARXISTS WILL ATTACK

Americans have big hearts. Traditionally Americans have tithed what they could to their church and donated what they could to service organizations, food banks, and the like. If they had additional discretionary income to give away, it went to the arts, preservation activities (land, oceans or animals), or, as many on the Left lament, college sports programs. This drives Marxists nuts, because they don't want disposable income (i.e., money!) diverted away at the taxpayers' discretion from social programs, public works boondoggles, or the government employment/pensions they want to advance.

The tax programs proposed by leftists such as Senator Sanders would limit itemized deductions with the effect of curtailing charitable deductions. The goal is to collect more taxes to fund government programs that replace the traditional role of charities. American's have always benefitted from the charity of the wealthy that's funneled through churches and non-profits to the needy. What the progressives want to do is remove the churches and non-profits from this role and become the new middleman. In the Left's view, God doesn't provide salvation. Government does.

In the Marxist's mind, taxes must be involuntary and high, and the revenues collected spent in accordance with whatever central planning goals they have in mind. So, to the Left, charity is only compassionate when it's funneled toward social programs they feel warrant it. But, since Big

Brother knows best, the Left wants to take your money and spend it how they, and not you, see fit. Therefore, because most people don't funnel their charitable contributions to where the Left wants, they instead want to raise taxes to divert more and more money from your paycheck—in the form of higher taxes. This is not just to add funds to their pot, but more importantly, it aims to lower your discretionary income, so you simultaneously give the government more, and you can't send as much money to places that—in the progressive's view—don't need it, like the Andrew Mellon Foundation or Notre Dame's football program.

In the Marxist view, charitable organizations—and the amounts donated—should not be a personal preference. Disposable income needs to be captured ahead of time (through taxes) and should be redirected from worthwhile entities, like a parish or the United Way, to where it's really needed—public works boondoggles, health care, welfare programs, government pensions, rent subsidies, and so on and so forth. The counter to that position is charity through tax exactions isn't heartfelt charity at all.

PUBLIC POLICY IS TRYING TO BECOME MARXIST POLICY

Marxism has made its way into American public policy through government overreach, including guaranteed government jobs, expensive programs, and leftist fiscal policies, such as a progressive taxation system. Leftists call for a fiscal policy that redistributes the perceived fruits of labor back into the proletariat's hands. They seek a more powerful federal government that will enact policies and make regulatory and judicial decisions to impose a fascist uniformity of the country's business, social, and political climates: Labor and industry on the same page, taxing and regulating the heck out of each other for the glory and honor of the state.

Conservatives view income as the fruits of one's hard work, dedication, persistence, and income from this labor, which should rightfully be kept, ought to be reinvested and spent as one sees fit. For the progressives they have a completely different view. They see income in Marxist terms—profit by the individual is evil, because labor and production are, in their eyes, a zero-sum game. You'll recall that socialist hero Eugene Debs ran on a presidential platform that no man should ever work to make a profit. In other words, if I have surplus disposable income, I've made a profit for myself and my boss and therefore I'm evil and selfish, because some member of the underclass is suffering as a result of it. Normal people understand that the economy is not a zero sum game. Everyone can profit.

Orthodox leftists live in a nineteenth century world where cash and resources were viewed as finite. To them it's impossible to envision, let alone justify, a laborer making a profit off his labor that helps a factory make a profit which assists investors in making a personal profit. This helps explain why they recoiled at Reagan's supply-side economic model. It was disruptive and flew in the face of Marxist-Keynesian demand side models that were largely accepted as gospel until that time. Our economic gains of the past 40 years are a direct result of the abandonment of left-leaning demand side models in favor of supply side models.

The Left believe income is a byproduct of society—we make a good living not because of our hard work, risk taking, delayed gratification, and education, but instead we make a good living because the state gives us license to do certain things (the manipulation of society) and the proletariat works their rear off to build and then purchase our products (houses, cars, TVs, etc.). So, for those in the housing industry, the tax logic goes like this: Since the state sanctions a development project (through entitlements) and authorizes (through permits) the construction of houses (through inspections), society is, therefore, able to buy houses, which provides good jobs for the housing industry, but with that comes an obligation to support (through taxes) society at large.

But not all taxes are equal. Why's that? One of the great successes the Left was able to legislatively achieve was progressive tax rates. This was an idea Karl Marx came up with and it goes like this: Because some people (factory owners, lawyers, etc.) are better at manipulating society for personal profit than others (factory workers, ditch diggers, etc.), they therefore have an obligation to pay increasingly more taxes to society as a price for the increasingly accumulation of wealth they steal from society. More taxes are therefore necessary for government to cure these abuses. To the Right, everyone making a profit to their abilities is perfectly legal and victimless. To Marx profit was an unfair crime. The term fair share came to mean income redistribution measured by how badly you manipulated society for your personal gain.

THE STRANGE DEVOTION TO THE LABOR THEORY OF VALUE

A great way to articulate the Labor Theory of Value is through the construction of new housing. In the Leftist mindset that persists in the city halls of towns like Seattle and San Francisco, the price (of housing) should ideally equal the cost (of production). In their view, homebuilders are unwilling to climb on board and forsake profit in the name of doing what's right. The idea of profitless production is something Marxists call the Labor Theory of Value. Yes, LTV would be inapplicable to for-sale housing in classical Marxist orthodoxy, because there would be no private property ownership. But, let me use housing as an example to articulate this theory, because it plays into contempt for capitalism and ignorance about how private industries work.

The Marxist thought process here is that housing and rentals aren't expensive, due to supply and demand or regulatory red tape. They're expensive because of greedy developers charging too much for housing or landlords taking advantage of the working class and overcharging for rent. In classical leftist thought, it's believed that if it costs $200,000 in land, design, labor and materials to build a home it should cost $200,000 for a member of society to purchase it. Homebuilders should only cover their costs, because the value of the work performed in production is what's important, not profit. Same with cars, appliances, iPhones or any other consumer good. If it costs $20,000 to build and sell a car, it should be sold for $20,000. Neither a penny more nor a penny less. A zero-sum game, where there is no loss or profit.

Naturally, builders are unwilling to build homes at cost or at a loss. Impact fees (basically a tax for the privilege to build in town) and other exactions do nothing more than raise costs. Leftist agencies want downward price pressure on housing costs but can't live without the taxes that put upward cost pressure on the industry. In an ironic way, if leftist agencies really want developers to sell or lease market rate housing at cost, and therefore at a more "affordable price," they should streamline the process and eliminate fees.

The Labor Theory of Value has been debunked, because it obviously ignores motivation, work ethic, incentives, and, of course, the law of supply and demand because, naturally, price or value is determined not just by supply, but by the demand of the consumer. Labor does contribute to cost, but so do the ever-evolving tastes and needs of consumers. (Few millennials know of the Volga and how it was never updated for 40 years, because consumer tastes in a Marxist economy were never a consideration. Besides, changing tastes would goof up the central planning model. In Marxist central planning, the government defines tastes and quantifies demand, not the consumer.) Marxists have a hard time letting go of labor being the source of all value. What Americans have learned for the past 200-plus years is that subjective individual evaluations create all value in a market, and this reality has been proven out, undermining Marx's economic conclusions and some of his social theories.

The progressive's tend to live in a fantasy world, where central planning can fix this. In the Marxist's view, housing is unaffordable not because of environmental regulation, bureaucratic red tape or NIMBYism ("not in my backyard") conspiring to create a supply/demand imbalance, it's expensive because developers build houses on oversized lots that are bigger and fancier than people need, and they charge more than they need to charge, leading to a profit, at the expense of the consumer. Due to unfairly high prices, banks then profit, because few people can pay cash for their homes, and therefore need to take out loans and mortgage insurance, that protects the lender. In the Marxist worldview, the key to affordable, for-sale housing rests on establishing policies that regulate, if not control, not just the demand and supply sides, but also the financing side of home ownership. They somehow think that if homes can be built cheaper, they would therefore be sold at a lower price, as if they were daily commodities. New home prices are set by market demand, not cost recovery. The cost to build the home determines the profitability of it, not the price of it. So, for rental housing, it's taxation in the form of fee exactions to fund public housing initiatives, or exactions through the entitlement process for inclusionary housing.

MARXISM NEEDS CHAMPIONS

Marxism needs champions to lead the cult of personality, and who better to drive home that message than pop culture personalities? There isn't a clear transcendent leader yet on the national political stage, because Marxism has no true base in America. The few politicians who are pushing this the hardest are not taken seriously by enough voters, but that's changing as millennials have an increasingly positive view of Marxism. Therefore, the Marxists need champions in pop culture and the media to advance the agenda and spread the message to the idiotic masses, and it's being cleverly rebranded as "democratic socialism," though it's still Marxist. If someone says, "If you want to change the world, be a journalist, a teacher, an activist, or judge," recognize that this is a common leftist dog whistle call from the '60s that leftists are still pushing today. Political correctness is a call for uniformity of identity and thought. (Read: Anti-America cultural and thought control.)

MARXISTS WANT MIDDLE CLASS VOTES BUT MIDDLE-CLASS DISCORD TOO

Marxism does not gain its fundamental strength from the underclass, although it certainly counts on the urban poor when Election Day comes. Traditionally, Marxist strength rises in response to disharmony in the middle class. This is why Marxists go out of their way to court labor unions and talk about how Republicans are ruining the American middle class. Labor unions are the quintessential example of American working-class laborers. These people aspire to join the middle class and provide a better life for their kids than what their parents gave them. Unfortunately, there's an old adage that everything labor unions touch, they ruin—the workplace, their industry as a whole, and local politics, for example. Marxism has ruined more than American labor unions, its ruined entire industries. Honestly, everything Marxism touches in America is ruined.

WHY DO WALL STREET AND TECH OLIGARCHS SUPPORT MARXISM?

Marxists teach young people that conservatives are intolerant, old fashioned and out of touch or out of step with modern society. A recent disparaging remark I overheard from a leftist, chastising an older conservative was, "Do you want your grandchildren to despise you?" There were essays written about the so-called creative class and how creative people will drive the new economy and, of course, how most of these people were progressives and gay and whatever. Wall Street and tech oligarchs support leftist agendas (godlessness, decriminalization of drugs, identity politics, homosexuality, etc.), because these behaviors resonate with millennials who desperately seek tolerance and acceptance of oppressed tribes. The issue conservatives have is not the people. It's the behavior. But, the Left has a hard time separating people from behavior because, to them, everything is about identity. Sex is not an activity; it's a lifestyle. Drug usage is not an activity; it's a lifestyle.

Most importantly, these types of behaviors are thought of by the Left as victimless personal choices and lifestyles and don't impact profits. As long as employees are coming to work each day, feeling good about themselves and knowing their employer does not object to their religious, sexual, gender blending or drug proclivities, then all is well. Objection to these proclivities is seen as draconian, repressive, and something only an old white man would have a problem with. As mentioned elsewhere in this essay, the Marxists have classified conservative, straight, Christian white men as the most significant part of the oppressive class they're at war with.

Chapter 12

PROGRESSIVISM TODAY—
PROMISES, MONEY, AND TAXES

MARXISTS ARE ALL ABOUT EGALITARIANISM AND income and social equality and the like. Their socialist view ignores the inconvenient truth that income sharing reduces individual incentives to work and rejects that incomes should be individualized. In short, they want power over a uniform egalitarian society. Critics of Marxism have argued that in any society where everyone holds equal wealth, there can be no material incentive to work, because one does not receive rewards for a job well done. They further argue that incentives increase productivity for all people and that the loss of those effects would lead to stagnation. High taxes, minimum wage, equal pay, prevailing wages, union guarantees, and so on and so forth are all income redistribution tactics, endorsed or mandated, by Marxists.

THE FAILED MARXIST PROMISES

Socialists make promises all the time. The further left they move, the more radical and extreme they become and, out of necessity, the more they need to rely on wild promises intended to resonate with broader and broader classes of people to stay in power. Because socialism has always been frowned upon in the U.S., it is seen as rebellious or taboo.

This edginess appeals to the have nots in society, and, consequently, controversial platforms need a charismatic cult of personality figures to lead the charge. This need for a "bad boy" or "bad girl" to, therefore, play the pied piper explains why an outspoken 29-year-old (AOC)— who had never previously run for office—can become the face of the progressive wing of the Democratic Party, almost overnight. A slogan used by Hitler was "Freedom and bread" and a promise was "A German husband for every German girl." Josef Stalin promised a society where there was better food and better working conditions. Mao Zedong promised farmers land to till. It's no wonder why capitalism isn't as popular with labor and youth—it doesn't make promises. Being young and unemployed and facing a complicated and uncertain future is scary. Traditionally, that's where family, faith, and friends lend their support.

But Marxism doesn't want interference from family or the church. It promises a heavenly utopia right here on Earth, with little to no effort, while living with capitalism requires hard work and risk taking. A Marxist society is portrayed as a wonderful place where everything sounds, well, promising. That is where everything seems easy, where those who "oppose" or "oppress" you are put down, and where everything from cradle to grave is taken care of by Big Brother. Those promises are never realized. Marxism always fails to deliver. It always leads to massive human suffering.

DO LEFTIST GOALS OF HIGHER TAXES REALLY EQUAL UTOPIA?

Marx introduced a progressive income tax in his political pamphlet: "The Communist Manifesto." A general consensus among Americans is that the best four countries to relocate to are the U.S., Canada, New Zealand, and Australia. Certainly, they are all English speaking, but coincidently or not, they have tax bites (income taxes as well as social security taxes) of between 18 percent and 26 percent, according to

Forbes. People often think of mainland Europe as a marvelous place to live, but at what cost? The taxes are significantly higher and with aging and declining native populations, the social security taxes are staggering and are only expected to rise. Sweden has a top income tax rate of 61 percent.

Per the OECD, which does an annual income tax calculation, if you factor in the total "tax wedge," which adds in the employer payroll contributions (such as the matching 6.2 percent of social security in America) the average Belgian is contributing 52.7 percent of his or her wages to the state, followed by Germany at 49.5 percent, Italy at 47.9 percent, and France and Austria coming in next at 47.6 percent. Compare that to New Zealand, which, due to its nonexistent social security tax, is at 18.4 percent, and that's for single filers without kids. As for a one-earner married couple with two children earning the average income, the tax is, wait for it, 1.9 percent. How can New Zealand be such a great place to live, if its taxes are so low? In the leftist mindset, only high-tax nations are great places to live, because high taxes provide high services. Could it be that people don't care for services just for the sake of providing service jobs? Could it be that lower taxes actually contribute positively to a great lifestyle? To the Left, this is heresy, because great communities exist because of great funding (taxes).

WHAT THE LEFT MEANS BY "DIVERSITY"

In local politics in San Francisco, there is a lot of diversity from sky blue to azure to sapphire to navy. Their idea of diversity is a lot like the political choices happening in the Soviet Union in the 1920's, after Lenin's death. Trotsky was left wing, Stalin was centrist, and Bukharin was right wing. Each was a Marxist and to Russians of that day, the spectrum those three represented was pretty broad. So, to latter day San Franciscans, political diversity is parsing the differences between former leftist mayors Diane Feinstein, Willie Brown, and Gavin Newsom. There is no royal blue or purple in their local elections, as any hint of red is a nonstarter—just blue to very dark blue. If you're not solidly blue, you are not in their corner and are unwelcome. The already-narrow spectrum of liberal to Marxist is the only acceptable diversity, and hence, words from their mouths are acceptable speech. In their world, conservatism is not diversity; it's hate speech.

WHO ARE THE "CONSERVATIVE DEMOCRATS" AND WHY ARE THEY DISAPPEARING?

Conservative Democrats have tended to have typical liberal values associated with eradicating poverty, adoption of tax-and-spend policies to stimulate the economy, strong secular education- and pro-union positions. They also may hold pro-life and pro-second amendment sentiments, while having more conservative positions on immigration, gay rights, and socialized medicine. Joe Lieberman, Eugene McCarthy, John Kerry, and Joe Manchin could be considered some of the more notable conservative Democrats. This strand of the Democratic Party used to be called Dixiecrats, then the Blue Dog Coalition, and the Boll Weevil Democrats. Gallup polls show that conservative Democrats, as a percentage of the American population, were as high as 25 percent in 2000, then down to 19 percent by 2015 and 13 percent by 2018, as the party moved significantly to the Left. Excluding certain African-American and Latin-American men, it's thought that this type of Democrat will eventually disappear, as leftists like Senator Warren and others will demand strict adherence by all Democrats to any and all leftist positions.

By today's standards, Senator Bobby Kennedy (RFK) would be considered a Conservative Democrat. RFK presented an interesting case about where many on the Left were in the '60s. RFK was a pragmatic politician, who was idealistic in his pursuit of social justice causes, but he also took time to examine and question policy issues. As an example, in 1967 & 1968, RFK went on a poverty tour across the nation with the intent of measuring the success of LBJ's War on Poverty programs but also to come up with new ideas to address rural and inner-city poverty. His ideas would have required some level of private business and charities working with the government to come up with responsible programs that could be measured. They would have required massive federal spending, but he knew government alone couldn't come up with all the answers. He needed commitment from local politicians, local charities, local businesses, and aid recipients. RFK expected to see the data and analyze the results, not hear ballpark estimates. He wanted his programs tied to welfare reform, school performance standards, and personal accountability, which was the type of carrot-and-stick strategies that you would normally hear out of a conservative candidate.

WHY DO MARXISTS REALLY WANT "FREE" COLLEGE TUITION?

The pretext the progressives offer sounds noble enough: Young people are saddled with too much debt and, therefore, are not positioned to afford mortgages or other grown-up expenses. Leftists have great allies in the white towers of higher education, and they certainly don't want fewer kids going to college. The real reason Marxists want free tuition is because most kids don't major in STEM fields—science, technology, engineering, and math—or in professional programs during their undergraduate years. They are not studying architecture or engineering nearly as much as they are majoring in the humanities, where 92 percent of the faculty is made up of leftists. (Whereas liberal professors outnumbered conservatives three-to-one in '68, it is now 12-to-one.)Liberals tend to teach sociology, women's studies, literature, African-American studies, philosophy, linguistics, art, music, journalism, history, environmental studies, childhood development, and education.

Leftists claim that the humanities are the best majors, because they develop critical thinking skills, but have you ever heard a biology major say, "I don't want to be a critical thinker, so I chose biology?" The American Conservative summarizes this as follows: "For all the debate about the current state of the university in general and the humanities in particular, here is what is trickling down to high school students: engineering majors become engineers, science majors become scientists, business majors become business people and humanities majors become activists."

The point: By enabling more kids to go to school and earn a degree debt free, the Marxists ensure that more and more students will come out of school as activists—and, more specifically, leftist activists.

TODAY'S MARXISTS THINK SUBSIDIES ARE SOCIALISM

It's common for American leftists to try and point out that socialism already is a daily part of our lives, so what's there to complain about? The most common assertion centers on the notion that subsidies to banks, the auto industry, or farmers are socialism. Or that tax cuts to corporations are socialism. This is comical. Socialism is government regulation in the means of production in private industry. Subsidies aren't telling a bank what interest rate to charge, how many small cars need to be built and where they get exported to, how to make a computer or how to make soybeans.

The progressives like to assert that tax cuts are socialism for the wealthy, because in their bizarre thinking, any and all government action means socialism. No. Not all government action is socialism. In fact, in America, very little government action is socialism. Socialism is a regulating action, but tax cuts are a deregulating action. How could tax cuts possibly be a socialist action?

Leftists tend to think conservatives are ignorant about subsidies and oblivious to the socialism already around them. However, they are the ones who are actually confused. Not only do leftists think subsidies are a form of socialism (they're not) and think tax cuts are a form of socialism (they're not), but they also comically think conservatives are selective in how they see and view socialism, as in, if socialism helps them (social security), they're quiet, and if it helps a minority (welfare), they are opposed to it. It's silly, but that's how the Left thinks.

THE ROBIN HOOD MENTALITY

A basic tenant of Marxism is: "From each according to his ability. To each according to his needs." It sounds very morally superior and fair—kind of like something Robin Hood would endorse, taking from those rotten rich and giving to the deserving poor. Except, people aren't naturally altruistic. They are selfish, and nobody willingly wants to give more than they receive, but they'd gladly take more than they give because, well, people are naturally selfish. Nothing comes close to articulating this more so than taxes, and a huge difference between the Left and Right in America is fiscal policy.

The Left believes people who are successful need to pay more because they have cleverly and successfully manipulated society to their advantage. Because they have manipulated society (i.e., they have taken home more than the value of what they have produced), they should rightfully pay society (income taxes) for that right. Sidebar: Ever notice how they don't use the word fair? They use the term fair share. Conservatives believe successful people make it in life—and often make it in spite of society's roadblocks—through hard work, risk taking, and perseverance. Conservatives believe in laws of supply and demand and a fair wage for a fair day's work, and nobody manipulated anybody.

Marxists try to portray their confiscatory fiscal views in this Robin Hood–like manner: The rich have manipulated society to where they have too much money, too many possessions, too much power, live in houses that are far too large, and drive cars that are far too expensive, all to the detriment of most of society. No amount of taxes on the successful, let alone rich, is too much, and income taxes are a great method of income redistribution. They play to heart strings and resort to scaring any reluctant elites by warning them the poor will revolt in some sort of income inequality uprising, if not appeased. By portraying the capitalists and most successful in society as undeserving, evil, selfish, and immoral, they play to the emotions of the have-nots in their never-ending Marxist passion play: Overplay the suffering of the oppressed, applaud the enlightened state of those who convert from the oppressive class, and bully everyone in the oppressive camp who doesn't convert into financial and class (racial) atonement.

What do they do once they get his money? Well, they want more. Former San Francisco Mayor and California Speaker of the House Willie Brown proclaimed that the initial budget you disclose to the public about a public works project is really just a down payment. If you tell people the actual cost, you would never get the support. So, you dream up an ambitious plan, state a somewhat reasonable price tag, and move forward. But, what if your plan is outrageously ambitious? What if the plan is so costly that it may never be implemented? So, to the Marxists in Sacramento marching forward with their ridiculous bullet train boondoggle, they will just keep spending taxpayer dollars, no matter how far behind schedule they are or how much the costs have increased.

The 380-mile California High-Speed Rail (CHSR) project, which was approved by voters in 2008, was estimated to cost $40 billion, but by 2012, the cost estimate had increased to $53.2 billion, and in 2018 it was up to $63.2 billion. Completion has been moved back from '22 to '33, if at all. Leftists like Brown feel that the way to see projects like this to fruition is to commit more and more money to it. The thinking is that you've gone this far, why not finish it up? Obviously, in Sacramento they have never heard of the spending warning that goes like this – when you reach the bottom of the pit, stop digging! In the case of the CHSR project, the solution has always been to throw more money at it and push back the completion date, rather than invest in cheaper transportation alternatives that people really need—like roadway improvements.

BEWARE OF WORDS LIKE FUNDING AND INVESTMENT

Funding is a Marxist dog-whistle word that means taxation. Investment in the Marxist vernacular doesn't mean financial or resource commitments to business, but taxes redirected (i.e., invested) into Marxist coffers for colossal and mismanaged programs and earmarks. So, beware when politicians say funding and/or investment as part of some promise for a magical utopian initiative. These two terms mean more taxes from you for big government to spend on programs, pensions, projects, and other leftist schemes.

PROMISING THE IMPOSSIBLE

Author and commentator John Hayward wrote, "Under socialism, promises are considered supremely valuable, but under capitalism, results are far more valuable than promises."

A classic leftist political stunt is to make outlandish promises only for their emotional effect on audiences, without regard for how they might be accomplished. This is sort of the Jerry Brown mentality of anything's possible because "Smart people will figure it out." Somehow the Left believes only politicians on the Right can be demagogues, who make promises they never intend to keep, but it seems to be primarily coming from the Left. The progressives express these empty promises, simply and theatrically, but remain extremely hazy about how they will achieve them, because usually they are impossible.

The most infamous example in American politics has to be former Louisiana Governor and U.S. Senator Huey Long. Senator Long was a Democrat and renowned left-wing populist who had a very brief political career, before he was assassinated at age 42, in 1935. Among other things, Long promised that if he were elected president: Every family would have a home worth $5,000, an automobile, a radio, and $2,000 yearly at a time when the average annual income was about $1,300 per year. He was vague about how he would make that happen, but people still supported him. Another kind of empty demagogic promise is to make everyone wealthy or solve all the problems. This is how the modern left operates to secure votes: Free college education, forgiveness of student debt, guaranteed government jobs and guaranteed minimum incomes, even for people who refuse to work.

WHY ARE YOUNG PEOPLE SO CAPTIVATED BY MARXISM?

There's a tremendous impulse by every generation of young people to change the world. Having high school and college students of my own, I know they can be rebellious, indignant, impatient, and unreasonably idealistic. They see their parents as living routine (i.e., boring) lives, tied to 30 long years of mortgages, child care and education costs, and other financial, professional, and societal commitments that preclude the spontaneous, independent, and irresponsible freedom, fun, and adventure they seek. Why save for a down payment on a condo, when they could spend that money on an enriching and extended sabbatical in Europe?

Millennials neglect to see that their parent's stoicism, faith, delayed gratification, risk taking, and hard work resulted in a hard-earned and quite often comfortable living. Rather than invest the blood, sweat, and tears and follow the example set by their parents, they fret about nebulous "isms" wrapped around equality, environmental and social justice, and quality of life, rather than focus on sensible American pragmatism, such as the virtuous dignities of the American ethos—marriage, child bearing, starting a career, serving your community, and achieving the American Dream.

Regrettably, too many young people simply don't know what they want to do in their lives. In past generations, it was find a job, work there for 40 years, and hopefully have saved up enough for a healthy retirement. Now kids are not thinking about career or family but are looking at their impact on the world in the context of social justice or change. They are influenced by cultural Marxism and post-modernism and think that travel to Europe means globalism is good. Consequently, too many young people are going to college, and of those who do, too many are studying the wrong major. Simply put, too many people are studying the wrong stuff.

There's a saying that goes, "Don't blame capitalism for your bad choices in life," which explains why those who have long since left school still wonder why BA degrees in comparative literature don't lead to six-figure jobs. All the while, they bitterly cling to leftist views about the way things ought to be. They blame racism, sexism, the "patriarchy," the hegemony, or other capitalist or Christian bogeymen for their underachievement in life. What's frustrating is seeing these adults tell America's youth that our communities, American society, and for that matter, the whole world sucks because of capitalism, all the while ignoring that liberty, freedom, and free markets are what made America great. They reflect on the old-school liberalism of their parents' and grandparents' generation and wonder where things went wrong. In their eyes, something more needs to be done. And it has to happen in their lifetimes. In comes a new and more radical yet seductive idea—millennial socialism, seeking its destruction.

Socialism is extremely seductive, because everything past generations needed to work hard for is suddenly cast as easier, fairer, more just, and of course "free." Who pays for it? Young people think the rich or their parents will. The government will. Anyone but millennials will. That's what they mistakenly believe. This is a rich country, they'll say. Just "Print more money," AOC says. Good grief.

By their late 20s, most young people outgrow the narcissistic selfishness and misguided ideologies taught on college campuses and on social media that goes like this: I don't care if Marxism ruins my parent's lives, or the lives of tens of millions of Americans, and ruins our economy. It's all about me. Marxism can get me a guaranteed income, free college, free health care, subsidized housing, and transportation for myself! I can finally get the social, environmental, and prison reform justice that I feel is desperately needed, which would include the prosecution of (conservative) speech I (as a leftist) disagree with. I can get rid of draconian social rules that those rotten Christians have imposed on society for centuries.

Thankfully, they get married, start careers, buy homes, have children, and eventually and rightfully, adopt more conservative and pro-capitalist views as they age.

Marxism comes in many forms, and some are less evil than others. Some policies are smaller and, hence, more tolerable than others, such as Social Security and Medicare in the U.S., and socialist safety net programs in homogenous nations, like Sweden and Japan, which are well managed and popular. However, what's worrisome to most Americans is the growth in empathy—if not downright support—for dysfunctional statist Marxism among American youth. By the way, Sweden isn't nearly as socialist as American's think it is. They pretty much backed away from it decades ago, but the myth that Sweden is the ideal socialist model lives on.

There is another famous saying that goes something like this, "If you are in your 20s and vote conservative, you have no heart, and if you are in your 30s and vote liberal, you have no brains." So true! Nonetheless, Marxists want to appeal to the delusional Marxist dreams of the college kids and hope that this generation—unlike the past two or three since the '60s—actually maintain their leftist views through adulthood. For the past 50 years, this transformational fantasy has never taken hold, but people like Senator Sanders and his ilk are counting on it finally happening.

The influence of Karl Marx's ideas on the West has been more influential than most notice, and for all American patriots, it needs to be stopped. The only solution is to understand what is going on, teach your children about the false promises of Marxism, and elect non-Marxists (preferably conservatives) to office.

As patriots and as defenders of our Constitution and all the freedoms, liberties, and protections it affords us, I recommend that we reject language coming out of the mouths of the Left that feeds a climate of fear and resentment or otherwise normalizes Marxist sentiments.

Chapter 13

PROGRESSIVISM TODAY— PEOPLE AND POPULATION

THE THREAT OF THEN CANDIDATE TRUMP BECOMING president in 2016 sent the Left into crisis mode. A prevailing solution they discussed to survive 45's occupation of the White House was leaving the U.S. I'm all for it. If you don't like America, don't change it; just leave. Snoop Dog, Lena Dunham, Bryan Cranston, Keegan-Michael Key, and Raven-Simoné promised to move to Canada. Chelsea Handler promised to move to Canada, if she couldn't move to Spain first. Canadian Neve Campbell threatened to go back, but never did. Barbra Streisand threatened to move to Australia or Canada. Cher vowed to move to Jupiter—not the city in Florida—the planet. Jon Stewart was willing to fly the rocket. Ruth Bader Ginsburg promised to move to New Zealand. Samuel L. Jackson wanted to move to South Africa. George Lopez was going to move to Mexico. Miley Cyrus, Whoopi Goldberg, and Al Sharpton wanted to live anywhere, but here. None of them ever followed through. What happened? Why didn't they move? Why wasn't there a mass exodus of celebrities?

You have to wonder if, deep down, they know America is the greatest country in the world, and despite our imperfections, there really isn't a better place to live. Was it a protest just for show? But, assume for a moment that these people really do hate it here. Then why do they stick around? If people hate America so much, why does everyone want to live here, and why do so few people flee for political asylum? (The number of permanent residence applications received by Canadian authorities was the same in 2017 as it was in 2016 according to The Guardian.) And when I say few, I mean few! In April 2018, The New York Times tried to find someone, anyone, who voluntarily left the U.S. because of President Trump's election, and they did! They found a single mom who left Seattle for Columbia, but it turns out it her move happened long before President Trump was even elected, and it was just for a general dislike of the GOP and, not necessarily, President Trump, because Secretary Clinton was the heavy favorite. Strange that someone in Seattle would have even heard of a Republican, let alone felt the urge to move 4,000 miles to Medellin to dodge one.

MARXISTS AND POPULATION

One of the bizarre dichotomies of Marxism is its position on population. Marxists want more people to bump up the voter registration rolls, but at the same time they want fewer people (abortion). The leftists specifically want more poor people to immigrate to the U.S. to serve as an ever-increasing underclass, centered in large cities, who are underserved, undereducated, and underemployed, and therefore in need of public assistance. This is done solely to create a large-enough base of a (voting) underclass to ensure leftists get elected. The Left has succeeded in obtaining permanent power in most major American cities and most of its largest states. When leftists take over, generally bad things happen to the local economy: Jobs leave, the tax base wanes, and more people become poor. So, to them, it's not about opportunity and economic growth; it's all about power. At the same time, leftists whine about man-made environmental impacts and fret about sustainability and what the world will be like if too many humans negatively impact our planet.

Illegal immigration puts a strain on the economic, political, and environmental systems. The Left likes to talk about the reckless environmental implications of urban sprawl and greenhouse gas and all that, but when it comes to immigration, all those issues that impact our carbon footprint never come up. Do the leftists really think that once immigrants come here, they'll stop having children or stop encouraging their extended family to come? Or not drive? Beto O'Rourke once suggested the endless stream of migrants showing up at the U.S. southern border shouldn't be a surprise and, better yet, should be welcomed, because they have no choice but to come here due to American excesses, which have damaged the earth to a point where everywhere (but America of course) is subject to crisis-level existential threats due to climate change. Think about that. Migrants need to come here because it's safe.

However, out of the other side of the Left's mouth, they say the U.S. is on a path to destruction due to climate change. If that was the case, wouldn't people like Beto suggest everyone flock to Europe or take high ground in the Himalayas? Pleas of migration to escape climate change are nothing more than a desire to increase the pool of left-leaning voters.

Here's an example of how climate activism relates to the Marxism trifecta—oppression, materialism, and humanism. Greta Thunberg, the 16-year-old climate striker from Stockholm, who was named 2019 Time Magazine Person of the Year, is a case study on the intersectionality of Marxism and climate alarmism. It goes like this: The capitalist patriarchy is creating an existential threat for humanity. As everyone has a moral responsibility to save our true god—Mother Earth—and time is running short, it's perfectly OK to hurl shame on those who deny this crisis. By believing they are saving the world, through their activism, one's life has purpose, as are efforts to hinder the issuance of voter ID cards, as well as efforts to push to allow locals to vote in local elections (such as the San Francisco School Board) and issuance of drivers licenses. A remarkable 11 cities in Maryland allow illegal aliens to vote, and according to political commentator Charlie Kirk, 10 states, plus Washington DC now allow illegal aliens to obtain drivers licenses. These are New York, California, Washington, Colorado, New Mexico, Nevada, Illinois, Washington, Washington DC, Hawaii, Delaware, and Connecticut. All 11 of these voted for Secretary Clinton in 2016.

Since '70, the U.S. population has increased from around 200 million, to about 330 million in just 50 years. So, for the first few centuries of America, most of our population growth was natural, meaning more births than deaths. With a few exceptions, about 250,000 to 400,000 immigrants annually entered the U.S. during the 75 years between 1890-1965. (The Immigration and Naturalization Act of 1965 significantly altered the numbers moving forward, through a policy we know now as "chain migration.") Now, approximately 90 percent of our population growth is through immigration with about 1 million legal entrants through chain migration and an untold number illegally. Estimates indicate that more than 100,000 illegal immigrants enter the country illegally each month. And, some sources put the illegal immigrant population at as much as 22 million. In another 50 years, what will our population be? 400 million? 450 million? Will the goal of open borders bring that figure to 500 million? What is our real population today? 350 million? Does anybody really know?

I find the Left's objection to the so-called citizenship question very odd. Why don't they use it as a rallying call to get a true count? If they add it and find out California's population is actually 50 million and not 40 million, and if every seat in the House of Representatives is worth about 740,000 people, that's 14 additional Electoral College votes and 14 additional seats in the House. Why wouldn't they want a true count? If California is really entitled to 67, rather than 53, Electoral College votes, wouldn't that be a win for the Left? It's strange that they would rather risk an unlikely undercount than a more likely windfall from an accurate count.

As to immigration, the fundamental questions to explore are, will enough white-collar jobs be created as a result, or will there just be demand for more service jobs to serve the massive underclass, and will we be able to create enough new viable farmland to generate the crops needed to feed that population? Since few native-born Americans want to be farmers, and most Americans are leery of eating produce from other nations, are we going to rely on immigrants and equipment innovation to fill the farming jobs and production capacity that will be needed? If so, are we just importing immigrants to fill the low-skilled jobs to service existing residents?

The environmental impacts of unmitigated immigration are astounding, such as natural open space converted to farmland and farms converted to residential housing. That's been the cycle for the past 100 years, as development migrated away from major cities. Not that there's anything wrong with that, but it's estimated that Florida alone will need to find as much as five million acres of farmland to serve their population in the next 50 years. Planting trees, cleaning up parks, preserving open space, and not using straws sounds wonderful, but is the thought of the environmental implications of servicing unfettered immigration even being considered? Even housing everyone in high rises in Manhattan, Westside LA, or San Francisco doesn't address the farmland dilemma, because immigrants are fueling suburban greenfield development. If sustainability, carbon footprint, deforestation, and other environmental concerns are really that important, maybe it's time for the progressives to rethink their position on unrestrained immigration.

One of the aspects of immigration that the Left doesn't discuss is the negative impact it has on working-class blacks. Whereas, every Democrat who has run for office in the past few decades always talks about providing job opportunities for blacks, they actually harm those exact same people, by allowing millions of low-skilled immigrants to enter the U.S. and compete for the same available low-skilled jobs. If they truly wanted to lift black America up, they would put a limit on immigration, because the actual effect of flooding the workforce with low-skilled immigrants means blacks may never be hired.

WHAT MARXISTS MEAN BY THE WORD OPPORTUNITY

Leftists want successful communities, and conservatives want successful communities. Everyone does. Unless you win the lottery or inherit money or live a life of crime, to be self-sufficient, let alone successful, it's necessary for people to take advantage of the most important opportunity that is guaranteed for every American, namely a free K-12 education. However, the word opportunity means one thing to most Americans and something completely different to those on the Left. A free K-12 education is a right, not an opportunity to the Left. A K-12 education should, therefore, be guaranteed. A K-12 education should yield certain expected outcomes, namely equal outcomes. See how this goes? Everyone wants to have an important role in their communities, and they want to make sure they have opportunities, but what the Leftists actually want is equality—specifically, equal outcomes arising out of those equal opportunities.

It's a mathematical fact that half of America's children possess below average IQs. Even if you raised test scores across the board, guess what? Half of America's children would still have below average IQs. For the party of science to deny simple math is pretty disingenuous. A long-held leftist dream of public education is a set of national standards (and equal funding) that ensures each child leaves school with a uniform, high-quality education (i.e., equal outcomes). This will never, ever happen. You can't guarantee equal outcomes for kids of such varying IQs, no matter how much money you throw at it or how much to teach to the least common denominator. It's a disservice to both high achievers and low achievers to teach to the least common denominator, but that's what the Left wants—equal outcomes due to equal investment, led by leftist policies that are driving public education.

Equal opportunity does not mean equal outcome, yet the Left wants to push an agenda that replaces what it considers opportunity in America with guarantees of equal outcomes. Its one thing to have equal opportunity, but the government cannot guarantee what is sought by the Left—social, racial, and economic "justice" and social, racial, and economic "equality." The American dream is predicated on average people seeing successful people and thinking, "I can do that." I'm willing to work hard. I can do this! However, the Left wants Americans to hate the rich—particularly the conservative rich—and resent their lot in life. They want the oppressed class to carry a grudge and have a desire to punish the successful. Success requires one to capitalize on opportunity and meet a need in society by providing a good or service that people will pay for. This requires initiative, ingenuity, entrepreneurship, risk taking, skill polishing, and hard work. The Left just wants equal outcomes without effort.

The idea of guaranteed outcomes is just as apparent in older rustbelt cities, undergoing gentrification, as it is in fast-growing cities in the sunbelt, where the underclass needs government to step in and level the playing field and ensure equal outcomes. The Left wants people to look at the successful people in society and always assume the worst—that they are exploitative racists who take advantage of the poor.

As noted previously, it's a mathematical fact that half of Americans are of below average intelligence. While it's possible to get a free K-12 education, it's impossible for everyone to be a millionaire. But, there is no reason why people can't have productive roles in society with a K-12 education. So, to redress this capitalist sin, leftists want to implement a Marxist "solution"—income equality—which means a redistribution of wealth from the successful and smart to the unsuccessful and dumb.

USING RACE AND IMMIGRATION TO SECURE A PERMANENT LEFTIST MAJORITY

At one point in time, about two-thirds to three-quarters of the world was living under Marxist control. Most of these nations make up what were once commonly called second- and third-world countries. The U.S., Western Europe, and a few first-world countries, such as Japan and Australia, weren't Marxist and were classified as first world. Leftists in America understand that to seize and hold permanent power in the U.S., it would be necessary to import as many left-leaning people as possible to establish a class of people dependent on social services and other safety nets to survive. The progressives don't seem to care about the implications these immigrants have on existing middle-class and working-class jobs. The goal is to win elections with a reliable underclass of voters from poor countries, who may very well harbor resentment toward white Christian America and/or a mistrust of the capitalist system.

The Left realizes that it's virtually impossible for anyone to openly criticize them, because to do so would imply racism. Immigrants from poor countries lean left and are almost all of color; once they are eligible to vote, they will be a reliable voting block for the Left. Yes, there are a few Cubans who have flown communism and quite a few doctors from India or PhD students from Africa who are welcomed by conservative America, but they are few in number compared to the millions of left-leaning, undereducated masses, who cross our borders legally and illegally every year.

The Left takes great joy in putting up road blocks to stop the Trump administration from securing the border. They know full well that the sheer number of immigrants can simply overrun the border and taking the proper time to vet each "asylum seeker" is impossible. Forcing demographic change for political purposes is just like eugenics—manipulating the population to achieve a political goal. If you notice this, you are labeled a white nationalist. If you oppose it, you are a white nationalist racist.

Latinos make up the primary base of leftists in California and will make up a majority of its population growth in the decades ahead. By empowering illegal aliens to vote or to lower the voting age only plays further into this wave of demographic change.

Remember, these immigrants aren't coming here for freedom. If they were, they would be voting conservative to ensure they were coming to a more libertarian society, but instead they are voting Democratic, which proves freedom isn't the goal. This was clearly seen in Orange County, California, which was a Republican stronghold for generations. But, in 2016 went to Secretary Clinton and, worse, all Republican congressmen from California were unseated by Democrat challengers. Immigrants are coming here for free stuff that the Left is willing to offer or promise (but unlikely to deliver on) in exchange for reliable votes.

The conversion of Orange County from red to blue, as well as voting transitions happening in Nevada, North Carolina, and Arizona, are textbook cases of weaponizing race and immigration to secure what the Left hopes is a permanent leftist majority. So, with California and New York in hand, Texas and Florida are the next two big targets to secure.

Humans are, by their nature, selfish and lazy. In this country, it's been proven that once an entitlement is secured by a class, whether it's for seniors, minorities, or immigrants, it's nearly impossible to take it away. Social Security has been described as the third rail of politics, because of the political suicide of anyone who suggests its reform or elimination. An increasingly diverse citizenry that is dependent on government programs and safety nets has created an electoral switch for Democrats that will be next to impossible for conservatives to reverse. President Trump won the rustbelt in 2016, by speaking to disaffected and mostly older white voters. How much longer before they become the minority in those states? Maybe two generations?

George W. Bush (Bush 43) secured a record 40 percent of the Latino vote in 2004, and it's gone down since. Senator McCain secured 31 percent in 2008, Senator Romney got 27 percent in 2012, and President Trump was slightly better, as he landed 28 percent in 2016. President Trump was aided by a higher-than-expected white turnout in battleground states. Moving forward, it will be difficult, but not impossible, for any conservative to win the presidency with less than 30 percent of the Latino vote. However, for the black vote, the results are showing conservatives are lagging since Bush's win in 2004. Bush 43 got 11 percent, Senator McCain managed just 4 percent in 2008, Senator Romney was at 6 percent in 2012, and President Trump secured 8 percent in 2016. African-American unemployment was at its lowest level ever entering 2020. As a result, it's expected that President Trump may double his percentage of the black vote.

Race matters to the Left, and a few percentage points in battleground states with a lot of black or Latino voters makes a difference. So, to appeal to the minority votes, they want to continue to encourage animosity by promulgating the view that white conservatives are indifferent to the plight of the immigrants and minorities in our communities and/ or are simply hopeless racists that should never be trusted, let alone voted for. Remember, to the modern American left, a racist is someone who is anti-Marxist.

MARXISTS NEED A BLIND COMMITMENT TO TOLERANCE AND EQUALITY

A way to keep the underclass in line, or as I call it, fat, dumb, and happy, is to provide cheap frozen food, subsidized housing, and cheap phone and Internet service. The Left doesn't want to stigmatize homelessness, drug addiction, or crime, because it advances their agenda to have drugs available. Drugs were a big part of the "If it feels right do it" mentality of '60s Cultural Marxism. They don't want to deviate from the narrative that the homeless or criminals are victims of an oppressive class. They are all victims of capitalism or victims of failed systems. So, to the Left, tolerance is a way to validate that you support equality. Intolerance only lives in the minds and hearts of the oppressive class.

WHY LEFTIST ELITES WANT TO FOCUS ON RACE AND NOT CLASS STRUGGLE OR INCOME INEQUALITY

To the Left, racism is a useful political tool. The liberal elites who live on the Atlantic and Pacific coasts have a vested interest in keeping any Marxist revolution focused on racial and identity oppression, rather than economic class, and the reason is pretty self-explanatory. If the villain (the oppressor class) can be described as white racists, rather than capitalists, the oppressed class will not focus on a more pressing question, which would be income inequality. If you ask them, and they are honest, the last thing rich elites living in the Upper West Side of Manhattan or Westside LA wants is Marxist wealth redistribution. Nobody wants to be taxed at 70 percent or wants their property confiscated or their business overly regulated; therefore, wealth redistribution isn't the most popular topic on the liberal's minds. But, what if the narrative changed, and the Marxist radicals with baseball bats and bricks began walking through a neighborhood, smashing windows or gashing tires on cars belonging to the liberal rich? That would never do; therefore, social insurance is needed.

An irony of socialism is that it inevitably results in extreme income and power inequality because a few party leaders end up controlling the state's political and economic power. The classic case is modern China where a relative handful of Chinese Communist Party (CCP) members control every conceivable form of power in a country of 1.3 billion. It's estimated that only 6% of the population are members of the CCP and less than 2% of the people are even worthy of applying each year. Of those only about 10% of those applications are approved annually. This is what a single-party ideocracy leads to: All animals are equal but some are more equal than others. In a bizarre twist the CCP sees the manufacturing profits they make via globalization as a form of internationalization Marx would be proud of. Chinese workers providing in-demand goods to the workers of the world. In exchange for boatloads of western currency of course.

By keeping the narrative focused, instead, on racial, ethnic, religious, sexual or gender identity, and/or immigration status, they are avoiding a much touchier topic, which could turn the tables against them. Once the radicals on the far-left stop focusing on racism, climate change, or other identity politics causes, they will turn their wrath on income inequality, and the liberal elite will suddenly be in the crosshairs. They absolutely do not want this to happen, hence the insufferable and relentless racism discourse. Their tolerance can be explained as such: So long as antifa focuses on white racists and not the windows of my business or my Mercedes-Benz, everything's good.

MARXISTS PORTRAY ALL CONSERVATIVES AND CONSERVATIVE PRINCIPLES IN RACIST TERMS

What a lot of conservative whites don't know is what exactly the progressives mean by the terms racism and bigotry. Most people think they are interchangeable, but they aren't. Bigotry in the eyes of the Left is easier to explain as it's the acting out on racist or discriminatory impulses. They reluctantly acknowledge that a black man can be a bigot if he says or does something improper to a Korean store owner. It's specific, clear and easier to define. Unfortunately, racism has expanded to now become a far more comprehensive description of a broad range of Christian-capitalist behaviors.

To them racism is not just doing mean things to people of another color. The Left saw that as too limiting and, therefore, outdated. People who act on those impulses are now called bigots. The word "racist" now means anyone who is anti-Marxist. It's the acceptance of the patriarchy and all the various institutions, laws, traditions and customs, known as the hegemony, that make up America. If you support an America as our Founding Fathers envisioned, you are a racist! An example the Left often cites is the criminal justice system which they claim discriminates against people of color and, therefore, it's racist. The Electoral College discriminates against people of color, therefore, it's racist. Voter ID laws, immigration processes and SAT and IQ tests discriminate against people of color, therefore, those are racist too. If you wear a MAGA hat, you are assumed to want to retain, rather than tear down and rebuild, the systems in our society that perpetuate and maintain an unjust society, you are therefore racist! Questioning let alone objecting to this new, and extremely offensive definition, is unacceptable to the Left. In their eyes only a racist would find anti-Marxist sentiments acceptable. And since William Reeves is a self-described anti-Marxist he is by their bizarre definition racist. I'm certainly not of course, but I'll gladly respond by saying that anyone who holds Marxist sentiments is a village idiot.

Remember, Marx and his band have always been about destruction and misinformation in order to aid the oppressed, by any means possible. So, to that end, what they did to redefine racist and racism was very clever. Disgusting, wrong and typical for those losers, but it's all about perception. The game they play goes like this: Most people aren't racists and certainly nobody wants to be called a racist. But, if you happen to support the Electoral College or the turning back of migrants at the border, for instance, you will be shamefully called a racist, because your attitude is oppressive and therefore anti-Marxist. So, to avoid that label, denounce the Electoral College and support open borders.

Because President Trump almost immediately took America on a 180-degree change from a leftist path of self-destruction to a conservative path of "Making America Great Again," of course, he was promptly labeled an existential threat. Correcting irresponsible President Obama-era policies by the Trump administration wasn't seen by the Left as necessary. It was seen as spiteful and racist. It was portrayed as a coordinated attack by white America to dismiss an articulate black man's brilliant accomplishments and take America back in a time machine to an era when blacks and women couldn't vote, or something like that. That isn't true, but the Left is fully invested in a march toward Marxism, and its relentless narrative says President Trump is trying to take America back to the pre-Civil War days, so therefore, he's mean, ignorant, heartless, evil, racist, and so on and so forth.

It, therefore, wasn't surprising that the Left wanted to portray President Trump as a right-wing racist, misogynistic criminal, even before he took office. In the eyes of the American left, being accused as racist is worse than being an accused murderer, because they see murder as an act and not a thought or ideology. Mix in the reasonable doubt standard, and the possibility that the murder may have been in self-defense, an accident, or mistaken identity, and murder is seen as regrettable and tragic, but not as bad as being racist. They see murder as heat of the moment, but racism comes from a lifetime of darkness in the heart. Murderers should be released from prison, but racists should be given life sentences. The Left broadly paints racism as any mix of unacceptable thoughts, words, and actions, and in the court of public opinion, there is no defense. Proof and context be damned. Perception is reality.

The easiest way to explain the pulling of the racism card is through examining one of the key distinctions between how progressives and conservatives think. Conservatives hate the game (leftism), but not the player (people who support it), whereas leftists hate the player (conservatives, the patriarchy, etc.) and the game (conservative values, capitalism, etc.). Because conservatives have contempt for leftist views, the twisted narrative the progressives advanced is that only a hater would hate socialism, and if you hate socialism, you must therefore hate socialism's fans and by default, you must be racist or sexist or whatnot. Leftism is based on irrational emotion, and their adherents believe that since they hate conservatives, the conservatives, naturally, must hate them in return.

There's a saying that goes "A racist is a conservative who is arguing with a progressive." Screaming "racist" or "xenophobic" at the first opportunity is a clever trick the Left uses to control a narrative, because it's hard enough to disprove something that you aren't and since leftists are now mind readers, it's effectively impossible to disprove that you have hate in your heart. Unless, of course, you willingly go through a leftist re-education process. Even University of Pennsylvania political science professor Daniel Hopkins admits that measuring prejudice is notoriously difficult.

Some even contend that denying racism is, in itself racism, as if one can be complicit of a thought crime for not openly renouncing the unknown thoughts of another. Describing our society as post-racist is hate speech to the Left, because it dismisses the most powerful of all oppression angles which is: America is inherently racist. Make no mistake about it. Racism is wrong, and it is bad, very bad. But Marxism is bad too. This is a not an argument of there being a lesser of two evils at play here as in, 'I'd rather have a racist friend than a Marxist friend.' Or, 'I'd rather listen to a racist than a Marxist.' What I'm saying is that they are both rotten, so I'll choose to have neither as a friend.

All leftists believe conservative whites in America are racist for upholding the existing patriarchy and hegemony and will retain a racist label unless and until they've proven they have gone through some Marxist detox program that centers on privilege awareness and atonement. Writer, radio host, and educator Dennis Prager has an interesting test to determine if a conservative is a racist or not:

Do you have more in common with, and are you personally more comfortable in the company of, (a) a white leftist or (b) a black conservative?

Would you rather have (a) nine white leftists or (b) nine black conservatives on the U.S. Supreme Court?

Would you rather your child marry (a) a white non-Christian liberal or (b) a black Christian conservative?

A white racist would prefer the whites in each case. I happened to answer "b" in each case, and I'd bet 99 percent of conservatives would agree with me. If it came down to nine white and nine black conservative candidates for a court appointment, of course, the more qualified applicant would be preferred. This is how conservatives think.

Marxism has historically appealed to the underclass, the poor, the immigrants, and the outcasts and non-conformists. In general, minorities, non-Christians, women, gays, and criminals/prisoners in America have sought out and advocated for economic models and political philosophies that, in their view, can and will improve their lot in life. Criticisms of these policies is taken personally, because if you are of a certain gender (male) or race (white), any criticism, dismissal, or questioning of any leftist agenda item or social program is labeled racist and/or sexist. It's not the validity of the critique that gets debated; it's the place of anger it must have come from that gets condemned. In other words, it's not the message that's the problem; it's the messenger who's the problem.

So, for centuries Americans understood that our freedoms and liberties are derived from Christian fundamentals and a relatively non-intrusive and preferably small government. In the 20th century, more and more Americans chose, wrongly, to believe that freedom and liberty derived from government—whether from legislation, regulation, or the courts—and, therefore, government policy can and should be leveraged to cure perceived social ills. White male conservatives dismissed these programs and policy goals as un-American, primarily because they were straight out of the Marxist playbook. The Left spun the narrative and objected to the objectors, because conservative men were inherently racist.

More and more, you hear leftist commentators on CNN or MSNBC say, "Only a racist would care about that," or "Only a white nationalist would want that." Why don't they ever, more correctly, say, "Only an anti-Marxist would say that?" Because Marxism is complex and hard to explain, let alone sell, but racism is simple to grasp, and it sells. Marxists and their lackeys in the media cannot separate contempt for policy from personal hate. So, to them, if you hate a leftist policy, you must be a racist or a white nationalist, because you must hate the oppressed individual who would benefit from that program or policy. This is a clever argument they utilize. Because normal people don't need or want government programs, and apparently only the oppressed class does, to complain about a program is to put down an oppressed class.

While conservatives show their more evolved manners by being able to "Hate the game but not the player" (i.e., contempt for welfare abuse, but not hate for blacks, or contempt for immigration abuse, but not hate for Latinos), the Leftists hate the player (white males), because of the game (conservative views or "patriarchal" American society or Christianity, or whatever). Progressives hate conservatives, because they (falsely) believe conservatives hate minorities or gays. They are convinced their hate is OK, because it's morally superior. Because they feel hate toward a class of people (white males), they wrongly believe white males must also harbor the same hatred toward them. That's simply not true.

Anti-rent control or anti-minimum wage positions, which have both been proven to disproportionately and negatively impact lower-income people, are cast by the leftists as anti-immigrant, racist, or anti-poor, and, therefore, the people who hold anti-rent control or anti-minimum wage views are, by definition, oppressors and, therefore, racists. Advocating merit-based selection, rather than on immutable characteristics, is deemed racist, even though it is exactly what King sought—judge on the character, not on the race. Opposing racial quotas for university entrance is racist, even though these quotas have been proven, ironically, to be discriminatory to minorities.

The point in this is that conservatives hate leftist policies, but not the leftists as people. Conservatives have contempt for leftist nonsense, but they do not hate. Leftists on the other hand hate conservatives and their policies, because that's what Marxism teaches: Thou must hate the oppressor. Most Americans believe we live in a post-racist society. The Left doesn't want to acknowledge this, because racism sells in the minority (and liberal) communities, and racial warfare is a key part of the class and cultural war being fought by the Left. Marxists take conservative's contempt and rejection of their ridiculous or anti-American views personally. So, to galvanize their base, Marxists portray common-sense conservative views in an unflattering racial context. They cannot, and will not, seek common ground or engage in healthy debate. Objection to Marxism and a rejection of false claims of racism is a declaration of war to them, and in the Leftist's view, there's no time for debate—only time for war.

IMMIGRATION

Outside of abortion and the death penalty, few topics are as polarizing as immigration. Republicans, particularly neocons and moderates, have publicly called for strong borders and respect for immigration processes, but have typically looked the other way, as millions have crossed our southern border in an effort to provide cheap labor to various blue-collar industries. Democrats have publicly wanted immigrants as part of a compassionate humanitarian agenda, but also have always looked at them as a gigantic pool of potential voters. In past decades, most of the people who crossed were Mexicans. Lately, the majority are from Central America. Because actual figures are impossible to tabulate, it is estimated that approximately 400,000 people crossed illegally in both 2017 and 2018. These are almost exclusively low-skill and low-wage earning people, who enter the workforce and displace low-skilled Americans, including high school students looking to work during spring or summer break.

About four million young people through high school or college graduation enter the work force every year. Adding 400,000 people to that total means the worker pool is actually 10 percent above what it's supposed to be. If you have an influx of prospective employees above what the economy expects or can absorb, of course, you're going to have downward pressure on wages. If the number of immigrants was slowed or stopped, U.S. companies would be forced to pay higher wages. You can see why some conservatives might not want to slow it at all.

The policy of inflating the labor pool is good for business. It lowers wages and creates consumers, which leads to profits and higher stock values. The irony here is that leftists call for ends to wealth inequality, and yet immigration transfers wealth from unskilled, and mostly young Americans, to the 401(k)s of older investors. It results in unemployed or underemployed low-skilled Americans, thus contributing to social ills, like substance abuse and homelessness, and economic ills, such as reduced tax bases and foreclosures. Remittances back to third-world countries lower tax revenues, because they divert economic spending from local businesses to foreign countries. (Oklahoma has taken the bold step to tax those remittances.) An abundance of unskilled workers in border and coastal cities attracts businesses to those regions and, thereby, negatively impacts small-town America.

There's one last point to mention. The flood of immigrants arriving at the border puts pressure on the president and Congress to reach an accord to grant amnesty to millions of existing illegal aliens. Amnesty leads to citizenship and voting rights. The flow of people arriving is unprecedented. Should we be surprised to know this is part of a political ploy? Of course not.

Another not-too-often consequence of immigration is the practice of sending remittances back to third-world countries. In Guatemala, remittances from expats totals about $9.5 billion per year and accounts for 12 percent of their GDP. Most of this money is being sent from the United States. This money could be reinvested back into American communities.

Former Housing Secretary Julian Castro and Senator Warren as part of their defunct presidential platforms wanted to decriminalize illegal border crossings by making it a minor civil violation, rather than a crime. Because breaking a law would no longer be considered a big deal, it would be illegal to arrest someone for breaking a law. Just hand the culprits a citation, like it was a parking ticket. As President Trump said, "a nation without borders is not a nation."

This is a double whammy for conservatives. Millions of pending, left-leaning voters and detrimental negative impacts on (conservative) small-town America sounds like a malicious, yet brilliant, long-term strategy, if you're on the Left. The only logical explanation for this endorsed immigration epidemic is to harm the American heartland. Remember, destruction is the only Marxist game.

HOW TRIBALISM IS HURTING THE LEFT

Once upon a time, people really believed the world would soon evolve into a post-racist society, where race is an afterthought. It seemed very plausible that we could soon judge people on the content of their character. Dr. King, and others, knew it would take years, and some communities and some states would come around faster, but there was an optimistic belief it would be accomplished within one and, perhaps, not more than two generations. Through the '60s and '70s, we slowly moved closer and closer to a post-racist society, until the Left realized they could benefit from division and that Dr. King's dream of colorless unity would not advance the oppression-oriented agenda. Unity would require a debate on issues and their merits, which was one the American Left was losing, so they opted instead to divide and (hopefully) conquer.

The Left made another calculated move. They realized that unity wouldn't achieve their dystopian goals, so they decided to divide America into tribal groups, and if you divide people into groups, it is much easier to win. The reasoning being that groups of people are easier to manipulate than millions of individuals. It is easier to win, especially when you've been inundating them with the idea that there are "others" actively working against them, as well as a system completely rigged to crush them. If the patriarchy could be defined as the oppressive tribe—a racist, old fashioned, and undesirable group of Americans (i.e., white, straight, Christian men and pro-life women, who were predominantly white) – that would be characterized as the villainy. All the other tribes the Left can think of could then be molded into the oppressed class, the underdogs.

Division is sown and promulgated by the Left because leftists need enemies. Since leftism is fueled by fear, envy and mistrust they need to point to villains and say, "you are bad and therefore the enemy". Usually the anger is pointed towards those who the Left feels ignores or otherwise dismisses a key tenant of Marxism: The notion that diversity is essential or somehow good for society. The Left wants to utilize the concept of diversity, as Gramsci and the others would, as a tool to diminish the dominant cultural narrative. The theory being that if countless cultures can be deemed equally essential to America's identity then maybe America's dominant culture–Capitalist Christians who speak English–isn't so special or necessary after all.

Here's the issue. When you celebrate diversity you celebrate differences and when you celebrate differences you advocate tribalism which leads to hate, envy and resentment of the dominant culture. Tribalism, and not conservatism, sows division. Don't let them tell you otherwise.

Blaming Trump for division is false, but totally predictable because he's an anti-Marxist who is exposing this and leftists find it extremely uncomfortable and unwelcomed. America is not great because of our diversity, it's great because for over 200 years people from around the world bought into a series of abstract 18th century ideals about liberty and freedom. The melting pot analogy was about conformance to those ideals. We are not a stew or an Italian wedding soup. We are a blended smoothie where you can taste, but not specifically see, the individual ingredients. Placing blame on conservatives for division is unfortunately one of the biggest lies in American politics.

The only way to bring America together is to drop the Marxist ideological theories of oppression, diversity and victimhood and re-conform to traditional American values. Regrettably that might never happen in my lifetime.

Latter-day leftist theory maintains that if these other tribes could be categorized and quantified into a collection of tribes that, although seemingly disparate, are nonetheless collectively opposed to the hegemony, they could theoretically form a powerful—Marxist—alliance. These tribes would be minorities, immigrants, gays, liberal whites, blue-collar laborers, the poor, the homeless, the disenfranchised, and non-Christians. Collectively, these cohort groups make up more than 50 percent of the American electorate. Although they each have different priorities and interests, the theory is that they each harbor resentment of America's Christian, capitalist and heteronormalistic patriarchy (aka the oppressive class). These ideas, coupled with the twenty-first-century phenomenon of victimhood in the culture, create the perfect petri dish for the progressive agenda.

The Left needs to foster division, and the anger and fear that accompanies it, because a fearful and angry people don't think rationally. A fearful and angry people can have that fear and anger pointed toward those they're told to be fearful of and angry at.

We've all seen and hear the "Us versus them" politics of the Left, especially the last few years: Rich versus poor, tolerant versus intolerant, straight versus gay, urban versus rural, and so on and so forth. But their favorite, and most effective, tool is race, as the hyphen has been fully weaponized.

IMMIGRATION AND THE MARXIST PUSH FOR RACIAL ANIMUS

President Johnson and other liberals of the mid-'60s could not understand why the rather impressive Civil Rights laws passed under his leadership had failed to immunize northern and western cities from rioting. At the same time, the Civil Rights movement itself was becoming fractured. In the mid-'60s, the Black Panther movement emerged; Black

Power advocates accused white liberals of trying to control the Civil Rights agenda. Proponents of Black Power wanted African Americans to follow an "ethnic model" for obtaining power, not unlike that of Democratic political machines in large cities. This put them on a collision course with urban machine politicians. And, on its most extreme edges, the Black Power movement contained racial separatists, who wanted to give up on integration altogether—a program that could not be endorsed by American liberals of any race. The mere existence of such individuals (who always got more media attention than their actual numbers might have warranted) contributed to "white backlash" against liberals and Civil Rights activists. Fourth, large-scale immigration, especially by Asians and Hispanics, is creating a generation of new voters whose resentment of the white majority and capitalism are of a piece. Ethnic identity can't so easily be disaggregated from ideology.

Black Lives Matters is a much more peaceful movement than the Black Panthers were. They are also disappointed in American liberalism and are seeking more effective leadership on the Left. Marxists see the BLM movement as an opportunity to capitalize on racial division in America.

HOW THE MARXISTS HIJACKED THE STATUE OF LIBERTY

Sure, millions of immigrants have come to the United States from other countries. However, the United States is not a country of immigrants. We are a country of settlers who become citizens and become part of our great nation. Steve Bannon said it best during an interview with Charlie Rose in '17 when he remarked:

"America was built on her citizens. Look at the 19th century. What built America is called the American system, from Hamilton to Polk to Henry Clay to Lincoln to the Roosevelts. A system of protection of our manufacturing, financial system that lends to manufacturers, OK, and control of our borders. Economic nationalism is what this country was built on. The American system, right? We go back to that. We look after our own. We look after our citizens, and we look after our manufacturing base, and guess what? This country's gonna be greater, more united, more powerful than it's ever been...And by the way that's every nationality, every race, every religion, every sexual preference. As long as you're a citizen of our country. As long as you're an American citizen you're part of this populist, economic nationalist movement."

In the view of many conservatives, we are not a country of immigrants, but a country of settlers. Settlers are different from immigrants, and settlers are not limited to those who came on boats from England 400 years ago. Settlers arrive at our borders every day. Since the 1600s, settlers created a nation ex nihilo—a Latin phrase meaning "Out of nothing." The expectation was that future settlers from all over the world would come in and adopt the rules, customs, and norms of the original founding settlers. Every immigrant that has arrived here since the 1600s is expected to be part of a perpetual flow of settlers who embrace traditional American values (hard work, piety, etc.) that date back to the colonial era. Latter-day immigrants are welcome to apply for residency and citizenship, legally. But, they are still settlers, and Americans have always expected them to think, and behave, like the settlers before them.

The Left struggles with this concept, because they see this as forcing third-world peasants, or non-Christians, to adopt the norms of a complicated constitutional republic. Therefore, the Left pushes back and uses the patriarchy card. Rather than encourage the settlers to be what they want and need to be, they try to tell existing Americans that they, and their forefathers, were immigrants, to shift the narrative from mandatory assimilation (by new arrivers) to mandatory tolerance (by existing citizens). They want to wrestle the moral high ground away from the American right, because it's, supposedly, basked in their tired racist tropes: White privilege and patriarchy. All the things we insist that settlers buy into—the founding principles of Puritan virtues, the Protestant/Calvinist work ethic, deference to the Constitution, respect for English common law and personal property, and adherence to law and order in general—are nothing more that constructs of an oppressive class: Marxism at work.

Leftists also want to use the term immigrant, because it's an easier term to grasp than settler—a term that suggests farmers and horses and buggies. The word immigrants seem so modern and relevant. Settlers sounds so old-fashioned, white, and Little House on the Prairie–like.

GROWTH OF THE PROLETARIAT POPULATION

Marxists need the underclass/proletariat class to grow enough in numbers and political clout to achieve their broader goal, which is European-style socialism implemented in the U.S. in the next 25 to 50 years and an inevitable leap into a communist governance world order in the next 50 to 100 years. The strategy involves political and cultural influences, but also maximizes policies, such as chain migration and open borders. It's been established that people will migrate to a less-favorable cultural locale, if the economic opportunity outweighs what is being left behind. The Left believes minorities throughout the world resent white capitalism enough that they will seek an overthrow of the existing capitalist system, once they have the numbers (votes) to do so.

To motivate their base, recruit new followers—often without them ever noticing it—and keep the notion of struggle at the forefront, there must be a daily crisis to rally around. It's always something, every single day. The Left cries that "President Trump eats two scoops of ice cream," or "President Trump doesn't put the toilet seat down," or "President Trump kills babies at the border," or "President Trump cheats at golf," or "President Trump is a dictator," or "Global warming is President Trump's fault." Marxists want us to believe we are in a perpetual state of war against oppressors—not necessarily with guns—but based on mob behavior in recent months, physical altercations are increasing, symbolically. So, to them, the end of the world is coming, and it's because of white men and, specifically, straight white men and, more specifically, President Trump, and the only way to save ourselves is through Marxism.

So, to prevent President Trump from destroying the world, our society must adopt everything that President Trump isn't—Marxist—to prevent evil capitalists like him from enforcing their will on the proletariat. Point: When someone mentions words like struggle, oppression, protests, demonstrations, and so on and so forth, it usually indicates a leftist agenda. Second Point: Even smart people say, and do, outrageous and dangerously stupid things. This explains why so many otherwise intelligent people on the Upper West Side of Manhattan voted against President Trump.

Chapter 14

PROGRESSIVISM TODAY—RELIGION, MORALITY, AND GOD

"Communism is by its nature anti-religious and considers religion to be the 'opium of the people' because the religious principles which speak of a life beyond the grave prevent the proletariat from pursuing the realization of the Soviet paradise in this world."

—Pope Pius XI from Acta Apostolicae Sedis, 1937

VINCENT MICELI IN HIS 1971 BOOK GODS OF Atheism, theorized that German theologians after Martin Luther began to see religion not as the seeking of knowledge about God Himself but finding God in man and for man. God could be discovered on earth and in men, and not necessarily in Heaven. The Protestants in Germany began to seek God in the humanity of Jesus Christ. People began to put faith in reason and science, rather than religion and "Developed a widespread spirit of skepticism and empiricism hostile to Christianity."

People in Germany and France began to see science, rather than God, as the way to explain the cosmos. Miceli theorized that as man opened his mind to new humanistic ideas, reason, and freedom of thought, he was able to liberate himself from the binds of orthodox Christian thought on God and the genesis of the universe. As his desire for knowledge and science increased, his need for God decreased.

In 1841, a German named Ludwig Feuerbach (1804–72) published The Essence of Christianity, and it laid this all out for everyone to read. It includes this quote, "The turning point in history will be the moment when man becomes aware that the only God of man is man himself." Miceli notes that shortly after publication, influential French philosopher Emile Saisset (1814–63) wrote: "Herr Feuerbach … offers Christian Europe a new God to worship—the human race." Marx in his manuscript The German Ideology (1845) cited Feuerbach's influence on both himself and Engels and claimed Feuerbach proved God is man's own invention.

In the eyes of the modern Marxist, the average citizen of the West, as a consumer, is the new proletariat, who is encouraged to worry about his social, rather than spiritual, well-being, and for whom life becomes the management of economic forces in his or her life. Does anyone even bother to counter such Marxist beliefs anymore? If they do, they are considered religious zealots or draconian and evil conservatives. Regrettably, Marxism is certainly gaining traction, because more and more people, particularly millennials, believe that the ultimate goal of life is economic well-being and social justice, rather than salvation.

As the focus moved from God to us, twentieth-century psychology began looking into the individual to help them seek self-fulfillment, freedom from guilt, and liberation from laws. Fueled by Feuerbach's contention that God was just a sick creation by man and influenced by Marx, psychologists like Carl Rogers, often thought of as America's top psychologist, and Erich Fromm advanced humanistic psychology. Fromm, one of the exiles from the Frankfurt School who ended up at Columbia, mixed the theories of Feuerbach, Marx, and Freud, as he pushed democratic socialism in America.

MARXISTS HAVE HIJACKED THE TERMS FREEDOM AND MORALITY

The two key aspects that drive left-leaning progressive thought revolve around very different meanings of the two words that built the foundation of the United States—freedom and morality. They claim: (1) Freedom is not the word we remember from our history books about the Revolutionary War, whereby, through our efforts, we liberated ourselves from the British crown to form a constitutional republic, but instead is a goal that we have not achieved as a society. We must truly liberate ourselves from oppressors to gain freedom, and this liberation is a perpetual political struggle (i.e., Civil Rights, identity politics, environmental crusades, egalitarianism, etc.). And, (2) The meaning of the word morality and purpose of moral thought has devolved from basic Christian fundamentals that guided our country for 400 years—and Western society for 2,000 years—to acts of overturning perceived unequal power structures.

LOOK TO THE STATE FOR FREEDOM

Marxism has redefined freedom from individual liberty to a secularist concept, where the state knows best. Marxists link freedom to political struggle (rights), where the state dispenses a communal morality. Liberty is no longer divine grace brought about by repentance and forgiveness, rather, it is the freedom to acquire goods and pleasure, enabled by social, political, and legal means, all brought on by the state. Never forget that the evil state that was run by Big Brother in the literary classic 1984, described not a right-wing government, but a left-wing one.

MARXISTS REJECT INDIVIDUAL RESPONSIBILITY

Marxism rejects individual responsibility and links all blame to the oppressive class. The oppressors are responsible, directly or indirectly, for all social injustices. The poor are poor because of discrimination, prejudice, lack of investment in communities, white indifference, and so on and so forth. Criminals are suffering in jail because of racism and injustice, brought by white supremacy.

MARXISM IS A CANCER THAT ERODES LOCAL NORMS

Marxism strives to chip away at societal structures that have worked for centuries. Structure is necessary to make civilization function and flourish. People rely on a certain level of organization and trust; however, Marxists reject structures that were created by individuals and ordained by faith. In the Christian societies, the notion of oppression doesn't exist. One is free to pursue life, liberty and happiness and pray to any God he or she chooses. Oppression is the fundamental motivator of Marxism, and oppression must exist (even falsely) for Marxism to flourish; hence, it is used to break down fundamental rules of how society rules and how it behaves. When you hear the words income inequality, racist, misogynist, fascist, and so on and so forth, you are really hearing a proletariat scream "oppressor."

CHURCH MEMBERSHIP

Jeffrey M. Jones, writing for Gallup.com in April of 2019, cited the following statistics: "U.S. church membership was 70 percent or higher from 1937 through 1976, falling modestly to an average of 68 percent in the '70s through the '90s. The past 20 years have seen an acceleration in the drop-off, with a 20-percentage-point decline since 1999 and more than half of that change occurring since the start of the current decade."

The numbers are hard to deny. Church membership has been declining since the turn of the century. So, for past generations, purpose and meaning in life could be found in familial and social structures that were usually centered on their faith. Sadly, young people today don't look to religion for meaning anymore. They look to left-wing causes to find meaning and emotional fulfillment. As an example, climate activism "Saves the world." Environmental activism might save a rare fish from extinction, prematurely releasing criminals absolves us of whatever racist reason they were in jail for in the first place, abolishing ICE or having open borders changes lives for the better, higher taxes helps feed the poor and shelter the homeless, and demilitarizing/emasculating the local police makes our streets safer, because criminals aren't on edge.

MORALITY IS WHAT THE STATE, NOT WHAT GOD, SAYS

Marxists do not view morality in religious terms. Morality has devolved into acts of overturning unequal power structures. It is no longer the alignment of mankind with the ways of God, or transcendence. Thus, political action (activism and social justice) is assumed to bring about change for the better. Whether improvement happens or not is questionable. However, when morality is only sociopolitical action, then relativism emerges; in that individual action is seen as the only catalyst for change. This is "historical materialism," where history is goal-oriented, and metaphysics (God, heaven, etc.) is an illusion. Marxism treats politics as religion because Marxism replaces religion. Political ideology becomes religion to the Left. This is most evident in what was once a simple matter as party identification. Unlike past generations where religion—and more specifically evangelical Christianity—provided the moral compass, leftists see partisan ideology as an indicator of character or moral standing and not of voting preference. Leftists, like Muslims when confronted with a challenge to Islam, believe an attack on a progressing law is a personal attack on their religion and by extension, an attack on them. This is why you see so much illogical rage.

Why the homeless are useful to leftists

The keys to making a meaningful dent in homeless, and I'm talking about the chronic ones that roam the streets of Los Angeles and San Francisco, like zombies, are mental health, drug rehab and accountability on the part of the families of these people. Sadly, the homeless are pointed to as the poster children for capitalism's failures in the eyes of the progressives, who say they are in their horrible condition due to a ruthless economic model, a broken patriarchy and a heartless hegemony that lacks willpower and compassion. They'll add they are that way because there are not enough social safety nets. And, they are that way because of not enough public funding for housing and programs. Or, they are this way because we demonize drug usage and, instead of legalizing and creating a less dangerous heroin, they become addicted to unregulated and underground products. So, they lie on the sidewalks, while leftist politicians and activists point at them, screaming at us for more money.

Marxists Want to Shift the Moral Compass to the Left

It's not uncommon for leftists to invoke a moral position, however questionable, to thwart debate on an issue. One common tactic is to claim "previously settled matters" are now the norm and question of that is considered immoral or racist. According to Senator Kirsten Gillibrand, "I think there are some issues that have such moral clarity that we as a society have decided that the other side is not acceptable." What she's most upset about is the leftist paranoia that "ultra-radical" conservative judges will somehow impose Christianity on our lives. (Honestly, I'd like to know of one radical conservative judge, but if she has names of "ultra-radicals," I'd like to know who they are.) The Leftist play here is that there has been some sort of liberal enlightenment in our society, where we have separated our religious views from our political views. It is sort of a pinnacle of moral clarity, where it is wrong to even consider any legislation or case that could, in anyway, impact any rights that have been claimed.

THE ONLY CONFESSIONAL THE LEFTISTS WANT TO ENDORSE

Marxism feeds on emotions, because hate, envy, and resentment are tremendous motivators. Nobody wants to hold resentful grudges, and everyone wants to feel good, right? What better way to feel good than to go to confession (your pocketbook) and apologize (denounce President Trump and your white privilege) for something someone you don't know did 150 or 200 years ago by getting "woke" and voting progressive—and pay reparations (in the form of taxes) for it. "Privilege acknowledgement" is a cleansing, they tell you. Marxists profess that "they" (our ancestors from 200 years ago) should have "known better" than to harbor pro-slavery or anti-immigrant stances, and the only path to redemption for modern society is a retroactive (and loud) denouncement of all things that symbolize what life was like from 1620 to, say, 1965, which is the American grand narrative—a constitutional republic offering liberties, opportunities, and freedoms not seen in any other country and based on common law and liberties rooted in conservative and Christian fundamentals.

Chapter 15

PROGRESSIVISM TODAY— DIVISIVE SPEECH

PEOPLE LIKE SENATOR KIRSTEN GILLIBRAND THINK society is on her side, as if 99 percent of Americans agree with her. It's been proven time and again that there is no majority in this country when it comes to abortion, gay marriage, or whether America is more liberal or more conservative. It's about a 50-50 split. She seems to be saying that being pro-life is somehow not acceptable and is exhibiting contempt for those who disagree with her. This was very evident on election night 2016, as the cameras showed incredulous faces at MSNBC and CNN and at Hillary's headquarters. How could people not agree with us? In their twisted minds, if those ignorant deplorables would just die, then society would be perfect. Just because you got a BA in humanities, a Masters in activism, and a PhD in hating President Trump doesn't mean you have the moral upper hand or are somehow on the right side of history. This is what debate and bipartisan dialogue is for. Because gay rights, abortion (women), immigration (Latinos), and civil rights (blacks) are traditionally deemed by leftist elites as unquestioned issues of and for the oppressed class, the Left simply doesn't want debate, because dissenting opinions, however logical they might be, are coming from the oppressors and are, therefore, heresy and unworthy of their attention.

It's not uncommon for the Marxists to take a position, claim a national mandate on the matter, and then declare that position to be a societal consensus. The game they play is to get enough influential people in Hollywood, for example, to advocate a position, and even if a small fraction of America agrees, the social media followings of the celebrity will get the message out to millions of young people. If, for example, abortion can be cast as reproductive rights, it puts a different spin on the matter. Americans like and respect rights. The word rights sounds like freedom. Reproductive freedom! Sounds American! This makes dissenting opinion tough, because it puts pro-life proponents in a position where they need to argue that a freedom, an individual liberty, or a right is wrong. The tragic comedy in this is that reproduction has already occurred long before an abortion takes place. Debating this inconvenient fact is, in the Leftist's eyes, unconscionably evil.

WHAT DO PROGRESSIVES MEAN BY "DIVISIVE SPEECH"?

Prior to President Trump, the Left assumed the nation was inevitably marching toward a world the Whigs and Materialists would have been proud of—a more scientific and less religious society, with a more liberal and less conservative worldview. This was certainly not the case, but the Left took it for granted that our society has moved to a point where adoption of leftist ideas, voting for liberal policies, and conformance to politically correct speech and behavior was normal. Then along came President Trump, and his election exposed a truth about the real America—we are not as ideologically similar as the Left had assumed we were, and America, particularly noncoastal elite America, is not ready, and may never be ready, to go down the socialist path. The silent majority stood up and said, "America is not a godless leftist nation." Conservatives finally spoke up and started wondering out loud for the first time since the '50s what the Left was up to. What exactly is the Left saying? Why is the Left trying to divide us?

President Trump, Conservatives, Republicans, Christians or other bogeymen the Left despises are not dividing America. Leftists bent on identity politics and diversity are. There has never been anything wrong with people of diverse backgrounds, colors and creeds assimilating and accepting the American ideal, while striving to achieve the American dream. There is a problem with telling people that they need to reject the American ideal, because of their background, color or creed. This quest to showcase differences is what's causing the divisions in America today.

It bears repeating, when you celebrate diversity, you celebrate differences and when you celebrate differences you are adding credibility to distinctions between Americans, based on race, gender, national origin, religious creed or sexual orientation. If you are celebrating identifiable distinctions, you are dividing the nation into tribes, and when people are in tribes, they tend to think and act in their selfish interests. The Left keeps claiming that President Trump wants to take America backward to another time in our history, when it's actually the Left that's taking America back to an era when only people of certain colors, creeds, political or socioeconomic classes associated with one another.

President Trump and Conservative America's resistance to the Leftist's cultural and political agenda was an unanticipated problem. Rather than admitting they miscalculated this, they began to call President Trump's anti-Marxist positions divisive speech, as if we were somehow united in a leftist big tent and President Trump is somehow tearing it apart. The irony of all this divisive speech nonsense is that the Left has wanted to drive a divisive wedge into our overarching ethos—a Conservative Christian nation—for a century, yet suddenly was turning the tables and accusing President Trump of being the one using divisive language. Why? Because President Trump is exposing and undermining the Whiggish transformation of the U.S. from a Christian nation founded on the principles of hard work, freedom, and liberty to an increasingly liberal society, sprinting toward a Marxist future. President Trump, the Left knows, is hindering this goal by saying, "We've had enough." Leftists, of course, don't hear, "We've had enough of this nonsense," they hear, "We want to take American back in time."

Part of the issue conservatives face in countering the Left's attacks is a relentless narrative from the Left that whatever is spoken out of the mouth of a conservative is automatically coming from a place of hatred. The policies are not judged on their merits. They are judged by who said them and how they were said and to whom. It becomes a game of "It's not the policy; it's the policy maker." And, "It's not the message; it's the messenger." A tactic used by the Left to shout down or otherwise silence conservative opinion and dissent is to dehumanize the oppressors through the old name-and-shame game. By calling them corrupt, illegitimate, privileged, bigots, sexists, tyrants and criminals, the oppressors are not people worthy of having a legitimate discussion with but are, instead, cast as inhuman. It's funny how organizations like PETA wants everyone to see animals as equal to humans, but the Leftists who support PETA want to see conservatives portrayed as less than human.

An irony is hearing the Left complain about the inherent corruption, authoritarianism, and moral bankruptcy in President Trump's world, when history has proven how truly corrupt and morally and politically bankrupt Marxism is.

Don't forget this militant leftist thought train, relative to silencing conservative views: Controlling speech can control thoughts, which can control behavior, which can control dissent, which can lead to favorable Election Day outcomes. The Left seems to believe that conservatives will eventually give up and get in line with their cultural Marxism (i.e., political correctness) and accept a Whiggish inevitability.

SHOUTING DOWN DISSENT

In 1985, Alexander Solzhenitsyn (1918-2008), novelist, political prisoner and Nobel Prize winner, reflected on 50 years of failed promises in the U.S.S.R., said, "Men have forgotten God; that's why all this has happened." Solzhenitsyn was a keen observer of the totalitarian tactics used by the communists, including a cycle of lies and the violent reprisals that would occur, if compliance was not achieved. He was one of the leading dissenters of his day and was a leading voice in explaining how leftist governments need to keep cruelty, ineptitude and other failures hidden. Dissent and criticism are unacceptable but abuses by the regime are tolerated by leftist sympathizers, who feel that transforming a society into a leftist utopia can be messy.

Leftists instinctively lack nuance and are incapable of finessing solutions or presenting a coherent counter argument, so they shout down or try to shame those who stand in the way of what they say is progress. Name-and-shame is a leading tactic activists employ. This belief that punishing or eradicating dissent serves the greater revolutionary goal helps explain why leftists tend to avoid criticizing human rights and environmental abuses in China. Once the Marxist regime is in place, the shouting down is replaced by punishment, physical or otherwise, which explains why Senator Sanders' volunteers feel conservatives should be sent to gulags, once the Marxists take over America.

WHY LEFTISTS THINK CONSERVATIVES ARE ALL RACIST AND DIVISIVE

First, a bit of clarity is needed. Racism and bigotry are used interchangeably by most people, but to some leftists, racism is the collective discriminatory policies and systems that make up the patriarchy, while bigotry would be the individualized meanness exhibited by a person of one race against another. So, to the Left, racism should, therefore, apply to the perceived injustices brought about by laws, policies and procedures throughout our society; however, that doesn't stop them from employing that word, to shame and dehumanize individuals. Racist just sounds harsher than bigot.

Leftists believe that if you are intelligent enough (in their judgment), evolved enough, and mature enough to reject racism, you are evolved enough and compassionate enough to fundamentally reject all forms of oppression. And, if you can reject racism, you are probably bright enough to identify oppressors and oppressive systems. And, if you can identify oppressive people, laws, norms, and customs (again, in the Left's judgment), you should, therefore, be attracted to socialism. By leftist definition, socialism is the fight against oppression, and since racists are oppressors, if they are oppressors, they are enemies in this existential fight. Further, what is irresponsibly dangerous are the ones who don't openly reject racism, because if they don't satisfactorily cleanse their soul to the Marxist gods of virtue, they are enablers who reject the lofty socialist ideal.

Where this logic fails is in this simple fact: just because you reject socialism doesn't mean you are a racist. The Left's simpleton view on conservatives is as erroneous as stating: Since all terrorists are Muslim, therefore, all Muslims are terrorists. So, to those on the Left, conservatives not being racists or sexists is a mathematical impossibility. If you voted for President Trump (i.e., rejected socialism), you must be pro-oppression, and if you are pro-oppression, you are anti-civil rights, anti-minority, anti-woman, anti-immigrant, anti-LGBTQ, and so on and so forth. This is why so many on the Left have concluded that all President Trump voters are ignorant, racist, sexist, or worse.

This is the basis of the GOP = racism narrative, pushed by the Left and taught to young people on college campuses. So, to put it another way, if you are not part of the solution (fighting oppression), you are part of the problem (an oppressor). In the Left's mind, there is no gray area. It's a time of war in their eyes. It's "Us versus Them". It's a call to arms. This is classic divisive speech brought upon us by leftists, who want to create division.

AN ANALOGY FOR DIVISIVE SPEECH

We're all on a boat floating toward prosperity. But then a leftist threatens to jump overboard and promises the group that it's better to swim to shore. A few others agree and say they've been on the boat for years and it's not fun anymore. The conservatives say, "Stay on the boat," and "Don't deviate from what works!" The Leftists don't hear wise advice. They hear oppressive overtures like, "What the hell are you doing, you fools!" Or, "Get back on board and get in line!" Conservative advice is not seen by leftists as sound common sense that may involve tough love but is instead seen as oppressive and unwanted finger wagging one would have expected in an anachronistic era.

AN EXAMPLE OF CULTURAL MARXISM IN ACTION TODAY

Generally, I'm not a fan of any historian, lecturer, and writer who was influenced by Marx and John Maynard Keynes, but Niall Ferguson was on point about one aspect of higher education. He once wrote that "Universities perform a number of functions. One function is to achieve economies of scale in research. Another is to ensure that the most intellectually able young people attain their full educational potential. A third is to promote the international exchange of knowledge." I sincerely wish those were the only three purposes for a university—besides fielding a football team. Sadly, college campuses across America have recently become better known as safe houses for leftist thought and the cultural Marxism, anti-capitalism, anti-Christianity, and anti-conservatism, which comes along with it. As much as universities like to speak about tolerance and diversity, it seems college communities (students, faculty, and administrators) see diversity the same way San Franciscans view local politics—in varying shades of blue.

In the summer of 2019, Colorado State University and American University unrolled language guides for the 2019–20 school year to foster "Inclusion, respect, and social justice." In the case of CSU, although it's not mandatory to follow, students and faculty were instructed not to use the words America or American because "America encompasses more than just the United States, and using these terms depicts the United States as the dominant American country." Thankfully, public outcry caused CSU to rethink those two words but that didn't stop them from doubling down on the purpose of their language guide. This is cultural Marxism at work, chipping away, piece by piece, at the grand narrative of American Exceptionalism.

As it pertains to how we describe ourselves, one only has to look at how others describe us: We are not United Statians. No one traveling abroad has ever had a European or Asian ask if you were a United Statian. Ever. We are Americans. They will likely ask, "Are you American?" Or, "Are you from America?" When we behave badly in Europe, or elsewhere, we are labeled "The ugly American(s)." Ask anyone in a European or Asian country where an American comes from, and I seriously doubt they would guess Argentina, Panama, or Canada. From north to south, people are generally called Canadians, Americans, and Mexicans. I suppose we could use our romanticized name and call our nation "Columbia" (the UK's romanticized reference, in case you're curious, is "Britannia") and call ourselves Columbians. But Columbia is its own country, and it's not our country. The Columbians come from Columbia. Americans come from America.

OUTRAGE MOBS AS A WAY TO ESTABLISH A "CONSENSUS"

> "Today's outrage culture insists that everybody who holds a view that's different from our own is not just mistaken. They must be evil and shunned. That's wrong."
>
> —Former UN Ambassador and former South Carolina Governor Nikki Haley.

There's an old saying that if the Left didn't have double standards, they would have no standards at all. Why is it that only the Left feels they have a right to be outraged? Again, it has to do with the perception of who the oppressive class is (conservatives) and who the oppressed class is (leftists). In leftist theory, only the oppressed group has the right to decide if they are offended or assaulted, and furthermore, conservatives have no right to feel offended, let alone feel justifiably victimized. When conservatives are harassed, they are getting what they deserve. Actor and Comedian Ricky Gervais once said of antifa, "It's interesting that people who believe that throwing a milkshake in someone's face shouldn't be considered assault are often the same people who believe that 'saying things' should be." The jingle for the antifa snowflakes should be, "Shakes and stones won't break anyone's bones, but names will always hurt me."

Latter-day progressive thought in America is often described by conservative commentators as "leftist" or "left leaning," as if American politics straddles a line where one or two degrees separates progressive from conservative thought, and progressivism is just the same old liberalism the Democrats have pushed for the past 50 years. I propose that "left leaning" is certainly not accurate. Progressivism, in its current manifestation, is actually Marxism for reasons discussed in this book. These so-called progressives claim that they aren't Marxists at all and that they are merely free thinkers, who are exercising their first amendment right to stand up to right-wingers, white nationalists, President Trump supporters, and anything accompanying the rotten hegemony that they ascribe to anyone who doesn't think as they do. They are self-described "activists," "resisters" and self-righteous defenders of the Constitution; however, they aren't actually red-blooded Americans who are just exercising traditional American rights to free speech and peacefully assembly.

Yes, dissenting opinion is an important part of the American political system, but they don't see themselves as the dissenters. They see themselves as not only holding a moral high ground but being correct, and they see conservative views as an illegitimate and oppressive relic of the eighteenth century. Furthermore, by definition, conservative speech diverts so from popular twenty-first century opinions that it is unacceptable at face value. Since they view themselves as being right, the shutting down of free speech by those they see as wrong is perfectly acceptable, even if it requires violence to do so. They are Social Justice Warriors (SJWs) who are a broad mix of students, writers, artists, faculty members, revisionist historians, and anarchists (i.e., revolutionaries), who are exercising age-old Marxists tactics by putting their disruptive words into destructive action.

Speaking of justice, here's a news flash for our SJW friends: Saying nothing is a crime anymore is not justice nor is it fair. Every crime has a victim. In the truly just utopia you desire, justice would be indeed blind, and everyone would have to stand on his or her own merits without a tilted playing field. Justice to them means giving the oppressed an edge. A leg up to help right old wrongs or balance the stats out.

The mob mentality that is so common these days is a traditional proletariat stunt, and regrettably, most young Americans don't know any better. Too many young Americans see conservative values as draconian, in large part, because that's what the Leftists want. Marxism is based on class warfare: A repressed class of laborers standing up and demanding justice against capitalists, but it's also based on what's known as cultural Marxism, where a repressed social group (the poor, the underclass, the under-represented, the marginalized, the misfits, the outcasts, and the minorities) are characterized as an oppressed class that is merely seeking justice against the wrongful powers vested in an oppressive system (justice meaning economic equality and equal power, not truth and fairness). Marxists want their adherents to self-identify as the victimized and oppressed underdog deserving of justice (on their terms, of course), but most American's aren't buying it. One can actually make an argument that they are nothing more than envious, if not also treasonous, anarchists.

HOW MARXISTS ATTACK THE FIRST AMENDMENT

There is a lot of misunderstanding about what the First Amendment says about Freedom of Religion. The short summary is that it prohibits the federal government and, by extension, the states from establishing or supporting a state religion, as in the case of England, with the Church of England (aka the Anglican Church) or Cambodia, where their constitution declares Buddhism as the official religion. Logic tells us the Founding Fathers did not go out of their way to include this for tolerance or diversity purposes, but rather were all part of various Christian faiths.

There were 118 different men who signed at least one of our three most important documents—the Declaration of Independence (1776), the Constitution (1789) and the Bill of Rights (1791) collectively known as the Charters of Freedom. Although Anglicans made up a slight majority of our Founding Fathers, 12 different faiths were represented by these 118 men, including French Protestants (Huguenots), Catholics, and Calvinists. King George III, as the head of the Church of England, was the antagonist during those years, and you'd have to wonder, if the

Founding Fathers were all Anglicans, would the First Amendment even have been written differently? I doubt it. Our Founding Fathers wanted to distance themselves politically and religiously from England. They succeeded.

The First Amendment does not prohibit religious beliefs and does not prohibit people from opposing or supporting laws that are consistent or inconsistent with their faith. Think about that for a moment. You are not prohibited from opposing laws that are inconsistent with your faith. This drives the Left nuts, and they try to twist the First Amendment to suggest laws trump religion. The classic example is many on the Left's contention that it is not unconstitutional, for example, to be opposed to an abortion bill or a gay marriage bill. The Left would like to frame the dissent conservatives bring forth on religious grounds in the context of an oppressive class (in this case I'll merge straight, white, conservative, Christian men) using unacceptable speech to harm an oppressed class. Is "unacceptable" the same as "illegal"? No. One is subjective, and the other objective. (Yes, murder is both unacceptable and illegal, but what we're talking about here is our beliefs.)

The deconstruction strategy the Left plays here is an argument that goes like this: Perhaps if conservative language we don't like could be cast as immoral (again the Left as the oppressed is the only side with the authority to judge), then it might not be too much to ask people to believe it's unconstitutional (i.e., illegal), even if it's perfectly constitutional. Leftists know darn well that nobody wants to be viewed—or accused—as out of touch, nobody wants to be accused of speaking illegally, and nobody wants to be outnumbered in an argument. Therefore, if dissenting opinion can be framed as illegal, wrong, out of touch, immoral, uncool, or unpopular, then debate could very well be chilled. That's the game being played here.

Leftist Mind Readers Think Trump Wants to Be King!

Besides being able to determine that every conservative is an evil racist, some on the Left are able to assess President Trump's psychological condition without ever meeting him, let alone diagnosing him, and still others are able to read his mind. Former U.S. Deputy Assistant District Attorney General Pamela Karlan, who served under President Obama, has somehow been able to determine that President Trump wants to be king, or something. Karlan, who many on the Left thought could have been a SCOTUS nominee under a Secretary Clinton administration, was invited to speak to the House Judiciary Committee during the President Trump–Ukraine inquiry. Karlan said, "When the president said 'do us a favor' he was using the 'royal we' there. It wasn't a favor for the United States. He should have said 'do me a favor' because only kings say 'us' when they mean 'we.'" This plays to the Leftist's belief that President Trump wants to run the country like it is a monarchy and he is the king. This nonsense is laughable, but strongly resonates with hysterical leftist fears of conservatives as a whole actually harboring neo-reactionary fantasies about a return to a strong far-right monarch that's seated for life.

Why Marxists Embrace Post-Modernism

> "'The myth of America as the greatest nation on earth is at best outdated and at worst, wildly inaccurate. If you look at data, the U.S. is really just O.K."
>
> —@nytopinion twitter post July 2, 2019

Over time, a relentless onslaught of Cultural Marxism has eroded our views of what it means to be an American. Marxism takes many forms, including the embrace of post-modernism, which at its core is the rejection of the grand narrative of American Exceptionalism. The goal is a coordinated skepticism or outright rejection of American greatness. A tenet of Marxism is to erase things from history that don't advance the agenda. American capitalist ideals of liberty, independence, freewill, and opportunity play to the American greatness identity that conservatives (and some Democrats) have, and these are threats to the mindless group-think mentality of Marxists.

Statements like "America was never great" is a Marxist statement, because it undermines American Exceptionalism and presupposes that a minority underclass, as the victimized oppressed class in their struggle, has been exploited, excluded, and screaming in pain for hundreds of years. American Exceptionalism respects the fundamental understanding that the government is by the people, of the people and for the people, with limited roles in our lives intended to maximize individual liberties and freedoms. Marxists, on the other hand, believe government serves an institutionalized purpose, and the citizenry is supposed to serve the government, because it knows best. As a result, the Leftists feel the government should play a more active role in the economy and in social policy and, thereby, should get into all aspects of our lives, such as health care. Socialized medicine is a really bad idea that once fully implemented, there is no coming back from. In short, when people talk about breaking down structures and ideals that have built America into the world's greatest nation, it's usually part of broader Marxist agenda.

Post-Modernism is feelings over rational thought and can best be described in practical terms, as a rejection of the "grand narrative" about America's greatness. Skepticism about the purpose and need for a war in Korea or Vietnam and doubts about man actually landing on the moon are examples. It grew from World War II through the '60s on college campuses and among writers and artists. The American grand narrative goes like this: The Founding Fathers set up the best political and cultural system the world has ever known, along with other unspoken truths, such as the Americans were on the right side of every war and the concept of American Exceptionalism, among other patriotic things. Post-modernism disavows all that and is a useful Marxist tool to introduce doubt into the minds of Americans. At its heart is skepticism that America is right, a questioning of American policies, and a rejection of Christianity and a criticism of the "American way." Naturally, conservatives reject post-modernism as it unnecessarily (and wrongly) calls into question truths and assumptions about what it means to be an American.

It is very leftist at heart. Marxists want to erode traditional views of America and what it means to be an American as part of a broader, borderless, one-worldist agenda. Any policy that chips away at American Exceptionalism is inherently wrong, and Marxism absolutely chips away at it.

An Obsession with Inclusivity, Social Justice, and Equality

Marxists are taught that all of world history is that of class struggle. Obviously, world history is the story of the bold, the brave, and the intelligent creating and sustaining flourishing communities. Besides the media and academia, many professional organizations and nonprofits go out of their way to chronicle history as a battle against oppression, rather than the celebration of success. The Left cannot point to one good thing that came out of 70 years of communist rule in the Soviet Union or the Eastern Bloc, so they need to find something, anything, to latch onto. They are obsessed with identifying and "fixing" social issues in America.

In April of 2019, 6,445 planners from across the nation descended upon San Francisco for the American Planning Association's (APA) annual national planning convention, referred to as NC19. Over the course of four days, there were more than 300 panel discussions and workshops, where much of the conversation was not focused on zoning, design, or land use law cases, but on equality, diversity, and inclusion. This movement away from providing resources on technical matters toward relentless essays and lectures on social justice initiatives is an emerging trend in the planning profession these days. Yes, APA had always been liberal, in large part, because most of their membership is employed in the public sector and/or have humanities-based urban studies, sociology or geography degrees. But, today's APA is darker than dark blue. In reading about NC19, I found the following quote from an attendee most interesting, "We were compelled to have conversations about decolonization and white supremacy."

When urban planning first emerged at the beginning of the 20th century, growing cities faced a number of problems they were not prepared for, such as transportation, public education, lack of public parks, and land-use incompatibility (homes next to factories), among other things. Since when has decolonization or white supremacy been a topic of subdivisions and land planning? Well, since public planning married social justice and urban design, I suppose. I disagree with planning theorist Wes Groom, who contends that planning shouldn't be narrowly focused on land use and development, but on "all social concerns." This is part of the social engineering socialists in America have been pushing for a century. This is part of the "central planning" Marxists want to establish in their utopian bureaucracy—using professionals as activists for change. Rather than solving for a more efficient land use yield, they want to solve for evasive solutions to social inequities.

THE EVER-EXPANDING DEFINITIONS OF "JUSTICE"

Justice should not be hard to define or explain to children. However, the term has been hijacked by the Left to reference not only criminal justice, but economic and environmental justice—whatever that means. A common cry from the Left is that the criminal justice system is inherently racist and unjust, because we have more prisoners per capita than any other nation. Why is that? Well, it's simple. We have the most effective and best-trained police forces that use the best investigative and forensic means available, coupled with prosecutors and judges that can't be bought off, unlike what you see in other countries, and guess what? You get high incarceration rates. Convictions are high, and incarcerations are what they are because criminals get caught. Duh! Crime exists in every culture in the world, and we have more people in prison because our police forces are the most effective. The fact that a disproportionate percentage of minorities get convicted is not an indicator of injustice, but proof that: (1) Crime doesn't pay like it can and does elsewhere, and (2) Lady Justice is indeed blind. She knows no color.

The latter-day Marxists use words like retributive justice, social justice, economic justice, distributive justice and environmental justice, among others, in part, to confuse us. What does all this mean? It means, "My group and I are envious of others, and we want to use legislative means to change the political and/or economic paradigm." Or, "My group and I know better than you, and you need to change for the benefit of the world." Never underestimate self-righteousness and jealousy as the basis for actions of others. Racism and sexism are bad, but unfortunately, racism and sexism have been overplayed by far too many people, with an agenda to push. Consequently, when it gets old and starts falling on deaf ears, it makes it hard for constructive dialogue to take place. There are certainly instances of discrimination based on race, but there are also some tired race card tropes that are used as an excuse for underachievement. If the Left could be just a little less disingenuous about race, intelligent dialogue could occur.

Now, if there's one thing the Marxists have taught their followers, it's that it's not their fault. Any perceived pushback by white males to affirmative action or other activist policy centered on identity politics is pounced on by the Left as an attempt by the oppressive class to uphold the patriarchy. It's a clever, but predictable argument. In the Marxist worldview, because the ruling class—whites, and specifically white conservatives—make the rules, only the oppressed class can pass judgment, and it's unacceptable (to a Marxist) for a white male to pass judgment.

Regrettably "justice" has become a Marxist dog whistle. The political and economic structure of our society was established 100, 200, 300, and 400 years ago. The fact that white Christians codified social norms and drafted the Constitution is not, of itself, evil or wrong. Breaking down society's structure was Marx's goal, but it's not the way to fix anything. Living and thriving within the rules is the foundation of a successful society, and that's why America is as great as it is. When leftist politicians use the word justice, what they are appealing to is not the unbiased eyes of Lady Justice, but identity, class, and/or racial politics. They want to orient the conversation to the negative context and focus not on justice (what's right and wrong), but injustice (the wrongs committed by whites). Class warfare is a classic Marxist tool that is being expanded by modern Marxists to include identity and race warfare as well, because the revolution can't be fought—let alone won—on economic terms, or cultural terms as well. What better way to advance that agenda than to continuously remind the underclass and marginalized why they need to be angry and jealous.

What the Media Ignores about Trump's Commitment to Poverty

The U.S. poverty rate stood at 22 percent in 1960, right before Michael Harrington's book, The Other America, came out. It fell to 19 percent in 1964 and 11.2 percent in 1974. The consensus was that the programs started by LBJ and continued by President Nixon were working. Since then, it's risen and fallen by a few percentage points with a high of 15.1 percent in 1993 and 2010 and a low of 11.3 percent in 2000. Currently, it's about 11.8 percent. The Department of Health and Human Services that administers Medicare, Medicaid, and subsidy programs, like Temporary Assistance for Needy Families, spent $29.6 billion in 1962 (in 2019 dollars) on their various programs. In 2019, the budget for this department was set at $1.23 trillion. Federal spending for the DHHS is now 416 percent higher in today's dollars than it was then, despite the population increasing only about 77 percent, from 186 million to 330 million, poverty being cut nearly in half (22 percent to 11.8 percent) and the number of seniors, as a percentage of the population, increasing by about 300 percent, from about 16.6 million to about 49.5 million.

The point is that spending on critically needed subsidy programs has outpaced population growth—including the senior demographic—while poverty has significantly been reduced. Furthermore, spending for Social Security is greater than Defense under President Trump, just as spending for Medicare and Medicaid collectively is greater than Defense under President Trump. These types of stats are not mentioned by the mainstream media, because they don't want to portray Trump as a champion of spending and especially entitlement programs. In the Left's bizarre world, Republicans only cut taxes and spend whatever they collect on Defense. Republicans, just like Democrats, are terrible at reigning in spending, and the deficit is spiraling out of control. President Trump, the populist, is no exception. Oh, and in spite of the '17 tax cuts, the 2020 federal budget is expected to be about 4.8 percent higher than in 2019 ($4.75 trillion vs. $4.53 trillion), despite inflation being under 3 percent.

THE LEFT THINKS THE NEXT DEMOCRATIC PRESIDENT SHOULD PACK THE SUPREME COURT

Perhaps nothing irks the Left more than President Trump being able to nominate two Supreme Court justices to the SCOTUS, not long after taking office. Studies by U.C. Berkeley and Georgetown this decade have evaluated exactly how liberal or conservative the ideological leanings of the justices really are, and the results are surprising. What they demonstrated is that, over time, each justice generally votes more and more liberal as his or her tenure goes on. Justices Scalia, Thomas, and Roberts all trended toward the middle. Justice Souter, appointed by President Bush (41), was once conservative, but is now as liberal as Justice Kagan. Justice Ginsburg, once a centrist, is now about as liberal as Thomas is conservative. Justice Sotomayor became significantly more liberal, especially during the Obama administration.

The point is that SCOTUS, despite the cries of the Left that conservatives hold a 5–4 edge, is far more centrist in their collective leanings now than it was in the '60s, '70s and '80s. Yes, conservatives held an ideological edge from the late '30s into the early '50s, and certainly the liberals held an edge from the early '50s into the '70s, and conservatives hold the edge today, but future shifts will happen, and besides, the chances of seeing an ideological outlier like liberal Justice Douglas, who served 36 years on the SCOTUS and would make Ginsburg or Sotomayor look like Thomas, again on the court, are probably over. Nine works. Leave it at that.

THE PARTY OF INCLUSIVITY ACTUALLY LOVES DIVISIVE CONCEPTS LIKE "WHITE GUILT"

Liberals, let alone Marxists, cannot win elections in the U.S. without enough whites voting for them. Relying strictly on white leftists, the working class, and underclass for political support isn't enough. American liberals, after World War II, believed that education and a Whiggish march toward science over religion, globalism over isolationism, and liberalism (pacifism) over hawkish conservatism would be the key to a Marxist future in America. However, 75 years later, that still isn't enough. If anything, America is more prosperous than ever, so new tactics need to be tried, including making whites self-identify as oppressors.

Mikhail Bakunin said, "Freedom without socialism is privilege and injustice," thus suggesting capitalism breeds privilege. A new term has arisen in recent years to replace what was once pejoratively called white guilt. It's called privilege acknowledgment and is intended to be a self-recognition and, if not, leftist peer-pressure that serves as atonement for the evils of "white privilege," which is a sin according to the Left. Guilt conjures up images of sadness and regret, and nobody wants to ponder those thoughts, because they are too depressing. But privilege invokes envy and anger. Privilege is seen as special, exclusive, and perhaps unfair, perhaps bought, or maybe illegally obtained. White guilt didn't move the needle, so white privilege was invented by American leftists to explain how whites generally lead safer, more successful lives at a more favorable rate, while other races don't.

White privilege is tied to the victimhood culture which you could argue is tied to Nietzsche's slave morality culture where cowards, the suspicious and the skeptics revolt against the oppressors through legislative or judicial means and the court of public opinion. White privilege was designed to help explain racism in a post-racist society. The theory goes that since institutionalized racism no longer exists something else whites were doing is to blame for underachievement by non-whites. Their non-activism and non-compliance was to blame. Privilege was therefore seen as oppressive and the opposite of victimhood. White privilege is seen by progressives as the worst trait someone can have. Privilege awareness is what was once pejoratively called white guilt. It is part of the act of renouncing white privilege and with it comes an obligation to renounce conservative beliefs. Conservatives who have contempt for this nonsense and who refuse to come around and cleanse themselves of the mortal sin of privilege are, as you can imagine, seen by the Left as the worst people on earth.

White Privilege is nothing more than voluntary self-flagellation. In short, it suggests whites are the beneficiaries of an oppressive system known on the Left as the patriarchy that aids them through every aspect of their lives to the detriment of the oppressed classes. White guilt was traditionally the private and personal lament liberals had about being socially safe and financially secure. White privilege is the recognition—the so-called privilege awareness aspect—and atonement for that lament. The thinking goes that you can somehow atone for the sins of the white man's construction by recognizing and acting on some type of obligation. The way to absolve oneself of white privilege is through privilege acknowledgment—a form of atonement for all of man's sins.

Marxism prevails when the oppressive class convinces themselves that they are indeed somehow guilty, regrettably privileged and undeserving of their standing. The Leftists assume if you are guilty about something, you are, therefore, wrong for doing something, and, therefore, you must repent and right those wrongs. Guilt, therefore, means action—penance rather than mere reflection. Marxists want the capitalists to feel embarrassed by how they achieved their social standing and wash away any perception of privilege as a means to address and cleanse those capitalists of guilt. By adopting views minorities hold, coupled with an acceptance of post-modernism, humanism, and Marxism, they can absolve themselves of privilege and sin and be "accepted" into the broader multicultural (i.e., global and egalitarian) society.

Remember, Marxism initially just sought absolute equality among classes. However, latter-day Marxists see the revolution as not just between economic classes, but between groups—cultures, ideologies, and races. This is the Cultural Marxism aspect. America was and is Christian, based on a Judeo-Christian tradition and Puritan work ethic (aka the Protestant work ethic or Calvinist work ethic). Marxists have equated this with a legacy of white hegemony and white patriarchy. In their view, to build a more perfect (i.e., equal) society, those outdated and racist values must be eradicated. The Spanish work ethic that was imported to the Americas is different from the one the British brought forth. The Catholicism the Spanish brought over is different from British Protestantism. Asian immigrants brought forth Eastern philosophies. In Europe, where Marx lived, Islam was spreading into Europe. Marx believed a borderless society, free of religious doctrine, racial preferences, and nationalist views, could break down traditional social constructs in the capitalist world. Marx didn't know it, but he was the father of political correctness.

While guilt is a tool to convince white America that they, as a culture, have a sinful past to atone for, most white liberals have accepted this as truth. Most conservatives laughingly reject it. America isn't perfect, but it's the best society humans have ever set for themselves. By asking white America to reject the grand narrative—because otherwise they cannot possibly join the New Age Marxists in becoming citizens of the world—you are asking white Americans to feel guilty, and if they eventually feel guilty, they will be willing to pay more taxes (atonement), be more active (penance), and accepting of the social justice agenda (resignation to the will of the Left).

Post-modernist efforts to bring skepticism and doubt to the grand narrative, coupled with fellow progressives' attempts to break down the traditional pillars of society in favor of a leftist culture bereft of religion, tradition, and history through bullying and shaming people into guilt should be seen as Marxist reeducation tactics.

THE HIJACKING OF THE FIRST AMENDMENT

Generally speaking, Marxists like rules when they advance their agenda. They like them even more when they harm conservatives. At the same time, rules are inconvenient when they get in the way, and consequently, some wording in our Constitution has been misunderstood to the benefit of the Left. Let's take a look at the most commonly quoted portion of the First Amendment. "Congress shall make no law respecting an establishment of religion, or prohibiting the free exercise thereof, or abridging the freedom of speech or of the press."

As part of a broader deconstruction of our Christian family values, the Left's attorneys have pushed for the legalization of pornography and other obscene material detrimental to our communities. The Left takes a position that there are no exceptions to the First Amendment clause, relative to free speech. The founding fathers envisioned the First Amendment as a protection for new ideas or new theories, but the Left has interpreted this as a free pass to get child pornographers or terrorists off the hook. Instead of speech that advocates for child pornography or terrorism being unconstitutional, the restriction of that speech is unconstitutional. We live in a world where leftists want to suppress constitutionally-protected speech, simply because they don't like it, or they don't like who's saying it. At the same time, they want to suppress dissenting views of leftist speech they support. They want it both ways.

HYPOCRISY

After his scathing monologue at the 77th Golden Globe Awards in January 2020 was immediately blasted by the Left as out of touch, right wing, and according to The Independent, "Overshadowing vital political messages," writer, comedian and actor Ricky Gervais responded by asking, "How the (expletive) can teasing huge corporations, and the richest, most privileged people in the world be considered right wing?"

"Vital." Now that's funny. If Christianity and capitalism are the arch enemies of Marxism, then conservatism and liberty are the arch enemies of cultural Marxists. So, to fight capitalism and conservatism, the Left needs their likeminded tribes to attack, shun, and ostracize the oppressive class, until it's eradicated. Senator Sanders rails about homelessness, housing shortages, and home pricing, yet owns, last I heard, three homes. Celebrity's virtue signal about carbon footprints, yet they are the biggest offenders.

Hypocrisy exists throughout the Left, from their private jets to their limos to their yachts to their huge homes, and all the other elements of their carbon footprints. But, perhaps the worst hypocrisy is in regard to the judgment Dr. King asked us not to have.

Many people of color are conservative, but since most conservatives are white, what better way for the Left to demonize the largest segment of a group, than to label them racists or Nazis? The Left is clever, because it's relatively easy to create a perception of someone or some group as racist, but extremely difficult for someone, even wrongly accused, of being a racist to disprove it.

The hypocrisy in this is the Left's blatant defiance of Dr. King, by judging a person on the color of their skin and making a further leap that unless, for example, a white person renounces his or her "privilege" and absolves themselves by joining their side, they are fair game to be labeled racist. In other words, all whites are racist until verified otherwise. They say outlandish things like, "Only a racist would deny racism is a daily part of American life," or "Only a racist would wear a MAGA hat," or "Only a racist would oppose solutions to jail overcrowding."

This game of (mis)association actually helps explain the disgusting contempt leftists have for black conservatives. Just like if a white man wearing a MAGA hat is supposed to be racist, because white history is boiled down to oppression, the Left's peculiar logic is that if they're black, they're supposed to lean left, and not right, because black history, even in the 21st century, is sickeningly reduced by the Left to slavery (oppression). In the Marxists worldview, it's imperative that blacks not only vote blue, but they must be open about it; otherwise, it would disrupt the narrative that they have been, and always will be, oppressed. If they don't vote in enough numbers, with "enough numbers" meaning a Republican win, it's because of systematic voter suppression by the patriarchy (an oppressor). If they happen to vote red, they are demonized—or the Russians are at fault!

The Left wants us to live in a colorless world, free of judgment and stereotypes based on skin color, but they constantly remind us that we live in a vile, racist world, where blacks are supposed to do this, and whites are supposed to do that.

HEGEMONY

Hegemony is a Marxist dog whistle word that ties what they call white privilege and patriarchy to conservatism and racism. In the Marxist vernacular, hegemony essentially means wrong (i.e., conservative) ideas that have been accepted by too many people (i.e., white voters) for too long. Wearing a MAGA hat is a great example. Marxists hate MAGA, and they think the way to flush this type of hegemony (i.e., their narrative is that MAGA equals white nationalism) out of society is to shame people into not wearing them. Leftists need more whites in more flyover states to move more leftward in their political leanings to achieve their goal of permanent takeover. So, to the Marxists, too many white people support President Trump, and too many of them wear MAGA hats. Therefore, those people, those conservative people, those bad white people, those deplorables are racist, xenophobic, homophobic, and I suppose intolerant Marxophobes.

The point here is that you'll hear, or see, the word hegemony occasionally in the news, and you need to remember it's a Marxist dog-whistle term, used as a pejorative to describe conservative people, conservative thoughts, and/or conservative actions that are culturally or politically unacceptable.

WHAT'S UP WITH MARXISTS AND THE GROUP THINK?

The Left spreads conspiracy theories and lies about conservatives and President Trump all the time, such as President Trump's a fascist and won't concede the 2020 election if he loses, conservatives want to take away human rights, Fox News is a mouthpiece of the Republican party and Breitbart is the mouthpiece of right-wing racists, and so on and so forth. So, with all the lies, mischaracterizations, and nonsense, it's hard to tell if Marxists really believe this stuff, or if they are simply, and blindly, following orders. Stick with the narrative. Stick with the plan. Stick to the talking points. "Group Think" is all about following orders, however ridiculous, however wrong, and however misleading, all in the blind faith that the Marxist agenda is somehow right, somehow morally superior, and somehow the destiny of America.

One of the issues the Left has with President Trump is that he has removed Group Think from his administration. Group Think is analysis and decision making by consensus where nobody takes responsibility and there is no feeling of individual accountability if things go wrong. It's the preferred method of analysis and decision making by the Left. To the Left, Group Think is good because it's inclusive and non-threatening. It's the counterintuitive belief that less mistakes happen and things run more smoothly when more chefs are in the kitchen. Including more people in the democratic or decision making process is good, or so their theory goes. Because everyone gets to touch it Group Think provides another layer of bureaucratic oversight. More reviewers mean more government jobs. Conservatives reject Group Think because it discourages prompt decisions, encourages destructive compromises and hides individual accountability when things go wrong. Also, conservatives believe group settings do not raise intelligence nor improve the quality of decisions as the mean IQ of the group is typically lower than the leader's. The rejection of Group Think is seen by the Left as racist and sexist because it eliminates a chance for inclusivity, and seems authoritarian because it takes people out of the information and decision making loop and thereby eliminates a checks and balance in democracy.

THE DISCONNECT THAT IS: "IT COMES FROM A PLACE OF ..."

Leftists often immediately dismiss criticism, opinions, or arguments from the Right, because, by definition, conservative speech comes from a place of hatred. The Left views conservatism as trying to uphold an illegitimate patriarchy, and, because conservative speech is anti-Marxist speech the only thing that can come out of a conservative's mouth is unacceptable speech, driven by hate. This is, of course, rooted in Marx's oppressed versus oppressor conflict. The oppressed is allowed to judge and complain and has a right to be angry at the thoughts and actions of the oppressive class, but the oppressor has no moral right to do the same. This is a clever trick to try and steal the moral high ground in any argument. Human nature says it's always better to give than receive blame, so the oppressed class complains and demands change, while the oppressor must listen and learn.

Conservatives usually have contempt for progressive speech, because it comes from a bad place—Marx. Conservatives view leftist speech as illegitimate, because it always ties to Marx, always ties back to Marx, and, by definition, flies in the face of fundamental American values.

THE FIRST AMENDMENT AND THE "RIGHT" NOT TO BE OFFENDED

The Left stifles unwanted dialogue many ways, but a common ploy is by claiming that there is a "right" not to be offended. Typically, speech is protected if it comes out of the mouth of a leftist (the oppressed class) but is offensive and unprotected if it comes out of the mouth of someone on the Right (the oppressor). In the Marxist worldview, acceptable speech is defined by the state, which is, of course, leftist. Absent the state's control of dialogue and messaging in America, the cultural Marxists have assumed the role of defining acceptable speech.

Since conservative speech is painted by the Left as part of the patriarchy and hegemony they hate and wish to destroy, it is automatically seen as wrong, racist, draconian, mean, or whatever. The Left does not want to debate the conservatives, because of the absence of substance to their arguments. Therefore, the Left tries hard to silence the Right, by claiming the unwelcomed speech is offending them and, perhaps, even illegal, and therefore the speaker should be censured, ignored, shamed or, even better, jailed! The rebuttal to this that conservatives need to use more often is that just because you're on the Left and dislike what a conservative has to say, or may be offended by conservative views, that does not mean you're right.

RIDICULE AND CONDEMNATION IS A ONE-WAY STREET TO THE LEFTISTS

Like satirists or court jesters, the oppressed class has a pass to claim a moral high ground to ridicule, critique, shame, or blame the oppressors with impunity. In the Marxist worldview, criticism is not a two-way street. The goal of criticism isn't to offer a better idea; it's to deconstruct. In Marxist theory, it is righteous and justifiable to shame the oppressive class, but impossible (and just plain wrong!) for the oppressed to be shamed by the oppressors. Hence, President Trump, as a rich, white conservative, is seen as fair game. You can criticize President Trump's personal behavior, but his policies are tougher on Russia and more anti-Marxist than President Reagan's or President Eisenhower's. The Left doesn't see this, or like this, because it doesn't fit the false narrative that President Trump colluded with Putin or is getting paid off by the Saudis or whatever. Truth and transparency in the exercise of our first amendment rights is a two-way street.

MARXISTS STRIVE TO ERASE EXISTING CULTURES AND NORMS

The ideas of Marx also have made significant and terrible strides in advancing the "culture war" by creating a mindset which encourages the West to abandon its own history. Christianity is seen as oppression, because it frowns on promiscuity, homosexuality, illegitimacy, and drug usage, and Marxists have made a seductive case to young people that modern-day Christianity is repressive and draconian. Those people who claim Christian allegiance do so, knowing that Marxists hold them in contempt. In Marxist thought, the problems of life are solved by technology (means of production) and/or through state policy. Its experts are the technocrats, those experts who seek to dictate how we are to think and live. Christian beliefs are viewed by the Marxists as superstitious and Christ as the opium of the people.

That goal, the one that seeks to erase our culture and chip away at American Exceptionalism, is to distort, erase, and disavow our history. This part of the agenda is essential to achieving their end game. The theory goes, if enough Americans can begin to doubt the grand narrative, to be skeptical, to impugn all that is special about America, they can be convinced that America is inherently racist, and it's not a big leap from there, to have Americans conclude that their nation is illegitimate.

THE DELIBERATE MOVEMENT OF THE OVERTON WINDOW

Traditionally, certain concepts went unsaid, and certain policies were not said out loud or published, because it was just understood that these topics were taboo. There were unwritten parameters of what was acceptable to discuss or advocate for, and for most of American history, these rules were followed. A political scientist named Joseph Overton was credited with explaining this phenomenon, and it was called the "Overton Window" in his honor.

It was intended to help clarify, for the benefit of the media and politicians, what the acceptable range of ideas were that the public might be willing to accept, without dismissing them. Policies and thoughts outside the window were deemed unacceptable. Overton's theory was that a viability of a political position depended on where it fell within a set of parameters, or a window if you will. Overton claimed that if a politician made recommendations or statements that fell within the window of acceptable speech, it would not be considered too extreme. As for instance, where it was once unthinkable for blacks to vote or own property and unthinkable for gay marriage to be nothing other than immoral or even illegal—as these were clearly outside the Overton Window—it is now acceptable public policy to discuss these topics, without fear of being censored, or voted out of office.

The transformation of an idea shifts from unthinkable propositions that are embraced by a few radicals who then, over time, advocate for it enough to be accepted by others in their ranks. Again, over time, the message gets refined to where the idea is deemed sensible by those outside the ranks to finally being popular enough to eventually be adopted into policy. The Overton Window defines a line, where a political party advocating for a new policy may want to test it, by crossing slightly over it, while trying to persuade the public to move to that new spot. It's historically been gradual. Introducing Marxist concepts, however outlandish, is an example of the Left, not just testing the limits of the Overton Window, but moving it to another wall in the house. Whereas, income inequality or 70 percent tax rates were not serious political topics, by AOC introducing them, they force the conversation as to where the window is and where the Left, and the Right, want it to be.

The Left Hates That President Trump's Win Smashed the Overton Window for Conservatives

Overton believed his theory did not test whether an idea was logical or effective—only if the idea was worthy of being discussed and advanced. So, for decades, the American Left—largely through the media—controlled the range of acceptable political discourse. Television programming pushed boundaries further and further leftward. Despite an expansion of the window over the past several decades in the arts and media, the constraints placed on politicians was still very limited until President Trump's election. After the 2016 election, the handcuffs came off. Intellectual (and moronic) debate expanded. Taboo topics were addressed. Methods of conveying positions were reinvented. Terms that were once seen as too touchy to mention without careful consideration of the context were weaponized. Racism, privilege, xenophobia, and illegal immigration became fair game. Stand Up America, founded after President Trump's victory, pledged to resist President Trump's dangerous agenda. Dangerous to whom? Those clamoring for a leftist America?

The irony of all this is the Left has wanted, for decades, to expand the window and propose fringe positions. To the Left, because all things are political, they wanted to control the narrative on social, race, gender, immigration, abortion, human rights, or sexuality-related matters. As the oppressed class, these people felt they, and they alone, were the only ones with the moral right to define those terms. In other words, because the Left kept moving the window to their liking, there were certain things a conservative could say about those topics, but expanding outside of it (i.e., regressing to another era in time) was unacceptable.

However, with President Trump in office, the conservatives in America are now doing the same thing the Left has done for decades, which is moving the window to a place on the house where they like it, by encouraging people to reclaim the cultural narrative, and call it as they see it, rather than cower behind political correctness that had moved the window in the first place.

MARXISTS USE "DOG-WHISTLE WORDS," TOO

Racist, xenophobic, Islamophobic, homophobic, closed-minded, neo-Nazi, and so on and so forth, are just a few of the common phrases Marxists will throw around to disparage conservatives. Supporting the hegemony, the patriarchy and the heteronormality of society is deemed racist and intended to discredit conservative thought. Rather than debate conservatives with productive counter arguments—which they mostly don't have—they rely on shaming, via name calling. The idea behind name calling is simple. Politics is complicated, and most people don't understand the progressive platform, for instance, but people do understand pejorative names, and if you shame your enemy, your base doesn't need to think through the whys of it. Since half of America possesses below average intelligence, the most impressionable of our society will be able to quickly judge, and condemn, anyone labeled as such.

New dog-whistle words have arisen in the President Trump era that Marxist's count on to condemn, without debate, and need to be explained. These words include patriarchy, white privilege, hegemony and heteronormality, and are intended to describe, contemptibly of course, certain people, certain socioeconomic classes, and certain political views the Marxists don't like.

To the Left, white nationalist is a dog whistle that means the object of their current scorn—usually a conservative—is a racist, but we'll label him something slightly less pejorative than that—for now—until the conservative sees the evils of his ways and shapes up.

Patriarchy means something that works in our society that Marxists really don't like. Marxists typically describe things that a male—and, specifically, a white, straight male—would prefer as patriarchal. Since straight, white men have held positions of power in America, they are part of the "patriarchy." Since Christian churches established the moral parameters Americans lived by for 300 years, they are part of the patriarchy. Women who preferred to have children and be stay-at-home moms are part of the patriarchy.

White privilege means two things. Outwardly it's: (1) The self-righteous blaming of white racism for someone's (usually, but not always, the speaker's) personal, and undeserved, achievement in life. Inwardly it's: (2) A strange self-loathing, sort of an acknowledgment of some shameful sense of guilt by many white American liberals, coupled with their incredulous view of why conservative whites don't feel the same. Remember, racism in any form is wrong, and Marxism is as bad or even worse: however, Marxism contains a wretched form of reverse racism rooted in the contempt progressive whites have for conservative whites. Marxism can never prevail in America, unless enough white Americans are seduced into its lies and/or otherwise guilt-tripped into accepting the lies as truth. Remember, truth is a virtue the Marxists don't have. There is no reason to accept a penance for a crime you did not commit, just to show the oppressed class you are righteous or responsible.

Hegemony is a pejorative word the Marxists use to describe ideas or cultural customs and norms they don't like, because they are seen as upholding the American ethos and thus blocking their objectives. Generally, leftists would define hegemony as "Wrong ideas that are accepted by too many people." More specifically, it is a dog whistle to draw attention (and scorn) to ideas and views that white conservatives have and, therefore, are wrong and unacceptable—as in the Marxists find it wrong and unacceptable. Latter-day Marxists have taken aim at this so-called hegemony by decrying what they see as the rotten heteronormality of American society—social, gender, sexuality, class, national identity, Christianity, along with children, family, and educational formation constructs that limit Marxist influence and advancement.

The phrase right-wing conspiracy theory is a classic dog whistle to their zealots. It warns their tribe that the Right has figured something out so everyone should be on high alert and ready to hide it, lie about it, re-define it or spin it differently. Remember, only a leftist with something to hide would use the phrase right-wing conspiracy in a sentence. Usually it means they're up to something and a conservative has caught on.

Chapter 16

PROGRESSIVES TODAY— EXISTENTIAL THREATS

NOTED CANADIAN AUTHOR AND RADICAL LEFTIST Naomi Klein is one of these New Age leftists who try to marry disparate matters into a larger agenda in order to broaden the base. In other words, the big tent can never be big enough. As an example, women's rights, black civil rights, immigrant rights, and gay rights have little in common, and their agendas were never synchronized until the Left brought those groups together under the Marxist idea of the oppressed versus the oppressor. Suddenly, all of these groups had a common enemy—conservative white males. Klein is just one of many leftists, who realized a long time ago that if you get someone angry about one thing, it's easy to get them angry about something else that they may not have normally even cared that much about—sort of the classic "The enemy of my enemy is my friend" mentality.

One of the reasons why conservatives are reluctant to acknowledge, let alone embrace, the "climate emergency" is the legitimate contention that it is nothing more than a Trojan horse. Conservatives see leftists as always seeking some purpose in life that doesn't involve important things like children, their church, their neighbors or their parents. Air pollution, acid rain, Greenpeace, genetic modification of crops, water pollution, denuclearization, over population and climate emergency are just some of the high profile external factors that have been tied to those big scary geopolitical forces the Left wants conservatives to relinquish control over.

Because those things have economic aspects to them the Right is therefore skeptical of activists and scientists with a green agenda and see them as "watermelons" – green on the outside and red on the inside. Klein is an example. She's a voice that, somehow, is trying to link climate change to economic change, and if you look closely the Green New Deal and Tom Steyer's Justice-Centered Climate Plan have little, if anything, to do with global warming. As most everyone knows, the economy has little to do with weather and vice versa outside of the inconveniences and disruptions periodically caused by fires, volcanoes, tornados, hurricanes, or polar vortexes. People go to work and assemble their widgets, whether it's 2 degrees or 102 degrees. Rain or shine, the banks and Wal-Marts are still open. For the most part, America is open for business, regardless of the weather.

If you look at the Green New Deal, you logically conclude that this not a scientific game plan to combat global warming. It's a playbook for the Marxist takeover of the American economy. Let's look at its policies: Health care, affordable housing and food, access to nature, guaranteed jobs with sustainable wages, family leave, retirement security, education and training, and investment in economically vulnerable communities. In short, the Green New Deal is a pretext for social justice goals. By requiring people to change behaviors, such as raising gas taxes, energy surcharges, and regulatory mandates (everyone has to have solar on their home), the government could wean the public away from fossil fuels.

The connectivity of otherwise disparate groups, shown by gay rights and union strikes, that had nothing in common until the Left married them, by telling the participants they are fighting the same oppressor—whether it's President Trump, the capitalists, or the patriarchy, or whatever. Next thing you know, they're locking arms in marches. They have nothing in common, except the advancement of a Marxist ideal: Fight the oppressor for the sake of fighting the oppressor. This is why teamsters support teachers' unions that are on strike and vice versa. Workers of the world, unite!

As mentioned earlier, half of America possesses below average intelligence. When it comes to the news and, in particular, geopolitical news, many people like simplicity. Nuances are complicated and boring. Most Americans like the issues boiled down to 140 characters or less. President Trump Is Evil or Dump President Trump are just a handful of characters to process. That leads us to Naomi Klein, an anti-capitalist who is linking climate change to global economic change. People like Klein are dangerous, because people aren't particularly smart, and she knows it. Check out this quote, "Climate can be our lens to catalyze this economic transformation that so many people need for other even more pressing reasons than that (i.e. climate change + economic change) may be a winning combination." And how about this gem, "This economic system is failing the vast majority of people. Capitalism is also waging a war on the planet's ecosystem." In other words, capitalism is failing and destroying the world at the same time, so let's get rid of it, before we all die! Crazy existential threats are doing nothing but playing to people's emotions and fears—a classic Marxist tactic. Who are these people?

WHAT IS THIS "DEGROWTH" MOVEMENT ALL ABOUT?

The degrowth movement is predominantly a French-based political, economic, and social movement that has existed in one form or another in Western civilization for a couple hundred years. The thinking is there was always someone out there who warned that there aren't enough farms to feed the world's population. It's got more attention in Europe over the past few decades, but is gaining momentum in leftist America, because, as you guessed, the degrowthers aren't concerned about farming, but they are concerned about the destruction of capitalism. Essentially, it's a leftist movement based on ecological economics, anti-consumerism, and anti-capitalism that strives to reduce consumption, in the hope of sustaining Mother Earth in perpetuity. It's odd, because it flies in the face of orthodox Marxism, because Marx was not concerned with quantity of goods—only the control of production. However, the degrowthers have linked their movement to Marxism, because of their focus on consumption, which they see as a byproduct of capitalism and wealth accumulation. In their leftist worldview, capitalism is unsustainable, because it relies on growth, and growth depends on the exploitation of resources, and since resources are limited and will soon be expended, capitalism is therefore unsustainable. In other words: Get rid of it!

MARXISTS TOUT THE "US VERSUS THEM" NARRATIVE

Nuances and complexities are not part of the Leftist talking points. Everything is boiled down to simple us versus them narratives, where "them" are the conservatives, the oppressors, the enemy. The conservatives' rejection of post-modernist thought is ignorantly spun by the Left and the media as not only an ignorant allegiance to white privilege and America's arrogant role as the world's peacekeeper, but a rejection of social change—specifically identity "rights" adjudicated into law over the last 50 to 100 years. Rejection of (or resistance to) change means a rejection of progress made by identity groups, meaning, more specifically, a rejection of progress made by blacks, women, and the LGBT community. Conservative beliefs in American Exceptionalism, and their rejection of an un-American concept, such as post-modernism and identity politics, is viewed in the Leftist's narrative as patriarchal, racist, and homophobic.

Utopian Schemes

Leftists love state planning, and they come up with endless ideas to reshape American society in Marx's image. Be wary of utopian schemes, they may push like Vision Zero—a goal of having everyone get around on bikes, busses, and trains, as part of some sort of Green New Deal initiative. Social equity is a stated goal of most Vision Zero plans, although it's unclear how taking cars and commercial vehicles off the street raises the standard of living for the urban poor.

Make no mistake about it. Schemes like this are simply wars on cars and single-family housing lifestyles. Equitable mobility is an objective of these schemes, as in everyone is supposed to walk or ride a bike or take a bus, but just don't drive a car. Road diets, a scheme to eradicate travel lanes off roads through restriping the lane to reduce vehicles and increase bikes, do nothing but increase congestion and, consequently, drive homeowners out of cities and into the suburbs. Vision Zero, road diets, or whatever they're labeled as, have nothing to do with safety or air pollution, but are initiatives to get people out of their cars and into high-rise apartments, near bus and train depots in existing urban areas. At its heart, Vision Zero's environmental goals are really a pretext to make suburban life untenable and eliminate cars—the symbol of American freedom and independence. Government mandates, programs, and initiatives that center on state planning, oversight, regulation, and that which rely on limited or non-existent skills, resources, and technologies are Marxist trademarks. Make a down payment and figure out the details on how to make it work later.

Everything Is an Existential Threat

The foundation of Marxism, whether it's socialism, fascism, or communism, is a belief that there is an urgent all-hands-on-deck revolution underway, a highly emotional and perpetual life-or-death struggle, where lives are on the line, a war against the oppressive class, the oppressive race, the oppressive culture, the oppressive religion, and the oppressive system. When you hear, "People will die if he is elected!" or "Impeach not only President Trump, but all Republicans, because otherwise the apocalypse will come at any moment," that's Marxism at work. "Climate change" apparently wasn't alarming enough. It's now referred to as "Climate emergency." That's Marxism in action. Painting the opposite side as not just an enemy, but an evil one who will kill you any day now, is classic Marxist dogma.

This clash is defined as being between two classes: The capitalists, who own the productive resources, and the workers, or what Marx called the "proletariat," who must work in order to survive. It may or may not involve lethal weapons, but violence—both verbal and physical. Violence against oppressors is deemed OK by the Left, which is why the media tends to underplay the behavior of antifa. Every single election, agency, or judicial appointment, policy and law is perceived in the context of a struggle. Immigration, health care, education, court and cabinet appointments, labor, women's rights, gay rights, black rights, and so on and so forth—everything is viewed in the paradigm of "struggle." The oppressors—typically white, straight Republicans—need to be portrayed as racists, xenophobes, Nazis, sexists, and so on and so forth to identify and give a face to a villain and ensure the oppressed class vilifies them, let alone votes for them. Everyone who fights for their causes, however stupid or misguided, is viewed as being part of a resistance, as being on "The right side of history." Think Black Lives Matter and antifa.

To most Americans, these are anarchists more in line with fascists of yesteryear. But to the Left, they are soldiers and the faces of the resistance, who are fighting the fascists in white America (conservatives). The only qualification for membership is a belief that you stand with, or are otherwise are part of, the oppressed class that is fighting the power.

Chapter 17

PROGRESSIVES TODAY—
LATTER-DAY MARXIST DENIALS

LEFTISTS WILL IGNORE THEIR HYPOCRISY AND deny they are dividing America. They deny their intolerance. They deny their engagement in revisionist history. They will deny that Marx was anti-Semitic and spoke of hatred. They deny that they ever engage in behavior that flies in the face of what they preach about environmental stewardship, whether it's traveling in their private jets, their limos or their yachts. They deny the incredible triumphs that America has achieved. They deny God, and marginalize those who performed great things in his name. They deny that a Cultural Marxism campaign has been going on non-stop since the '30s. They denied the presence of communists in Hollywood in the '40s and '50s. They deny that there is fetal pain during abortion. They deny that there is a link between drug usage and crime. They deny China is America's biggest threat, instead maintaining that Russia, with an economy the size of South Korea, and smaller than California, Texas and New York is the biggest threat. And, currently, they deny the successes of President Trump, including his lawful victory over Secretary Clinton.

DENIALS ABOUT PAST MARXIST FAILURES

Leftists can be counted on to accuse conservatives of denial, whether it is climate denial or social justice denial, privilege denial or whatnot. However, these same leftists are in absolute denial over some inconvenient truths about the history of the Democratic Party and Marxism. Through revisionist history, they will contend they were once the party that supported slavery, fascism or Jim Crow. They will deny that their religion has been a destructive failure everywhere it's been tried. Latter-day Marxists normally respond with, "It's been tried but never the right way." Or, "that wasn't socialism. That was fascism, Marxism, communism or totalitarianism." Or, "It's never been tried in a nation as rich and diverse as the U.S." Or, "We're not Marxists! We're Democratic Socialists". Or, "We're Justice Democrats." They deny that 20 million people died in the U.S.S.R. or that 70 million have died in China or more than 6 million at the hands of Hitler, that 1.5 to 2 million Cambodians died at the hands of Pol Pot and the Khmer Rouge and countless millions at the hands of the Kims in North Korea or throughout Africa over the last 100 years, as a result of Marxism. Those deaths were a result of totalitarianism, fascism, dictatorships, evil, etc. The truth is, those deaths were a byproduct of the disease that is Marxism and not because some isolated, vile dictator like Stalin or Hitler hijacked Marxism.

Leftists will deny, and maybe become quite angry, when presented with some extremely inconvenient truths. Marx was not an atheist, as most people presume, but a Satanist bent on the destruction of the Christian world order. Gentile created fascism to be the truest and most practical form of Marxist governance. And, Hitler and his band of National Socialists were actually leftists, not right-wingers. Want to see a leftist triggered? Present them with one of those facts, let alone all three. Marx was not a warm and loving humanist who wanted to help the workers of the world. It's hard for people to come to grips with facts that fly in the face of all they've been taught. This is especially true for the leftists, who would rather silence you than debate you on these types of points.

Most on the Left have no knowledge of history beyond their last Starbucks, and, strangely, and, wrongly, believe Trumpism is Nazism and, therefore, by definition, bad. They probably believe George Wallace was a Republican. And, since the media and cultural elite say President Trump and conservatives are bad, we should listen to Senator Sanders and adopt socialism to save ourselves from President Trump and his base, because socialism isn't racist like President Trump and Hitler. This is, of course, a total joke, because, as you learned earlier Nazism was German National Socialism! Yes. Socialism folks!!!

In the modern left's view, fascism has little interest in egalitarianism, it persecuted underperformers and society's misfits, advocated for a strong military, appealed to national identity and supported capitalist industry. These sound like American Conservative things, but whether they do, or don't, they do not take away from the fact that socialism is on the left, and not the Right side of a political compass. People on the Left may want a strong national identity, tight borders and a strong military. Look no further than North Korea for proof. The bottom line is that the fascists were committed socialists who believed in a highly regulated single-party political system that demanded conformance and compliance from everyone.

THE OLD "IT WORKS IN SWEDEN" TROPE

A wild claim from the Left is when they say the only reason socialism hasn't work is because everyone has been doing it wrong. Marxists like to point to Sweden as an example of how Socialism "works," yet they conveniently ignore the caveat that Sweden is a small homogenous society or the reality that socialism has been dialed back significantly in Sweden since the '80s, as people realized privatization, lower taxes and deregulation were needed. Any government will flourish when every citizen thinks, looks and acts the same. This is why certain socialist programs do well in Japan too. Do the leftists really think most Americans will agree that Medicare For All (aka "M4A") and 70 percent tax rates are in our best interest? No. Some will. Maybe just enough will. They hope 50 percent +1 do.

THE DENIAL OF EUGENICS

The Left also believes racial cleansing is a right-wing phenomenon, but what exactly happened and why is a practice known as "eugenics" tied to the Left? Let's review some indisputable facts first. Abraham Lincoln was a Republican. Marx felt slavery in the U.S. was a great socialist model – cradle to grave care of the oppressed by an oppressor class. Republicans supported the Reconstruction effort after the Civil War and Democrats didn't. Jim Crow laws were enacted and enforced in states with Democratic legislatures. Members of the Ku Klux Klan were the storm troopers of the Democratic South. Since slavery and a voluntary diaspora were not options to rid America of blacks, northern intellectuals undertook eugenics. It was a progressive phenomenon embraced by American leftists as a solution to urban ills and, therefore, as a means to improve society. Mental hospitals and prisons were public options for eugenics. Planned Parenthood was devised as an alternative for those not institutionalized.

These days, Planned Parenthood is associated with feminism and choice, but it's important to understand the genesis of that organization and historical ties between eugenics and German fascism. Margaret Sanger (1879-1966) was a nurse, racist and eugenicist. In 2016, she opened the first birth control clinic in the U.S. and was the founder of what became known as Planned Parenthood. Sanger was a member of the New York Socialist Party and early feminist, who felt women needed to have control over whether or not they have children. She was also a eugenicist who believed a woman could best serve the state (socialism), if she could first serve herself and that only women who were healthy enough, and could financially tackle motherhood, should have children. In short, eugenics was a science for quacks, racists and social engineers in the first half of the 20th century. The pretext was to discourage the unprepared from having offspring. The real reason was social engineering, through racial population control.

Leftists will deny that Hitler has any ties to not just socialists but progressives or liberal democrats. Madison Grant (1865-1937) was a lawyer and zoologist, who was a leading thinker in the Progressive Era. (He went to, wait for it, Columbia Law School. There's that school again!) He wrote a book titled, "The Passing of the Great Race: Or, The Racial Basis of Human History" in 1916. His Nordic Theory was considered profound and was adopted as fact by the Nazis. Hitler wrote to Grant and stated, "The book is my bible." Whole sections were incorporated into Mein Kampf.

GEORGE SOROS AND DARK MONEY

Leftists and their media collaborators have always liked to demonize the Koch brothers and other conservative activists working behind the scenes, but the media doesn't seem to have any concern about the amount of money and motives of the ones who work for their side. In fact, the media denies that leftist dark money even exists. Guys like Tom Steyer and Michael Bloomberg were running as Democratic presidential candidates and aren't necessarily behind the scenes anymore, but George Soros is someone worth mentioning. Soros is an 89-year-old Hungarian Jew, who grew up in Nazi-occupied Hungary. He ultimately migrated, after the war, to London, then later to New York City, and he lives the life of a billionaire, as the patron saint of Marxist fundraising in an armed estate in a tax haven (Curacao), where he can avoid U.S. and EU regulators and, of course, taxes.

To leftists, he's an ATM machine who can be relied on to fund their increasingly dangerous agenda, and for conservatives, he's the world's largest donor to anarchist and Marxist causes. Soros is a major source of financial and policy influence through various organizations he bankrolls. Is what he does illegal? Likely, no. About 10 years ago, a pair of Supreme Court decisions made it legal for non-profits, unions, trade associations and others to make untraceable political donations. These donations were called dark money. Since then, more money has been raised through dark money sources than political action committee (PAC) fundraising, because the latter needs to disclose donors.

Do conservatives dabble in the dark money game? Yes. But, it's an America First agenda. The difference is that Soros is a globalist, who longs for a future where the influence of the U.S. is minimized or eliminated. Sort of an America Last agenda. He's said, "The main obstacle to a stable and just world order is the United States." An advocate for a borderless world, his Open Society Foundation is devoted to the eradication of national sovereignty, especially in the U.S. and Israel. He sees the Syrian refugee crisis as good for Europe and wants to create a world free of Christianity, capitalism and, above all, American Exceptionalism. Among other things, Soros opposes Brexit, supports Media Matters for America, which is sort of a counter-information organization bent on discrediting conservative news, and supports American Bridge 21st Century, an opposition research group for democratic causes. He bankrolls various leftist causes in America and has been accused of destabilizing the Catholic Church by supporting gay marriage, abortion, and physician-assisted suicide.

So, to men like Soros, things like racism, misinformation and anarchy sell. It's one thing to encourage responsible dialogue on race, gangs, crime, drugs, etc. It's another thing to encourage the dangerous concept of de-policing urban areas. Where most people might support candidates running for legislative seats on a city council, state assembly or the U.S. House of Representatives, he cleverly supports far-left attorney general candidates. He's a member of the so-called Democracy Alliance, which is a group of leading leftist policy makers and donors that includes Steyer, Speaker Pelosi and Senator Warren. This club is a funding clearinghouse, working tirelessly to implement strategies to combat what they would describe as President Trump's terrifying assault on Presidents Obama's achievements, the Constitution, Mother Earth, the media, and so on and so forth. According to their website, they state, "We play a leading role in fostering the infrastructure necessary to advance a progressive agenda for American."

Sometimes the contributions aren't even dark. According to opensecrets.org, of the nine donors who disclosed their contributions for the 2020 election cycle and donated at least $5 million, seven are liberals, including George Soros. Ironically, a goal of the Democracy Alliance is to get dark money out of politics, but according to Speaker Pelosi, you need dark money to get your candidates elected, so they can eliminate dark money from politics. So, when someone says this or that is a Soros-funded program, initiative or organization, or something or other has ties to Soros, you now know it's on the far left.

EPILOGUE

EVERYTHING THAT MAKES UP THE PROGRESSIVE agenda has its roots in Marxism. Globalism, open borders, secularism, if not the outright disavowal of religion, egalitarianism, progressive taxes, gun control, environmentalism, regulation, government programs, deflection of accountability from the individual to society, conformity of thought, destruction of the hegemony, denial of American Exceptionalism and identity politics, are all out of the Marxist playbook.

Marxism has been carefully honed over the past 200 years. So, from Kant, Hegel, Hess, and Marx; then through Gramsci, Gentile, and Marcuse; and finally, through Alinsky and the so-called democratic socialists, it cleverly influences or outright directs all American progressive thought. The cultural Marxism agenda we are seeing pushed forward by Hollywood, the media, and academia is obviously rooted in Marxist thought, as is environmentalism and militant feminism.

Whereas, Marxists used to keep a low profile, they are coming out into the open with unsustainable, if not downright crazy, ideas to solve whatever social, economic, political, or judicial ills they wish to address, but usually taxes and big government are at the bottom of it. The Green New Deal, drafted immediately after the 2018 mid-term election, is just an example of this. Individual accountability is being replaced by the state stepping in to fix things that are really not your fault, because the world is out of your control and you need Big Brother to help manage your life.

REMEMBER: PROGRESSIVISM IS MARXISM, NOT LIBERALISM

Most progressives see themselves as liberals, but many liberals do not categorize themselves as progressive. Basically, "classical liberalism" in its purest form, going back some 300 years, promotes freedom and individual rights. Classical liberals could indeed be conservative, and their goal was freedom to engage in commerce with limited government interference (laissez faire) and respect for the rule of law and private property. Classic liberals sought to move away from monarchies to democratic structures. In France, those who supported the king and a slower pace of social change sat on the right side of the chamber, and those who sought the faster change classical liberalism promised sat on the left.

Liberals were not necessarily Marxists and may even be centrist in their views, but they embraced much of what Marxists sought. Progressives see themselves as liberals, but they are actually Marxists, who have moved far left from typical American liberalism. Progressivism is not a spin-off of classical liberalism or an offshoot of American liberalism. In actuality, it's the antithesis of classical liberalism, and their radicalism does a disservice to the legacy of true liberals like JFK.

Progressivism promotes egalitarianism, the redistribution of wealth and the concentration of power, the reconstruction of the economic system, borderless one-worldism, the discrediting of faith and the erosion of American culture. This unattainable objective demands an ever-growing, invasive, ponderous, inefficient, centralized government. That is not liberalism. Progressivism's natural enemies are limited government, free markets, private property, and the rule of law—ideals that

American liberals and conservatives can agree on. Progressives are not implementing a liberal agenda, as they claim. They are promoting a Marxist agenda.

Liberalism, like conservatism, is also about individualism; however, progressivism, like Marxism, is not about individualism. It's about conformity and uniformity. It's about having a number on a uniform, being a machine, and doing what you are told, without dissension. But, people are not machines. They are individuals with different goals, dreams, and aspirations. They have different IQs, different skills, different tastes in food, and different levels of motivation. When you kill dreams, as Marxism does, you kill the individual. This is the big differentiator between progressivism and liberalism.

SIMPLY PUT: MARXISM DOESN'T WORK

Karl Marx's worker-led takeover never occurred in the West and certainly not in America, because labor never had a strong-enough base to overcome the Protestant work ethic, rooted in our capitalist system. Christianity is simply much stronger in America and a bigger part of people's lives than it is in Europe. Saul Alinsky understood that Marxism could not win on economic or political terms alone. In his book Rules for Radicals, he talks about fighting for power on a different front—the cultural front. He rightly believed the keys to the economic and political systems are held together by our shared—and strong—American ethos— the American cultural hegemony, if you will. So, to tear down those shared values, to undermine our history and our culture, and to instill beliefs that the "have nots" are systematically oppressed, is their agenda. Their aim is to achieve a cultural Marxist, if not an economic Marxist, takeover that will create a new leftist American cultural hegemony.

Marxism has been a worldwide failure, and you'd think that by now, support in Western democracies for it would be gone for good. The violence in the streets of Venezuela and on the farms of South Africa; the corruption and persecution of political and religious foes in China, Bangladesh, and Cuba; and the perpetual starvation and poverty in Benin, Laos, and North Korea should lead Americans and, in particular, American politicians to label it as toxic. However, the dream of a socialist utopia lives on, as seen in the wide support of Alexandria Ocasio-Cortez (AOC), Kamala Harris, Corey Booker, Bernie Sanders, and Elizabeth Warren, among many others. Their words and actions are alarming, and the belief among these actors is the twisted notion that "Socialism is great, but it just hasn't been done the right way yet, and luckily for you, my fellow Americans, vote for me and my fellow 'progressives' because we know just the way to do it right."

The Marxists want you to believe the world will end any day now (with President Trump firing nukes) or certainly within 12 years, as AOC and her band of Kool-Aid drinkers would like you to believe. Global warming (or is it climate change or is it climate emergency?) is portrayed daily as an existential threat, and if you listen to the Left, President Trump pulling out of the Paris accord means he's now single-handedly responsible for every hurricane that lands on our shores.

There is a conspiracy theory making the rounds in leftist circles that President Trump may not accept the results of the 2020 election, if he happens to lose. Even if President Trump wins fair and square, the Left will not recognize a mandate by the people. They will portray his reelection as dangerous and instill fear that President Trump will have unchallenged power to undermine the leftist gains (rolling back Obama administration regulations, nominating conservative judges, etc.). So, Marxists resort to scaring people, by suggesting the reelection of President Trump will (not could but will) bring the world to an end. According to Rufus Gifford, who served as President Obama's Finance Director for his 2012 campaign, "Scaring people is absolutely appropriate, because the threat is real." Yikes!

All of this is a coordinated effort to push their base to the edge. History has proven scared and angry people are not likely to think rationally, and the Marxists know this.

I've told my children that dreamers make movies, and daydreamers watch them. Dreamers have vision, and daydreamers have fantasies. Dreamers work hard and produce, and daydreamers complain about why the world is not an idyllic paradise, because they are not getting their fair share. Dreamers turn ideas into jobs that benefit society. Daydreamers feel entitled and wonder why society isn't fair. It's far easier to watch a movie and even critique a movie (daydreamers) than write or produce one (dreamers).

Criticism is a foundational element of Marxism, rooted in the envious hatred daydreamers have had for Christianity and capitalism for the past 200 years. Marxists like to criticize President Trump, not just because he's against them, but because it's easier to complain than debate, or find fault than find a compromise or a solution. Opinion is what the Left likes to do best—like talking about a movie they just saw. Sadly, they can't handle it when the spotlight is turned on them to explain themselves, because they prefer to watch, judge, and pontificate and not listen and understand. They stubbornly refuse to acknowledge, let alone unlearn the particularly vile cultural Marxism they have been indoctrinated with, and this chasm, caused by the wedge Marxists have used to divide us, will only get deeper, unless and until, the Left realizes that the problems in America are actually a Left problem and not a Right problem.

CPSIA information can be obtained
at www.ICGtesting.com
Printed in the USA
LVHW040718190621
690450LV00004B/10